Two
Truths
and a Lie

Two Truths and a Lie

A Murder, a Private Investigator,
and Her Search for Justice

Ellen McGarrahan

 RANDOM HOUSE | NEW YORK

Two Truths and a Lie is a work of nonfiction. Some names and identifying details have been changed.

Copyright © 2021 by Ellen McGarrahan

Published in the United States by Random House, an imprint and division of Penguin Random House LLC, New York.

RANDOM HOUSE and the HOUSE colophon are registered trademarks of Penguin Random House LLC.

LIBRARY OF CONGRESS CATALOGING-IN-PUBLICATION DATA
Names: McGarrahan, Ellen, author.
Title: Two truths and a lie / Ellen McGarrahan.
Description: New York: Random House [2021]
Identifiers: LCCN 2020009767 (print) | LCCN 2020009768 (ebook) |
ISBN 9780812998665 (hardcover) | ISBN 9780812998672 (ebook)
Subjects: LCSH: Tafero, Jesse, 1946–1990. | Murder—Investigation—Florida. |
Crime and the press—Florida. | Judicial error—Florida.
Classification: LCC HV8079.H6 M388 2021 (print) | LCC HV8079.H6 (ebook) |
DDC 364.152/3092—dc23
LC record available at https://lccn.loc.gov/2020009767
LC ebook record available at https://lccn.loc.gov/2020009768

Printed in Canada on acid-free paper

randomhousebooks.com

9 8 7 6 5 4 3 2 1

First Edition

Book design by Jo Anne Metsch

FOR PETER

Murder is an act of infinite cruelty.

—RAYMOND CHANDLER

Contents

AWAY   xi

PROLOGUE: Six Minutes Past Seven   xiii

PART ONE: FLORIDA   1

1. A Real Strange Situation   3
2. By Glue and by Dream   10
3. The Most Dangerous People   20
4. No One Is Going to Talk to You   26
5. A Squealer, a Liar, and a Mute   35
6. The Fugitive   45
7. Don't You Worry That Someone Is Going to Kill You?   63
8. So Much Blood   79
9. The Missing Pixels   86
10. Fifteen Miles, Seventeen Minutes   102
11. Everything. It Was All Gone.   111
12. The Personification of Death, If I Chose   121
13. The Closest Thing to a God in Prison   129

14. Naw, He Ain't Shot Him 137

15. A Very Uneasy Feeling 143

16. Grace 149

PART TWO: BUT WHICH TRUTH? 157

17. Investigation 101 159

18. But Which Truth? 180

19. If Anybody Moves, They're Dead 196

20. The Playground 202

21. The Kingdom of Lochac 208

22. Investigator Strait 223

PART THREE: GONE GHOST 227

23. The Boxes 229

24. Shattered Glass/Shiny Gun 237

25. What Kind of Strange Fate 244

26. Metal Rods, Running Through 264

27. On the Road 269

28. Michael J. Satz, State Attorney 282

29. The Truth 301

30. The Heat 304

HOME 315

EPILOGUE: The Price of a Lie 317

Acknowledgments 327

Away

Prologue

Six Minutes Past Seven

The road out of town was narrow and dark, and I did not see the prison until it was right in front of me. Five-thirty in the morning. Starke, Florida. May 1990. A bleak building, boxy, wrapped in razor wire and washed white by flares. I drove past the prison gates as instructed and pulled into a grass parking lot. The other reporters were already waiting, silhouettes in a mist floating up from the night fields, and as I walked over they were talking about clothes. *Wear what you would wear to a funeral,* one reporter said his father, a preacher, had advised. He looked solemn and shiny in his clean dark suit. I was back in my car scrambling out of my blue jeans and into my black jeans when two lights swept across me. The prison van, arriving to take us inside.

In the prison entrance hall, steel bars spanned floor to ceiling, wall to wall. Beyond them, the prison slept, cold and bright and pin-drop quiet. A guard with a gun checked my driver's license and press credentials, then I passed through a metal detector and into a room where a prison matron told me to get my hands up over my head. She patted underneath my shirt, skin to skin. She took away my shoulder bag, car keys, and wallet, and handed me a yellow notepad and two pencils. I carried those down a linoleum corridor to a briefing room, where tiny desks stood in tidy rows, like school. The prison spokesman was friendly and had a metal hook for a hand. Last meal: scrambled eggs, fried pepperoni, toasted Italian bread, two tomatoes, steamed broccoli, asparagus tips, strawberry shortcake with fresh strawberries and whipped cream, whole milk, and hot Lipton tea, he said. Yes, the governor was aware of the complexities of the condemned man's case. The innocence claim. No, the governor had not issued a stay.

As the spokesman talked, a banging began, metal on metal like a hammer on a pipe. The noise grew louder, clanging, clanking. A huge slamming sound, and the room blacked out.

Standard procedure, the spokesman said, through the gloom.

For every electrocution, Florida State Prison switched to its own generator to make sure there was an uninterrupted flow of power, he explained. When the lights came back on, they were yellower, weaker. I made a note: *These people know what they're doing.*

Then we got back in the van and rode around the prison yard to Q-Wing, and the electric chair.

Q-Wing was one small room, very brightly lit. The electric chair stood directly inside the door. It was enormous. Old, oak, bristling with electrodes and leather straps. It was so close I could have reached out and touched it except for the Plexiglas separating the witness area from the death chamber. On this side of the Plexiglas were four rows of seats, facing front. I chose a spot over by the window, third row back. The ivory-colored venetian blinds that covered the window felt reassuring in their vaguely residential way. The sun was up now, the sky outside the pale white of dawn. On the wall behind the electric chair was a junction box with a thick black wire snaking out of it. On the other wall was a clock. The clock hung just above the compartment where the executioner sat with the electrical controls. By law, every single thing about the executioner was secret. I tried, but there was no way to see into the booth.

On the wall clock, the minutes ticked past. Half a minute now. Seconds.

At seven A.M. exactly, the door in the back of the death chamber burst open.

Three men. Two in uniform. One shackled, struggling.

He was white, this prisoner. Wan and wiry. Dressed in a light blue button-down shirt and dark blue trousers, in stocking feet. Bald, because guards had just shaved his head. A square face with a strong nose, full lips, wide-set long-lashed dark brown eyes. He was forty-three years, six months, and twenty-three days old. His name was Jesse Tafero.

Jesse Tafero was bracing his feet against the floor and bending backwards toward the door he'd just come through. But the guards were strong and they were ready for this. They had him by the armpits, and they dragged him into the chamber and slammed the door shut behind them. Then they turned him around and made him look at the chair.

Before this moment, I had never laid eyes on Jesse Tafero. I'd never spoken with him. The only photograph I'd ever seen of him was a mugshot, taken the day he was arrested for the murder of two police officers, back in February 1976. The arrest that had landed him here.

Whenever the governor of Florida signed a death warrant, the editors at *The Miami Herald*, where I was a staff writer, called up the paper's capital bureau in Tallahassee and asked who wanted to be put on the witness list. When Governor Bob Martinez signed Jesse's warrant, I was new in the bureau, the youngest journalist there, and the only woman. I volunteered. I knew nothing about prisons. I'd grown up in Manhattan, spent summers on Cape Cod, went to private schools. Five years earlier I'd been deconstructing *The Executioner's Song* in literature class at Yale. But the State of Florida was using taxpayer money to carry out death sentences and my beat assignment included the Department of Corrections, so it seemed to me that witnessing was part of my job as a reporter. I wanted to be a good reporter. I also thought I had the whole death penalty thing figured out. A delicate equation of actions and forfeiture and gain and loss, plus the law is the law, was my opinion. It did not seem impossibly complicated to me. And anyway, almost every death warrant was turned down by the courts at the last moment, everyone said, so no need to get too worked up. My bureau chief, for example, had never witnessed an execution and he'd been covering the state government for seven years.

But now the guards were strapping Jesse into the chair. Thick leather straps: arms, chest, legs. The electric chair faced the witnesses, and as we watched Jesse, Jesse was watching us. Beneath his shaved scalp his dark eyes burned. He was starting to look at the witnesses in the front row, one by one, I realized. He was going to stare right into the eyes of every single person who had come to see him die. I did not want him to stare at me. But when his eyes finally reached me—the guards were yanking the straps tight— I decided, Well, it's probably polite. I met his gaze. Locked in. One, two, three, four, five, six. Then his stare moved on.

He is defiant, I wrote on my notepad. He also looked afraid.

Now the guards were pushing a microphone in front of his face so he could say his last words. My hand was shaking and all I got was "I think it's very unfair. I think it's time that everyone wakes up to see that the same laws that can go against crime can go against you tomorrow." Then the guards tied a leather strap across his mouth and dropped a leather mask over his face and screwed the thick black wire from the junction box into a metal headpiece and clamped that down tight onto his shaved bare skull.

A pause.

At six minutes past seven o'clock, they pulled the switch.

My buddy Tex had witnessed two executions for his job with a wire service. He told me it was going to be no big deal. We had been out drinking at an oyster bar near St. Marks National Wildlife Refuge, a marshy stretch of mudflats and alligators on the Gulf of Mexico. "They sit up straight when the juice hits them, and then they slump forward and they're dead," Tex told me, in his molasses drawl. "The worst part about it, babe—and I mean this—is the long, boring drive back home."

That is not what happened to Jesse Tafero.

When the electricity hit Jesse Tafero, the headset bolted onto his bare scalp caught fire. Flames blazed from his head, arcing bright orange with tails of dark smoke. A gigantic buzzing sound filled the chamber, so deep I felt it inside the bones of my spine.

In the chair, Jesse Tafero clenched his fists as he slammed upward and back.

He is breathing, I wrote on my yellow notepad.

The executioner, anonymous in the booth, turned the power off. Jesse, in the chair. Nodding. Breathing. His chest heaving. Then—the buzzing again. Flames. Smoke.

His head nods. His head is nodding. He is breathing.

My prison-issued pencil dug into the page so hard that the paper ripped.

I can see him sigh.

Outside again, the daylight was a hammer. The van dumped us back out onto the field opposite the prison and drove away. I stood there trying not to blink. It had taken seven minutes from the time the executioner first turned the power on until Jesse was declared dead, and three separate jolts. Usually it took one jolt, one minute, no nodding, no flames, no smoke, no heartbeat, no sighs. I went back to my motel room to file my story, working at a table next to a window. One of the radio reporters who had been at the execution sat with me because he didn't want to be alone. I propped open the door to my room so we could smoke cigarettes together while we wrote. My computer was a Radio Shack TRS-80, a Trash 80, about the size of a cereal box with a screen that displayed eight lines of text, and I typed fast on deadline and transmitted my report down to the city desk using rubber cups fastened around the handset of the motel room telephone. Twice it cut off before finishing. A buzzing on the line, the operator said.

I did not know this then, but I had picked up a ghost.

That summer, after the execution, my house in Tallahassee was robbed. I came home from the *Herald* one day to find my front door jammed open and everything I owned trashed on the floor. I moved instantly. My new place was in a forest by a set of railroad tracks, deep in a ravine. When the freight trains came through, the ground shook, a low rumble like a far-off growl, a sound that kept catching me off guard. Every morning, I ran up the hills of the city in the punishing heat. In July, I went back to Florida State Prison for a test of the electric chair. The prison officials had determined that a kitchen sponge they'd used in the headset during Jesse's execution was to blame for the fire, and to prove that the chair was working they hooked up a metal colander to the same wire that they'd bolted onto Jesse's head, put the colander in water, and turned the power on. The water boiled.

After I saw that, I stopped being able to run uphill, and then to run at all. When I tried, my breath turned to lead. I'd been seriously dating a reporter—beautiful, hilarious—from the *Herald*'s city desk, but I abruptly broke up with her and took up with Tex, getting wasted on beer with him on Saturday afternoons out on St. George Island. There was a high bridge out to the island, and I found that if I hit the top of it at the right speed there was a moment when the road disappeared and it felt like flying, white pylons flashing past and blue water shining all around. The heat out at the shore was so intense that on the drive home I sometimes stopped and threw myself into the Wakulla River, water the color of tea, cottonmouths in the trees.

Go see another one, Tex told me. That'll get it out of your mind.

In August a serial killer stalked Gainesville just as the University of Florida was starting its fall term. Four young women murdered, one young man. Mutilated, decapitated. I was sent to cover the story. Everywhere I went in Gainesville, people told me I fit the profile, meaning I too was a young woman with dark hair. Like the victims. Like a lot of other people also, I said. An old man at the city morgue insisted: *You could be next.*

The following spring, I spent my days rereading my battered college copy of *Les fleurs du mal* in the rotunda of the capitol during the legislative session instead of taking notes in the committee meetings, which I decided were soul-crushing rodeos of blowhards and existentially irrelevant concerns. As opposed to French poetry, you see. It was all lies, I told my bureau chief, the one who'd never witnessed an execution. Liars and lies.

Being a journalist was what I'd wanted to do. From the time I first read *Brenda Starr* in grammar school to editor jobs on my high school and college papers to an investigative reporting internship at *The Village Voice* to a local news stint at a small Massachusetts daily to political reporting at *The Miami Herald*, I had devoted myself to finding the truth, making it public, holding the powerful to account. But after witnessing Jesse Tafero die, I could not tell if any of that shit mattered, at all.

It was purely by chance that I started working as a private detective.

In the winter of 1992, I packed all my belongings in my car, drove out to California, and got a job in construction. Tile setting. It wasn't anything I'd ever thought of before. In this new life, I had a hose, a shovel, two five-gallon buckets, a pair of leather gloves for carrying things, and a pair of rubber gloves for cleaning up. My job was to load sand, lime, and cement into a mixing pan, add water, shovel the wet mud into the buckets, and lug the buckets upstairs without tripping over my own feet or gouging the walls. I liked it. With tile, a small mistake at the beginning could turn into a much bigger mistake at the end, one that would be impossible to change since everything was literally set in stone. I respected that. The zero-bullshit factor of the physical world. My new girlfriend had a big red dog, an Akita mix who looked like a giant fox, and he became my dog as well, riding shotgun in the front seat of my powder-blue Volvo sedan as I went from one high-end residential job site to the next. Palo Alto, Mill Valley, Hillsborough, Sea Cliff, Sausalito. A new world of Port-O-Lets, pallets, shards of Sheetrock everywhere like shattered snow. The hills above the Berkeley flatlands had burned to the ground the previous autumn, and on jobs up there I found myself in a blasted wasteland of melted glass and twisted metal. That felt familiar to me. I moved into a stilt house out on a marshland, and after work I watched night herons hunt in the shimmering shallows below my dock. I envied those birds. Their ability to tune everything out—and fly away.

Every day now ended in a layer of fine gray dust on my skin. A shroud, slowly lightening as it dried to white. At work I earned my pay sweating, with my heart pounding, my arms and legs on fire. *I am alive.* I listened to the radio, turned up loud. I hated the hard-rock music that played on every job site radio and then I started to love it—the foolproof brainwashing of merciless repetition. Some of the clients spoke slowly to me, enunciating their words carefully as they stared at my cement-covered clothes. Others were kind; one blistering afternoon a homeowner appeared with a bowl of plums, cold from the refrigerator, burstingly sweet. A few of the job site guys were jerks, but I let it roll. Mostly I was invisible. It was all okay. I knew I was making myself pay penance for sitting in a folding chair like a spectator at a sports match and watching a man die. I just did not exactly know why.

One Friday evening, not quite two years after the execution, I was watching television in my living room. On ABC, the news program *20/20* was beginning, with Barbara Walters in a bright yellow suit. Suddenly a close-up of my front-page *Miami Herald* story about the execution—my byline, right there—flashed onscreen. "3 jolts used to execute killer." An announcer asked: "Could the State of Florida have executed an innocent man?"

On my couch, I froze.

The day Jesse Tafero's death warrant went up on the bulletin board at *The Miami Herald*'s capital bureau, I'd read through a stack of news clippings about the crime that sent him to death row. It was a complicated tale.

One morning in the winter of 1976, Jesse; his girlfriend, Sunny Jacobs; two young children—Sunny and Jesse's baby daughter and Sunny's nine-year-old son; and a friend of Jesse's named Walter Rhodes were asleep in a beat-up Camaro in a highway rest area. Just past seven o'clock, two police officers on routine patrol stopped in the rest area to check out the Camaro. Moments later the officers were dead.

Jesse and Sunny and Walter—with the children—fled the scene, crashed at a police roadblock, and were arrested. Walter quickly told police that Jesse and Sunny murdered the officers. Walter testified against his friends at trial and his testimony helped send both Sunny and Jesse to death row. But not even a year later, Walter confessed that he had committed the murders himself. Then he recanted his confession. Then he confessed again. Then he recanted again. He confessed again. He recanted again. Confessed again. Recanted again.

Before arriving at the prison for Jesse's execution, I tried to figure out if Jesse and Sunny were guilty—or if Walter was. There was not much time. The death warrant Governor Martinez signed in mid-April had scheduled Jesse's execution for early May, and I was starting from zero. I had never so much as read Jesse Tafero's name before. I raced through the old news clips in our office files, then ordered more from the *Herald*'s main archives and scoured those too. I requested interviews with Jesse and with his girlfriend, Sunny, but they told me no. And in late April, I drove down through a grove of orange trees to the prison where Walter Rhodes was serving out three life sentences, because Walter had agreed to talk to me.

This was the week before the execution. It was my first time inside a prison.

Prison was not like it is in the movies. There was no bulletproof glass panel, no telephone. A guard ushered me down an empty corridor into a conference room. In the center of the room was a table, and at the table was a prison inmate dressed all in blue, waiting. The guard left the room, closing the door. I was alone with a convicted murderer.

Standing close by the door, I took a good long look at him.

Walter Rhodes, chief prosecution witness and possible liar, was tall, broad-shouldered, lean, and ripped. Jet-black hair, onyx eyes, skin tanned to an amber brown. A young Clint Eastwood, a young Montgomery Clift. His gaze was smooth and smoldering, I thought, steely, like the inside of the barrel of a gun. Not that I'd ever seen one of those.

I knew I needed to ask Walter Rhodes about Jesse Tafero and Sunny Jacobs. About how Jesse and Sunny said that it was actually he, Walter, who had killed the officers. And about his confessions. All those confessions. *Is Jesse going to the electric chair for crimes you committed, Walter?* That was what I was there to find out.

The first thing I did, though, was sit down across the table from him and light a cigarette.

"I guess I'm gonna have to tap my ashes on the floor, which will probably piss off the Department of Corrections," I told Walter, trying to sound cool. "Well, what I wanted to talk to you about was—how do you say his last name?"

In the two hours that followed, Walter Rhodes did not confess to me. He said the only thing he'd done at the highway rest area was stand with his hands in the air—"surrender in any language"—while Sunny and Jesse murdered the officers. Still, it was a heavy conversation. We discussed karma and destiny in addition to the murders, and as the interview drew to a close, I decided Walter was telling me the truth when he said he was innocent. I knew it. I could *feel* it. I rushed back to the office and wrote a story about Jesse Tafero's impending execution that did not so much as mention that Walter Rhodes had ever confessed to the killings at all.

"He is a psychopath," Jesse's girlfriend, Sunny Jacobs, was saying now on *20/20* in my California living room, about Walter Rhodes. Onscreen, Sunny was small and delicate. A pixie. Clear brown eyes, shiny brown hair, pink lip gloss. She grew up in a leafy New York City suburb, *20/20* reported. Wealthy parents, summer camp, swimming pools. Now she was behind bars for the murder of two policemen, put there by someone who had later confessed to the killings himself. Her voice was sweet and soft and she looked directly at her interviewer with a calm and unblinking gaze. "I think he believes every word that he says, each time that he says a new story," she continued, about Walter. "It's been my experience that anyone who has really dug into this comes back finding out that I am not guilty—I did not shoot those men—and that I am as much a victim as they were."

And Jesse? the interviewer asked. "Did he still maintain he was innocent?"

"Yes," Sunny said, her voice a whisper now, raw with emotion.

"Right up until the end?"

"Yes. Yes. And we didn't say goodbye, we just kept saying 'I love you' until we had to hang up."

I walked across the room and snapped the television off.

Three years passed. In the winters the king tides came, flooding the boardwalk with silver water. In the summers the marsh behind my house dried out and turned to gold. Then one morning I blew out a disc in my spine picking up a hundred pounds of cement. Shortly after that, my girlfriend announced she was in love with someone else. I got a job writing again at a San Francisco paper, and found a tiny apartment in the city. After work now, I sat and watched the fog coming in over the hills from the ocean, opalescent, effacing, erasing. Absolving, I hoped. I started dating a photographer I'd met on a job site years before, when he was laying hardwood floors and I was starting out at starting over. We had nothing in common and we didn't like each other much. That seemed best.

I was driving to work in San Francisco one day when an interview program came on the radio. The guest was a woman who said she was a private detective.

I listened for a little bit.

Yeah, right, I thought. Sure. A private detective.

A few weeks went by and I was hanging out at the Lone Palm on Guerrero with my friend Tim. Bourbon in highball glasses, red neon bleeding in through the windows, rain coming down hard outside. Usually Tim and I just complained about our love lives, but this time talk turned to the subject of work. Tim was a newspaper reporter, like me, and he'd stumbled onto a brand-new gig. He was working part-time as a private detective for an agency over in Pacific Heights. That's so weird, I told him. I just heard that show on the radio.

It's a blast, Tim said. A license to go through the world sorting truth from lies. The detective was looking to hire a woman, because women make good private eyes. Here, he added, writing the detective's office number on a bar napkin.

I don't think so, I told Tim. I might be at loose ends, but I am not fucking crazy.

That whiskey-soaked napkin came home with me anyhow. And one afternoon soon afterwards, I decided what the hell. I called, as a lark. Then, when the detective didn't call me back, I decided it wasn't a lark, it was a test. If you can get the job, you can have the job. I called him again. And again. When I finally reached him, though, he yelled at me. "You're calling me during the dinner hour. You have heard of dinner, yes? A time when respectable people have a reasonable expectation of privacy?" But then he'd paused as if a thought had hit him, barked an order to be at his office the following morning, and slammed down the phone.

The address he gave me turned out to be a gilded Victorian

mansion at the top of a hill overlooking San Francisco Bay. The detective answered the doorbell himself. A serious man in a very good suit. I immediately regretted my flowered dress, ponytail, and cowboy boots. Upstairs, in an office with a spectacular view of the old prison on Alcatraz Island—glowing like a Roman ruin in the sun—I told the detective the truth: I was thirty-two years old, I lived alone, a runaway New Yorker with a degree in history, a newly found and hard-won respect for the law of gravity, and a dawning suspicion that I might not ever turn into the person I'd been brought up to be. Proper and all that. Where was I headed? No clue.

Somehow we got on the subject of my fifth-grade teacher, Sister Frances Marian, who'd had her own theory about the way the universe worked. An elderly nun facing down thirty-seven children in a New York City classroom, she didn't go in for forgiveness or redemption or grace. Her thing was consequences. *That is going on your permanent record,* is how she put it. She had me believing that somewhere there is a piece of paper where every single thing a person has ever said or thought or done is written down.

I think she had a point, I told the detective, in his office. Not about the paper. About the existence of an objective reality, one that is wholly independent of what we might want it to be. What actually happened. I believe in that, I told him.

He hired me. "You are motivated by guilt, which means you will never stop until the job is done," he pronounced. I felt insulted and intrigued. How had he known? The job sounded impossible, in any case. I would be talking to strangers. Showing up unannounced on their doorsteps and asking for a moment of their time. It wasn't gumshoe stuff. No divorces, no cheating spouses. His clients were celebrities, Fortune 500 companies, *world leaders*—these last two words delivered in a hoarse growl that was somewhere between a shared confidence and a direct threat. Oh, and my dress was fine, my hair was fine, but the boots would be off-putting to elderly witnesses. With that, he sent me out on the road.

I never came back. Instead, I became a private detective. It freed me. It saved me.

And then it brought me full circle, to the mystery I'd tried so hard to leave behind.

After the execution, I kept running into Jesse Tafero.

The first time was the *20/20* program hosted by Barbara Walters in her yellow suit. "Has a mother of two spent sixteen years in prison because the real killer lied in court?" *20/20* asked. "Sonia Jacobs and her boyfriend both claimed to be innocent. He was executed, and yet some believe this man"—a picture of Walter Rhodes flashed onscreen—"is the actual killer."

Six months after *20/20* aired, Sunny Jacobs was released from prison. The United States Court of Appeals for the Eleventh Circuit threw out her murder conviction, ruling that the State of Florida had hidden a crucial piece of evidence in the case: a polygraph report that cast doubt on Walter Rhodes's truthfulness at trial. A damning lie detector test.

The appeals court ordered that Sunny be given a new trial, but since Walter had by then confessed to the murders many times himself, the state gave her a plea deal instead. Sunny Jacobs was free. Jesse Tafero, convicted on the same evidence, was dead.

"They were both innocent," Jesse's mother, Kay, told the Fort Lauderdale *Sun-Sentinel* after Sunny's release, in October 1992. "I'm never going to get my son back. They killed the wrong man."

Sunny Jacobs walked out of prison into a blaze of flashbulbs. A death row prisoner set free—it was a major news story even without Jesse's fiery execution just two years earlier. On the courthouse steps, Sunny let out a piercing cry. It was Walter Rhodes who murdered the police officers, she told reporters. But even so, Sunny had "no angry words" for the prosecutor who put her behind bars. "Being bitter is a waste of time," Sunny said. "And I happen to know, none of us have any time to waste." Later that day, Sunny's childhood rabbi spoke to the press on her behalf, calling her "a wonderful soul" who spent her time in prison meditating and inspiring fellow inmates. "She learned to get rid of negative things and let go of the pain in her life," Sunny's rabbi said. For her first night out of prison, Sunny's friends gathered together in an ocean-view room at the Fontainebleau in Miami Beach, where Sunny drank champagne and took a bubble bath, the *Sun-Sentinel* reported. "I don't know who I am. I am a newly created person," Sunny said. Jesse's mother called the moment bittersweet. "I would like to see them both out together, but I'm just happy for her," Kay Tafero said.

In 1996, ABC aired a TV movie about Jesse and Sunny and Walter. *In the Blink of an Eye* was a docudrama that showed Walter Rhodes framing Jesse and Sunny—young, trusting, and in love—for his own terrible crimes. "A true story of justice compromised," the *Los Angeles Times* called the movie. "Those arguing against capital punishment frequently point out cases in which the condemned are later found to be innocent. Sunday's ABC movie, *In the Blink of an Eye*, is about one such case."

In 1998, two noted death penalty scholars wrote a law review article about Jesse Tafero stating as fact that "a prosecution witness"—Walter Rhodes—had perjured himself on the stand and was "the real killer." The title of their article: "The Execution of the Innocent."

In press interviews—the stories always mentioned Jesse too—Sunny talked about having nightmares about being on death row again. Even so, she refused to be consumed by the past. She said her practice of yoga and forgiveness helped. "I figured if people could survive the concentration camps, then surely I could survive this," Sunny told the *St. Petersburg Times* in 1999. Now that Sunny was free, one paper reported, she worked in a convent, teaching yoga to nuns.

I watched it all. I read it all. I tried not to, but the news reports seemed to find me and stick like glue. Like quicksand. Sunny and Jesse. Jesse and Sunny. Every single thing I read and saw about them haunted me: two young lovers sent to death row on the false testimony of the true killer. I wanted to put the execution behind me and just get on with my life, but the news reports kept bringing that morning back. Jesse, masked, gagged, shuddering, flames shooting out of his head. Every time I saw his name, the world fell away and I could hear the buzzing in the death chamber. Feel it inside my own bones like it was still happening. I hated that feeling, but it never asked my permission. It just arrived.

I'd been tricked, obviously. Taken in by good-looking Walter Rhodes. There were not many hard facts to be had in the flood of news stories about the case, and not too much detail either about Jesse and Sunny and Walter—who they were, how they knew one another—so it was difficult to tell what exactly went down out there at the highway rest stop that morning, but no matter. The whole thing was incredibly upsetting. The calm, controlled, rational private detective I was becoming examined the news stories, looking for clues. But it felt like there was a whole other part of myself still back in the death chamber, watching Jesse Tafero die.

In 2002, *The Exonerated* made its debut off-Broadway. Billed as a documentary play about wrongful convictions, with every word drawn from court documents and letters and interviews, it was an immediate smash hit. "Someone else committed their crimes," *The New York Times* announced, calling the play "an artfully edited anthology of interviews with six former death row prisoners who were all discovered to be innocent of the crimes for which they were incarcerated." One of "the exonerated" was Sunny Jacobs. Telling her own story of innocence, and Jesse Tafero's too.

It was now more than a decade since Jesse's execution. During that time, I'd completed my training as an investigator, passed rigorous professional exams in two states to earn my private detective licenses, and opened my own detective agency. I'd spent tens of thousands of hours as a private eye investigating all kinds of cases: capital murders, extortion by kickboxers, cigarette trafficking, fires at sea, environmental pollution, bank fraud, theft of corporate secrets, and the dealings of syndicate kingpins. My entire professional life was all about tracking down facts. But even so, the facts of this mystery at the center of my own life continued to elude me. *Discovered to be innocent.* I accepted that. I believed it. I trusted the television specials and the news reports and the rave reviews of this new play. But: Discovered how? Discovered when? I wanted to know. I needed to know. Because I was having trouble figuring out how the eyewitnesses fit in.

Maybe it was because I was now a private detective, but after reading all the latest news stories about Jesse and Sunny and Walter, I'd gone and dug up some older clips too. And those older stories mentioned something that the more recent reports did not: Two independent eyewitnesses who'd seen the murders firsthand. Two truck drivers with nothing to gain either way. At Jesse's trial in 1976, those two truck drivers swore they saw Walter Rhodes standing with his hands in the air as the fatal gunshots rang out. Maybe it was no big deal. Eyewitnesses are unreliable, as everyone knows. But I was having trouble letting it go. If the eyewitnesses saw Walter standing with his hands in the air as the shots were fired, then how could Walter have killed two policemen? That question was starting to haunt me. I wanted to stop thinking about Jesse Tafero. About the ashes on his dress shirt afterwards, fallen down from his scalp. Was this burned man innocent? I had to know. Every time I read or heard his name now, I trembled. A hard shudder, brittle. Dark like a gravestone. I needed that feeling to stop.

And there was one other thing. It was something everyone agreed about—prosecution, defense, the eyewitnesses, even Jesse himself. As the first shot rang out that morning, the doomed officers had Jesse up against the police car. Restrained. Jesse Tafero, the man who went to the electric chair, could not possibly have acted alone. Someone else had to fire first. It wasn't the police officers—their hands, tested after their deaths, were clean of gunshot residue. So who did? Double-crossing Walter Rhodes, according to the current news reports. Perjurer, murderer. But that's not what the two truck drivers told the jury back in 1976. Their eyewitness testimony said the first shot had to have come from the woman who was famous now as a sweet, spiritual, tragically innocent yoga teacher: Sunny Jacobs herself.

One Sunday morning in November 2011, I was at my breakfast table, having coffee and reading *The New York Times*. I'd gotten married and moved east to Chicago; outside, the wind blew leaves along empty sidewalks, a first icy breath of winter. I opened the newspaper and took out the Style section, my favorite. And there was Sunny, surrounded by Hollywood actresses, smiling out from a color photograph splashed across the top of the society wedding page.

> Most married couples will tell you that the things they hold in common helped cement their relationships. For Sonia Jacobs, 64, and Peter Pringle, 73, married in New York last Sunday, common ground was the decade and a half each had served on death row before their convictions were overturned for the murders that they steadfastly maintained they did not commit.
>
> "We have each lived a nightmare," Ms. Jacobs, in a gold dress and matching pearls, whispered to a friend minutes before marrying Mr. Pringle, his snow-white beard aglow against the backdrop of a black suit and matching bow tie. "Now it's time to live our fairy tale."

I could feel myself starting to tremble.

Eight years ago, after reading those rave reviews, I'd gone to see *The Exonerated*, the play that had made an international star out of Sunny. And after seeing the play, I had visited Walter Rhodes. Again. To ask him, straight up this time, not as a dazzled young reporter but as a professional investigator: *Did you kill Florida Highway Patrol trooper Phillip Black and Canadian constable Donald Irwin?* Because that is what the play said, Walter. *Tell me the truth.*

But Walter Rhodes had not been a friendly prison inmate this time around. My attempt to confront him was a total disaster. And afterwards, I'd shut down. Just: no. I stopped talking about Jesse Tafero and Sunny Jacobs and Walter Rhodes. I stopped reading about them. I tried everything I could to put all of them the hell out of my mind. Shredding my files. Never mentioning my own experience as an eyewitness to an electric chair execution to anyone, ever. Silence, always. To erase, to disappear. Them, me. But even so, in my own home, here at my own breakfast table, on a Sunday morning no less, my ghost had found me. "Mr. Rhodes confessed to murdering the two officers," the *Times* said.

I am an idiot, I thought. A former reporter who should know better. A private detective who cannot let go. Gunfire, two mortally wounded police officers, all this pain.

Old murder cases are like coffins. Buried deep, holding a world of hurt. I knew this from the death row cases I'd worked on over the last two decades as a private eye. I was not going to lie to myself about it. You have to be careful, opening them up. You may find things you cannot forget. That you'll wish you'd never seen.

I knew, too, that trying to figure out the truth of Jesse Tafero's case would mean bringing murder back to the doorsteps of Trooper Phillip Black's and Constable Donald Irwin's families. I was not sure I had the right to do that. Reawakening the very worst part of the past—prying it open, picking it apart—when everyone else has put it away. Selfish. Arrogant. Self-important. Damaging. Futile, in any case. For naught.

Shivering at my breakfast table in Chicago, I don't know yet that when I finally do visit the widow of Trooper Black, she will greet me with kindness. She will tell me that Phil Black was a gentleman and a "really, really great father" to their little boy, who was just seven when his father was slain. "I would like to know the exact truth of what happened as well," Grace Black will tell me, her eyes steady and serious on mine. "If that is what you are doing, you have my blessing." From the depths of her loss, a shining generosity.

But I don't have the benefit of her benevolence yet. Right now, with this newspaper story in front of me, I only know that I have arrived at a turning point.

I've tried to ignore this mystery, this misery, which has grayed the edges of so many days. My unfinished story. I've tried to plead with it, to appease it, to surrender to it, to concede its points to it, to argue with it, and to bury it. But I keep waking up in the middle of it, this rattling echo, this old sorrow, these dead bones. I need it to go away and leave me alone.

It never has. It will not. It has become part of you.

There is only one way for that to no longer be true.

I'm a private detective. This is a mystery. I know what I have to do.

But I've never worked inside my own life before. Never dared to face my own shadows.

And I am afraid of ghosts.

PART ONE

Florida

A Real Strange Situation

Fort Lauderdale, Florida. January 2015. A dead-end street beneath a power plant, just west of downtown. Except for the metallic buzzing sound in the air around me, the day is empty and dusty and bright. I am standing in the middle of the street, listening to the power plant and staring at an apartment building. Single-story, chipped stucco, asphalt for a front yard. I've got an old newspaper clipping with me from the days immediately after the murders—"Witness Testifies Tafero Didn't Shoot"—and I dig it out now to double-check the address.

Yes. It started here.

In the winter of 1976, Walter Rhodes lived in this building. In Apartment B, up on the right, second door in from the street. One afternoon around Valentine's Day, just after *Taxi Driver* hit the movie theaters and as heiress Patty Hearst was standing trial for bank robbery out in California, Walter took a call in Apartment B from his friend Jesse Tafero. Jesse asked if he could come crash with his girlfriend and kids for a few days. Walter said okay. And on about their third day here together, Walter and Jesse and Sunny and the children came out of Apartment B, down this cement walkway, climbed into a red Ford Fairlane, and drove off. For Jesse Tafero, that trip ended in the electric chair.

There are some things I need to make clear, here at the outset. I'm a licensed private detective but I don't carry a gun. I've never slapped a witness or slept with one, although there've been some who deserved it and a few who tried it. All my life I've been mistaken for someone else—*Don't I know you? Haven't we met?*—and what people assume about me is usually wrong. I'm not going to lie: That used to piss me off. Once when I was a newspaper reporter, the press secretary to the governor of Florida asked me who I'd slept with to get my job. I wrote a whole newspaper column about how sexist and outrageous and unacceptably ubiquitous his attitude was. But not long into my new life as a detective I realized all that bullshit was now working in my favor. Being underestimated, talked over, talked down to, ignored, pitied, patronized, flirted with, hit on—all superpowers, to a professional investigator. No wonder women make good private eyes. For nearly twenty years now, I've earned my living by speaking to strangers, but in my own life I'm shy. And I don't know how I feel right now, standing here, except that I cannot believe it is real.

Four days ago, after I finally got up my nerve to do this, my husband and I shuttered our house up north, threw some clothes in the car, and headed off into a blizzard so fierce it took five hours to drive fifty miles. Trucks skidding off into drifts in Michigan, snow blowing across the road in Indiana, rain pounding down in the mountains of Tennessee. All the way along, I tried not to think about what I was getting myself into, but the electric chair flickered in the back of my mind. Now I'm in South Florida for the first time in a quarter century, standing on this street, looking at this building, and feeling—nothing. It's weird. Nothing at all.

Up at Apartment B, there's a doorbell, an aluminum threshold, and a window so dirty I can't see inside. I stand still for a moment, staring at a pile of cigarette butts on the ground. It's not that I'm expecting to trip over a bullet here and solve the case. But this threshold is the threshold Jesse and Sunny and Walter crossed, setting off. This roof is the last roof Jesse Tafero slept under as a free man. An investigation has to start somewhere, and I like to touch base. It's a form of superstition, possibly. The hope that the past will be present in a place.

And I don't have any other clues. This building. Some old newspaper clippings. A few court records. Seriously. That's it. With those as my starting point, I have to find the truth about two heartless murders committed almost forty years ago on the side of an interstate highway in a rest area that has long since been completely torn down. Obliterated. Erased.

Detective work is, in its essence, a form of time travel. It's being in two places at once—now, and then. Now being me, with all my fears and flaws. Then being the split seconds those shots rang out in the rest area. That is the instant I need to get back to. To own my life again. That.

I raise my hand. I knock.

But no luck. There's no sound. No one's around.

At the Fort Lauderdale courthouse the next day, I write the names *Jesse Joseph Tafero, Sonia Jacobs Linder,* and *Walter Norman Rhodes Jr.* on a piece of scrap paper and slide it to the clerk who sits behind a pane of bulletproof glass. It's a gorgeous day today—I drove along the Atlantic Ocean on my way here, cobalt waves beneath a clear blue sky—but this office is windowless with overhead lights that buzz and snap. I hate the buzzing. I've spent the morning calling my clients to tell them I'm taking some time off. I don't say why. Nobody wants a haunted detective. I've given myself three months here in Florida, from now until the end of March, to figure this case out. It's day two and already I feel like I'm running behind.

Now the clerk is coming toward me with a stack of boxes on a cart. Broward County's official court file for case number 76-127SCF, *State of Florida v. Tafero et al.* The case is thirty-nine years old and the boxes look alarming. Onionskin documents, faint purple mimeographs from the 1970s, mold on the pages, staples rusted in place. But somewhere in this mess are the undisputed facts of this mystery, the facts that have always been accepted by everyone as true. Every case has them, even this one. I reach into the box, take a file folder, and begin.

February 20, 1976. A Friday morning, about seven o'clock. In a rest area off Interstate 95, a beat-up green two-door Camaro is parked tight alongside a grassy curb. The car's windows are cracked open, its hood is bashed and rusted, the door on its passenger side is jammed shut, its front bumper is falling off. The sun is up but the day is foggy and the rest area is covered in white mist.

Inside the Camaro, lanky Walter Rhodes is asleep in the driver's seat. He's dressed in a silky blue shirt, corduroy trousers, a wide leather belt, and sneakers. He has dark shiny hair in bangs across his forehead and a mustache that is midway between male model and porn star. At his feet, a loaded gun.

Over in the front passenger seat: Jesse Tafero. Jesse is asleep too. He's wearing a tan leather jacket, a dress shirt, tan slacks, and white slip-on shoes. He has wavy brown hair, a mustache, thick muttonchop sideburns, and a dark beard. Around his neck, on his smooth bare chest, he wears a green-and-gold Buddha on a chain.

Jesse's girlfriend, Sunny Jacobs, is in the backseat, also asleep. Sunny is delicately built, five feet tall and one hundred pounds, with wide brown eyes and long hair. She's got on a green pullover sweater, loose on her thin shoulders, and bell-bottom jeans. With her are two sleeping children: nine-year-old Eric and little Tina, ten months. A denim bag with pink baby pajamas is at Sunny's feet.

Just past seven o'clock, a marked Florida Highway Patrol cruiser pulls in off Interstate 95, Trooper Phillip Black at the wheel. Trooper Black is starting his shift this morning with a routine patrol of the highway rest areas. Waking people up, checking they're okay: He's told friends that he considers it one of the basic duties of his job. Black is tall and fit, with short brown hair and a square jaw; clean-cut, friendly, helpful, and popular, he's a central-casting version of a handsome state trooper. He's also a former United

States Marine who picks up his young son from school after his shift ends and stays a moment to help tidy up the classroom too. Today he's wearing his Florida Highway Patrol uniform: light brown shirt and trousers, black epaulets, belt, and shoes, a cream Stetson hat. Black has a fully loaded .357 Magnum service revolver strapped in a holster at his waist. And this morning, Black has a friend riding along.

Donald Irwin is a Canadian constable who, along with his wife, has been spending the week as a guest of the Black family. Both officers are white, thirty-nine years old, and married with children. It's the last day of Irwin's Florida vacation; tomorrow he and his wife are heading home to the Ontario cold. As a ride-along, Irwin is here as an observer with no official police powers, so he is dressed in civilian clothes: a white knit T-shirt, gray Levi's, brown shoes. He's wearing gold-framed aviator eyeglasses. He is unarmed. Irwin has been a police officer in Canada since 1958, and in those eighteen years, he has never once fired a weapon in the line of duty or come face-to-face with a gunman.

In his cruiser, Black pulls alongside the Camaro. The two cars are side by side now, with the cruiser on the left. Black parks, and he and Irwin step out into the morning mist. As Irwin hangs back, Black walks over to the Camaro. Two young children, asleep in the backseat. A fragile-looking young woman, sleeping with them. Walter, asleep in the driver's seat. There's a handgun at Walter's feet. A Smith & Wesson 9mm semiautomatic, black steel with a wood grip.

Trooper Black reaches into the Camaro and takes the gun.

That wakes everybody up.

Black asks Walter for identification. Walter hands over his driver's license and then steps out of the Camaro. Black takes Walter's license and the gun, goes to his FHP cruiser, and radios in.

TROOPER BLACK: We've got a real strange situation here. Need some 28s and 29s. First one is . . . on a weapon, Smith & Wesson, uh, it's a .38 automatic, serial number is A187854, that

will be A Adam 187854—correct that to a 9mm semiautomatic. Then run one on a Walter Norman Rhodes, R-H-O-D-
E-S, Jr., W/M, DOB 9-2-50. Then run a 10-29 on 10-169558,
10-169558, and we believe there's a weapon under the front
seat and we're having trouble getting the two people out of
there, we'll let you know in just a second.

The two people that Black is "having trouble" with are Jesse, in
the front seat, and Sunny, in the backseat with the children.

Dispatch radios back: Walter Norman Rhodes Jr. is on parole.

Black orders Walter to get up to the front of the cars. Next Black
stands at the open door on the driver's side of the Camaro and
talks to Jesse and Sunny. Minutes pass. Then Black radios in again.

TROOPER BLACK: *10-24 Lauderdale.*

10-24 means *send help.*
The radio goes dead.

Outside the courthouse, dusk has fallen. Gone is the Kodachrome
afternoon; in its place, a black-and-white world, night sky and
streetlights, shadows and glare. I find my car in the gravel parking
lot and head back along the ocean to the bungalow my husband
and I have rented for the winter. A fifties throwback with jalousie
windows and terrazzo floors, it's nothing like home. I live in Michigan now; we left Chicago a year and a half ago, trading the clash
and clamor of the city for a house by the lake in the pine woods. It's
quiet there, and dark, no streetlights, just foxes in the fields at
night, bare branches, a silvery moon. Here in Florida, the very
sunshine feels flagrant and outrageous. And I don't recognize this
place at all. Back when I was a reporter, I spent a lot of time in Fort
Lauderdale. Drinking, dancing, running around. After the execution, that all fell apart. I haven't been back since, and now, twenty-
five years later, nothing looks familiar. Everything is bigger, taller,
faster, brighter. I'd always worried that maybe no one would talk

to me if I ever came to ask them about this. But maybe that won't be the problem. Maybe no one will even remember.

"One of them is lying about the murders," I tell my husband, when I get home. Peter is making dinner. He's a private detective too. That's not how we met, though, or why we're together. "It's either Walter or Sunny. I am going to find out who."

"Holy God," Peter says. He has stopped cooking.

"It's not entirely impossible," I say. No reason for him to look so shocked.

"No, outside. Behind you. Turn around. That building right behind us is on—"

I whip around.

"*Fire,*" I say.

In the distance, a high wail. Sirens. Getting closer.

2
=

By Glue and by Dream

Two fifty-seven the next morning. I am wide awake. It was past midnight when the fire trucks and their flashing lights departed, and I've given up on sleep and come into the living room. A breeze has picked up off the ocean and the air smells of salt. Before turning in last night, I started watching a movie, and when I open my laptop here it is, onscreen. Paul Newman in a prison uniform. *Cool Hand Luke,* from the book by Donn Pearce. Yesterday at the courthouse, I saw Donn Pearce's name in the case file. For forty days in 1976, the file said, Donn Pearce worked on the case. He was Jesse Tafero's private investigator.

Each of our days is connected to the other by all sorts of personal artifacts, attached together by glue and by dream. That's from his book. Donn Pearce lives in Fort Lauderdale. I am going to talk to him later today. To try, anyway. *And those lives, long since dead, sound like a distant melody played on a muted saxophone.*

Nineteen years ago, after I went for that first interview with the detective in his mansion in San Francisco, he sent me down to Los

Angeles and out into the desert alone. It was a test. I had a rental car, a list of names, a paper map, and some quarters for the pay phone. To call back to the office, not to call ahead. We never call ahead, the detective said. Get out to the house, ring the bell, tell them you're a private detective, and ask for a moment of their time. Don't lie. Don't make promises. No bribes. No favors. No threats. All of that shit will backfire in the courtroom. There are so many ways to fuck up. Do not fuck up.

Right away I hated it. Standing there on the front doormat in my polka-dot dress, business card in hand. The witnesses on my list were retired mechanics who'd built fighter planes during World War II, and I needed to ask them about the toxic chemicals used in the factory. Chemicals that had dripped down through the sand and polluted the water underneath the entire basin. *No. Not interested. Not willing to get involved.* With the sun beating down through my windshield, I got turned around in the glare, and did not even notice that I'd driven farther out into the desert until the dust cloud in my mirror got too big to ignore.

I braked hard, came to a halt, and stepped out of the car into the heat. I took my map and spread it across the hood of the car. Back to the main street, turn right, down two more and right again—I was concentrating so hard that it took me a moment to feel it.

This. The big emptiness. Sand and sky, arcing, the low roar of the road in the distance, the echo. I stood up straight and took a better look around.

Nothing. As far as I could see.

I felt a rush of awe. Rising, alive. And surprise. I could not believe it. I had finally, finally found it. The place I'd been searching for since the day I saw Jesse Tafero die.

Away.

I spent the next two decades on the road.

Grand Bahama Island: sawgrass and pine, wild dogs in the underbrush, and half-built buildings falling down, gray like bone.

Seattle: caviar at a marble-topped bar in a candlelit restaurant, the waterfront outside rain-swept and lavender beneath a lowering sky. Biloxi: boiled peanuts out of the can for dinner in my motel room as I tried not to look at the floral bedspreads, the same dark roses as there had been at Starke. I learned that you can't tail someone by driving in front of them, that it's a bad idea to fall asleep in your car when you're trying to serve a subpoena, and to always make sure you stay between the witness and the door. There were four of us operatives working for the detective, and sometimes we did cases together—getting our instructions over a speakerphone like a scene out of *Charlie's Angels*—but mainly I was out on my own. Days upon days, I spoke to no one but the people I'd been assigned to and my boss the detective, who yelled. The detective yelled when I did a bad job and when I did well too. It was strangely motivating. When I started out, cellphones were a new luxury technology, email was not oxygen yet, and at home I was living alone. But the solitude suited me. And the velocity. That felt necessary, like rain.

Today I arrive at the courthouse to find that the clerks have stacked my tattered file boxes next to a spare desk and reserved it for me. I am still going through the documents, learning the basics of the case. "See? We try to keep it nice here. Try to keep it positive," a court clerk says. A long scar runs across the back of his head, baseball-stitched, as if someone had cut his skull open, lifted it off, and sewed it back on.

10-24 Lauderdale.

As Black's shout sparks out across the airwaves, the Florida Highway Patrol rushes to his rescue. *Lauderdale, all units.* But the first trooper who reaches the rest area finds Trooper Black and Constable Irwin unconscious on the ground next to the Camaro, bleeding hard from gunshot wounds to their heads. "Send some help," the trooper pleads, into the radio. He's weeping. Black's cruiser is gone. Stolen.

A short distance north, a security guard is waving the police cruiser through the entrance gate of a retirement village, not noticing that it's Walter Rhodes in his groovy shirt at the wheel. In the village parking lot, a kindly gentleman in horn-rimmed eyeglasses sees the police cruiser come in. Someone in the village is having a medical problem, he thinks. He starts over to see if he can help. He is holding the keys to a late-model orange and cream Cadillac. The cruiser rolls up to him, and Walter and Jesse step out, guns drawn. "We have to get a child to the hospital," Jesse says, taking the keys from his hand.

Fifteen minutes later, out on the far western edge of the county, the Cadillac bears down on a police roadblock. Walter is at the wheel again. Sunny and the two children are in the front seat. Jesse is in the back, next to the frightened owner of the Cadillac, now a hostage. They don't see the roadblock—three police cruisers, sharpshooters leaning on the hoods of the cars—until they're right on top of it.

As everyone else in the Cadillac ducks down, Walter accelerates straight into the gunfire. A rifle shot hits the left front tire and the car starts to spin. Then a shotgun blast tears through the driver's-side door of the Cadillac and slams into Walter's left knee. The Cadillac veers off the road, crashes headfirst into a dump truck, and comes to a halt surrounded by police officers who have their rifles drawn.

The officers pull Walter and Jesse out of the car, throw them to the ground, handcuff them, and place them under arrest.

On Walter Rhodes, officers find a fully loaded handgun stuffed down the back of his pants. "I didn't shoot anybody," Walter says.

On Jesse Tafero, officers find a fully loaded handgun in a holster on his right hip, along with two clips of ammunition. "I didn't kill nobody, I don't know nothing," Jesse says. "Oh shit."

Leonard Levinson, the Cadillac's owner, the hostage, tries to get out of the car but a trooper raps his shotgun sharply on the window and Levinson stays where he is. The officer thinks Levinson is "terrified."

The officers at first treat Sunny as a hostage as well, but as they are leading her and the children away from the Cadillac, Sunny bursts over to where Jesse is lying handcuffed on the ground. "I'm with this man," she tells a trooper. The trooper frisks her and puts her and the children in the back of a police car. The roadblock commander confiscates Sunny's designer purse from the Cadillac. Inside is a loaded .38 caliber revolver. "Please don't kill me," Sunny pleads.

Westbound from the courthouse, the Fort Lauderdale traffic heads directly into the sun. I still don't remember this city. A few tiny flashes here and there, maybe. That thatched-roof bar on Dixie Highway—was that where those pool parties happened on Sunday afternoons? Now the route to the address I found for Donn Pearce is threading through an anywhere landscape of gas stations and strip malls as the residue from my window wash turns the world blind. Jesse and Walter both had loaded guns on them when they were arrested that morning. And Sunny had a loaded gun in her purse. Interesting. I had not known that. I hang a left onto a street shaded by live oak trees; entering the gray-green light beneath their branches is like diving below the surface of a pond. I don't need to look at the house numbers to know which belongs to Donn Pearce. On this block of lookalike bungalows, his must be the mansion built of coral rock and draped in Spanish moss, ethereal, fantastic, alive.

Pay attention to what the house looks like, the detective in San Francisco told us. *Write it down.* It's not because your house is a window to your soul. It's because that way, if you claim you've never met me, I can ask: Is there a collection of vintage Coke cans in your kitchen? Do you have a three-legged dog? It's habit by now. I've knocked on a lot of doors. Hi, your name, my name, I'm a private investigator, can we talk. But low-key, mild-mannered. A mirror. A blank slate.

Four years after I started as a private eye, I founded my own firm with my friend Freya. That's not her real name. We'd worked together for the detective in San Francisco. Freya is a diplomat's daughter, brought up all over the world, effortlessly elegant in her faded Levi's, brilliant at talking to absolutely anyone anywhere. Married to a rocket scientist, a real one. Right away, we were busy. We never advertised. Our clients found us strictly by word of mouth. Big, complicated cases—ships catching fire in the middle of the night, cigarettes spirited across state lines, secrets stolen from companies and offered for sale—that had us flying off to Alaska and counting mile markers along two-lane blacktops in Texas and being waved past security guards inside skyscrapers in New York City, *Hello I'm so sorry I just need one minute of your time.*

We worked on criminal cases. On murder cases. An investigator on a murder case gets to know the whole show. The trial facts, yes, but the secrets too, details so high-octane and hideous that they never make it anywhere near the courtroom. Donn Pearce was Jesse Tafero's private investigator. If I can convince Donn Pearce to talk to me, I'm figuring, I'll have my answers and be off back home tomorrow to the snow and my pajamas, where I belong.

Okay, I tell myself. Notebook. Pen. Keys. *Hello, Mr. Pearce? My name is*—and, right, here it is, the fast stab of pure dread I feel every time I face a new door. Every single time, for almost twenty years. I jumped out of an airplane once—skydiving—and it feels just like that: *Oh God why am I up here what am I doing what happens next?* I never know what happens next. But I realized a long time ago that the trick is to just jump anyway. Don't spend too long looking. It's a long way down.

A calico cat is at the front door as I climb the steps. I ring the bell. I hear the sound of a heavy object being dragged over gravel. I turn around. A large man is coming up the driveway, sweating. He is lugging a garbage can.

"Hi," I say, walking back down the steps toward him. "Is this the address for Donn Pearce?"

"Why?" the man says.

Instantly a rotor blade starts up inside my rib cage. Metal, sharp. It's my usual anxiety plus—a lot. *Shit.* I have spent the last decade trying not to say Jesse Tafero's name out loud to anyone. Ever. Part of my failed attempt to not care. Now I have to say it. Right now. It feels absurdly personal. Confessing my obsession, to this stranger. *Welcome to my ghost story.*

Inside, Donn Pearce is having lunch at his kitchen table. With him is Big Momma, a tabby cat. Donn's best-screenplay Oscar nomination for *Cool Hand Luke* hangs on the wall behind him, signed by Gregory Peck.

"This lady is here to talk to you about a case you investigated," the man from outside says. He's Donn's son.

"I just saw you on *To Tell the Truth,*" I tell Donn, slipping into a chair and getting my notebook out. I found the old TV show online, from 1966, watched it before coming over here. Donn handsome and self-assured in a dark suit. Merchant seaman, short-order cook, safecracker, convict who spent two years on a chain gang— that's how the show described his career, pre-*Luke*. And after *Cool Hand Luke*, Donn was a private detective in South Florida for two decades. He got a special dispensation from the governor to carry a gun.

Outside in the driveway, Donn's son had warned me that his father's memory is not so great anymore. Now he writes *Jesse Tafero* and *1976* on a piece of paper and slides it across the table to his father.

Donn studies the paper intently. I watch him, hoping. But then he shakes his head.

I feel crushed. Literally. It's like two hands have taken my rib cage and are squeezing hard, one on each side.

"Well," I say, after a moment. "I really appreciate the—"

"One second," Donn's son says. He leaves the room and returns holding a cardboard box. "There might be something in here," he says, handing it to me.

The box is full of paper, a couple of hundred pages total, typed and stacked in date order. Each sheet an investigative report written by Donn Pearce, every single one so sharp it could cut glass. *It was clear that she does not want to testify, that she was frightened and she was lying.* Another: *The witness is likeable, but violent.* Wait, here's a report from 1976. In what feels like slow motion, I reach into the box.

But it's a divorce case involving an errant wife in a red dress, a set of translucent bedroom curtains, and a damp douche bag. Not Jesse Tafero.

"How in the world did you get all this?" I ask Donn, looking up from the report.

"It's a game of playing dumb," Donn Pearce says, about investigation. "I'm no dummy but I let people think I am—that's the job. You know everything and you don't know anything, and you have to decide when to flip the switch."

I nod.

"But I never pulled a punch," he continues. "There's a lot of bullshit in the job, but there was no bullshit coming from me. I built a reputation on that. I hit the nail on the head. If it meant someone went to the electric chair, then they went to the electric chair."

"Right, but how do you know?" I ask him. Bullshit versus notbullshit. "How can you tell one from the other?"

Well, okay, Donn says. First off, he's seen all of life, up, down, and sideways, and having been in prison himself, he knows how to handle even the toughest situations. But really, there is just one key. Do I want to know what it is?

I do, yes.

"I *absorb*," Donn says, his eyes alight.

As he says it, I can feel it. He's absorbing right now. Everything in the room is running downhill toward him. I suddenly know how moths feel when the porch light comes on.

"Also, you have to be tough with yourself, and what you know, and how you screwed up too," Donn Pearce adds.

Did I screw up? I must have. I know that.

A thunderstorm shakes the house around midnight, and I wake early to sunlight as clear as rainwater. Out on the front lawn, white ibis stilt across on hairpin legs, stabbing the grass with curved beaks. It's very odd, I tell Peter. We're walking over to the beach along a sidewalk lined with hibiscus and bougainvillea, past tall hedges whose leaves shine in the breeze, evergreen. I was so scared of coming here and now I'm kicking myself for not doing it sooner, I say. Getting started feels like such a relief. Even the ashes from the fire next door look fine in this light, just an anthracite incident, no harm done.

At the ocean, Peter takes off for a run while I wade into the clear shallows. After reading the files yesterday at the courthouse, and spending time with Donn Pearce—*you have to be tough with yourself*—a memory has surfaced that I'd long ago put away.

That morning, on the way out of the death chamber, I walked along the Plexiglas directly past Jesse in the electric chair. His body was sitting bolt upright, his head wrapped in a black leather hood. Dead. I'd just seen him struggling and staring at me and speaking his last words and, as the guards moved in to gag him, slowly closing his eyes. I got in the van with the other reporters and rode out past the barbed wire to the grass lot where we'd started. There, a small group of demonstrators was waiting, including a Catholic nun. I made my way over to interview her. She told me that executing people was not a solution to violence. I listened, I took notes. I wrote her name down. I was trying not to blink. Every time I blinked, I saw flames, and smoke.

The nun reached out and put her hand on my shoulder.

"What do I do now?" I asked her. Not as a reporter. As me.

"Bear witness," Sister Helen Prejean told me.

Around me, the beach is starting to fill up with sunbathers. I've brought along some copies from the courthouse and I take them out now. They're sworn statements from Jesse's friends, part of a petition his legal team was putting together in 1989, trying to save his life. Other than seeing him die, I don't know the first thing about Jesse Tafero. But to find out what happened in those split seconds at the rest area—to bear witness—I need to know everything. I need the permanent record. For Jesse, and for Sunny and Walter too.

Jesse Joseph Tafero. Brown hair, brown eyes. Six feet tall, 145 pounds. Born in Jersey City, New Jersey, in October 1946 to Jesse Senior and Kathleen, who went by Kay. Jesse Senior was a used car salesman. Kay was a miner's daughter, born in rural Wales. She came to Pennsylvania with her father as a young girl. After Kay and Jesse Senior married, Kay joined a women's club in Neptune City, New Jersey, where she helped with the refreshments and the afternoon teas, always as "Mrs. Jesse Tafero." Jesse Junior was their only child and Kay doted on him.

Little Jesse was sickly, Kay wrote in her statement. Frail. It worried her. So when a doctor told them little Jesse needed warmth, they sold up and moved to Miami. It was the mid-1950s, a boom time. Flamingos, flower gardens, swanky hotels out on the beach, with diving shows in the afternoon and Frank Sinatra at night. The Fontainebleau. The Eden Roc. Everyone decked out in black tie, the women with their beautiful jewels, luminous in the neon night. In Miami, Jesse's father bought a used car dealership just south of the Little River. But they were poor, and Jesse was ashamed of that; he was teased at school for his old clothes, which embarrassed him. His father beat him and locked him in closets, where Jesse screamed and cried to no avail, his mother wrote. The family attended Catholic church, and Jesse was an altar boy when he was young. "Jesse has never in his life been a violent person," Kay Tafero wrote. "He just wanted peace and quiet."

When I look Kay up, I find she died ten years ago. But there are other people who knew Jesse I can try to talk to. I decide to start with a friend of Jesse's named Marianne, mainly because she lives near our rented bungalow in Fort Lauderdale. But also because she was a Playboy Bunny and her affidavit doesn't mention Jesse being an altar boy at all.

3

==

The Most Dangerous People

"Marianne?"

The house is a buttercup-yellow cottage with a white Mercedes in the driveway and a pot of pink geraniums on the porch. I am on the porch as well, and I am having second thoughts. My skydive anxiety, as usual, plus it's hot out, there's no doorbell, my skirt is sticking to the backs of my knees, and I am not ready, it's too soon, what am I doing here, I need to be better prepared, I should leave and come back later. Or never. *Hi, Marianne, remember your friend Jesse? Well, I saw him die.* That feels crazy. Because it is crazy. I think I'll just—

"Who is it?" a voice calls out, from behind the door.

"Marianne?" I say.

"Yes? Who is it?"

"Marianne, I need to talk to you about someone—"

Okay.

"Jesse Tafero," I call out.

A moment. Then the jangle of keys in locks.

A woman in a pink polo shirt and slim sand-colored capri

slacks stands in the doorway staring at me. Big blue eyes, dark blue eyeliner, a bombshell figure, cotton-candy lip gloss. Blond hair tumbles in thick ringlets down past her hourglass waist.

"Yes, I knew Jesse," she says, in a sweet whisper.

And she opens the door wide so I can step inside.

I am in a front parlor with two velvet armchairs and a fireplace. After the heat and light outside, the cool darkness is like stepping into a stone church. Around us, the house stretches away, oriental carpets and beveled-glass French doors and good antiques. On the wall to my right hangs a portrait of a young woman in farmer's overalls, blond curls tied up in a red kerchief, denim straps strained to bursting over her bare breasts. She looks, I notice, just like Marianne. She is holding a daisy and smiling.

Marianne has taken a seat in one of the velvet armchairs, and when I tear my eyes away from the painting I find she is watching me. This friend of Jesse Tafero's. "I was just thinking about Jesse when I heard you at the door," Marianne says. She seems so much less surprised than I am that I'm here.

It was 1973, Marianne begins. Back in those days, she owned a bar in Miami called the Gold Dust Lounge.

I've taken a seat in the velvet armchair across from hers and am balancing my notebook on my lap. I'd been thinking we would inch delicately toward the reason for my visit today, but no. We're into it. That happens sometimes.

The Gold Dust was an after-hours bar in a basement opposite the Playboy Club, over on Biscayne Boulevard near the beach. It had live music—cool jazz, saxophones—and dancing and drinks until two A.M. A fun, popular place. This kid named Jesse used to hang out at the Gold Dust, and one night he asked Marianne for a job. Jesse was twenty-seven then, a good-looking, soft-spoken young man. Always in chinos, never in jeans. Marianne was older, thirty-seven, married. Jesse seemed too fragile for the real world, Marianne thought. So Marianne had him help her around her house. Odd jobs, for pocket money.

"Jesse was very, very sensitive," she says.

When she says that, I sit still for a moment. Absorbing.

Last weekend, Marianne says, she spent a day cleaning out her house. No one lives forever, is why. She's in her seventies now and she wants to save her children from having to go through her things after she's gone. In a back closet, she found a box of letters from her children, and some from Jesse too. Letters Jesse wrote to her from death row. She spent yesterday reading the letters from her children and destroying them. It's time to let go, she tells me. This afternoon she had just taken Jesse's letters out, to read and destroy them too, when she heard me at the front door.

"It's so funny you came by today," she says.

"I almost didn't," I tell her.

She reaches over and puts her hand on my arm. Her touch, like her voice, is soft and warm.

"Did you ever talk to Jesse about what happened?" I ask.

"He verbally told me he didn't do it. He said, 'I did not do it.'"

Marianne goes opaque for a moment. A candle, blown out. Then she stands up and walks into the next room. When she comes back, she's holding a piece of paper. It's my newspaper article "3 jolts used to execute killer."

"Have you seen this?"

"I wrote that."

Marianne looks at me, then looks down again at the paper.

"Did he scream?" she asks.

"They gagged him."

We sit there for another moment. Marianne gets up again, and this time she comes back holding a stack of envelopes with bright red prison postmarks.

"Do you want these?" she asks.

That night, I sit at the dining room table in our rented bungalow with Jesse's letters from death row. Outside, there is a wind through the palm fronds, a deep rush and rustle as they sway. As I open one of the envelopes, a Polaroid falls out. A thin pale man in prison whites. He has a thumb looped in his waistband, a pair of wire-rimmed amber-lensed sunglasses dangling from his collar, and a gold watch on his left wrist. Jesse Tafero. He's smiling. There's a letter with the Polaroid, dated March 1988, which would have been right after Jesse won a stay on his second death warrant. The letter is about the warrant and the run-up to his execution, the one that was called off.

"The whole situation was such a nightmare," Jesse writes.

His penmanship is all slashes and loops, and it takes me a while to decipher, this faded blue ink on paper turned brittle with age.

Hearing that his death warrant had been signed was difficult, Jesse is saying. And the warrant meant each new dawn brought him one day closer to the date set for his death—a countdown, a pressure cooker, a "definite physio-psychological torture experience" that made him feel kinship with slaves and revolutionaries and even "Christ himself." And every moment, the prison around him rang and echoed with the cries of one hundred caged men screaming and cursing. A high-pitched noise riot twenty-four hours a day.

At times he felt hopeless, he confides. But coming close to death also put him in touch with "deep, intuitive and valid insights into the meaning of things like courage, love, friendship, faith, wisdom"—those words all in one line across the bottom of a page, keeling sideways like sails pushed by a gust of wind.

And now, having survived the warrant, still alive, Jesse feels optimistic. Determined. Courageous.

"Things will all go right," Jesse's letter says. "I'm sure."

After I read the letter, I put it down on the table and sit for a long moment, listening to the wind outside. My ghost has taken on color. I feel—I'm not sure. Sad. So sad.

Later, I can't sleep. I tiptoe into the living room and switch on my laptop. After reading Jesse's letters to Marianne, I'm curious about her.

"Two Bombs Rip Home of Underworld Figure." A story from my old newspaper *The Miami Herald* floats up onto my screen in the dark room. It seems to be about Marianne.

In 1967, a bomb blew up a "sleek red high-powered speedboat" docked at the home of Marianne and her husband, blowing two doors off the house and shattering every window, the story says. Another bomb wrecked the "sky blue Cadillac" parked in the car-port. Two days later, a third bomb sent the family's cabin cruiser to the bottom of Biscayne Bay. The boat was named for Marianne, "a 101-pound Playboy Bunny," the *Herald* reported. "Rubble and shattered glass" covered the house and the lawn, but no one was hurt.

"Jewel fancier John Clarence Cook" is how the *Herald* described Marianne's husband. Cook was a master of disguise and the best jewelry thief in the business, according to a sworn statement from the man who planted the bombs, I'm reading now. Cook pulled off high-profile heists in Belgium and the Bahamas and Miami Beach, and one night he was said to have escaped police in his speedboat, a volley of gunshots across the dark waters as he fled with his run-ning lights out. A few years before the bombings, FBI agents inves-tigating the theft of a priceless sapphire and other precious gems from the American Museum of Natural History in New York City tailed John Clarence Cook around Miami. Three beach boys—one of whom was a suave stunt diver famous for his act at Miami Beach hotels—had confessed to the daring theft, and the sapphire, a cabochon rock nicknamed the Star of India, turned up in a bus station locker in Miami, but some of the other jewels—including a one-hundred-carat ruby—were still missing. When the FBI staked out John Clarence Cook after the heist, Cook rammed the agents' car.

As I'm scrolling through the old news stories, a short wire report catches my eye. In January 1975, Marianne was arrested by federal narcotics agents who alleged she was part of a drug-smuggling ring.

Odd jobs. Pocket money. Miami, the 1970s.

I am a fucking moron. Of course: *cocaine*.

Twenty-four million dollars in smuggled drugs, operatives in Colombia and Miami, eighteen people indicted as federal Drug Enforcement Administration agents tried to smash the ring. The wire story has a quote from one of the DEA agents and I read it over and over, trying to square it with the gorgeous, sweet, soft-spoken woman I met yesterday.

"These," the agent said, "are the most dangerous people I've ever encountered in my years as a lawman."

4

=

No One Is Going to Talk to You

Pine trees, a green car, a white sky. Blood.

It's the morning after my conversation with Marianne. I am at the dining room table again, next to the pile of Jesse's letters. I am not reading the letters. I'm staring at my husband's computer. On the screen is Friday, February 20, 1976. The day exactly. The sunlight and shadows of that morning, flickering.

Look, there's the Camaro. Dusty, dirty. There's Constable Irwin, on the ground, under a yellow tarp. Trooper Black has been taken away in an ambulance, but his cream Stetson is still where it fell, right by the Camaro's front tire—next to a small shiny gun. And blood. So much blood. Bright red and so thick, like paste. A thick bright red pool at the driver's-side door.

"How did you find this?" I ask Peter.

Peter shrugs. He searched the video collection of Miami Dade College. The Wolfson Archives. Newsreels. "But I've never seen it before," I say, almost in protest. It's been all around me in the ether this whole time.

I hit pause, rewind, and watch it again. My stomach feels like it is filled with burning cement. And again. And again. I'm looking for the truck drivers, to see if they're on this tape too. Their statements are in the case file at the courthouse: the eyewitnesses.

At the rest area, it's close to seven-thirty in the morning now. Mist covers the ground still, shrouding the cars and the spindly pines. At the south end of the lot, a truck driver is pulling in to check the lights on his tractor-trailer. Pierce Hyman is fifty years old, from Jacksonville, Florida. He's working for Pilot Freight. As he brings his big rig to a halt, Hyman can see a Camaro and a Florida Highway Patrol cruiser parked side by side, up at the north end of the lot, near the entrance ramp that leads back onto the interstate. There's some action going on up there. Hyman sees Trooper Phillip Black standing at the open door on the driver's side of the Camaro, bending forward, looking inside the car. There's a man in a brown jacket sitting in the driver's seat of the Camaro. That is Jesse Tafero. Another man stands outside the Camaro at the front of the cars. Walter Rhodes.

Now Hyman watches as Trooper Black straightens up and walks over to his FHP cruiser. Black is at the cruiser for a couple of minutes, on the radio. Then Black walks back toward the Camaro. As Black approaches, Jesse stands up from the driver's seat and gets out of the Camaro. A sudden scuffle. Black grabs Jesse. Constable Donald Irwin steps in to help. Black and Irwin have Jesse pressed up against the cruiser; they are trying to restrain him. Now Black is backing off and drawing his gun. When Black does that, Hyman sees Walter Rhodes, up at the front of the cars, "put his hands in the air." Then:

> The trooper was standing at about the door of the Camaro. The shots appeared to come out of the back of the car, through the left side. . . . I heard the patrolman say "Oh my God, I've been shot."

Pierce Hyman is not the only independent eyewitness to the murders. Truck driver Robert McKenzie sees them too. McKenzie is thirty-two and driving for Food Fair, in Miami. He's in the rest area on his morning coffee break, in the cab of his tractor-trailer rig. Through the mist, up ahead, McKenzie can just make out the cruiser parked next to the beat-up Camaro. He sees Trooper Black standing at the door of the Camaro, talking to Jesse, who is sitting in the driver's seat, sideways, with one foot on the ground. He sees Walter outside the car, walking around. Now Trooper Black is bending down to look inside the Camaro. Black stays like that for a while. McKenzie thinks the trooper must be talking to someone in the backseat of the car.

McKenzie's coffee break is over. Still watching, McKenzie puts his truck in gear and starts easing toward the highway entrance ramp. The route takes him close to the Camaro. There's Trooper Black, stepping in toward Jesse to frisk him. Jesse, jumping backwards. Constable Irwin stepping to assist. The two officers push Jesse up against the cruiser. Now Black is backing off and drawing his gun. Black points his weapon directly at Walter Rhodes. Walter puts his hands up in the air. "The guy reached his hands up," McKenzie says.

Then: *I heard five shots. And the officer fell instant, and then the other guy fell right behind the officer.*

McKenzie cannot see who fires the gun. But he is watching Jesse and Walter as the shots go off. They are both standing outside the Camaro. Neither one of them has a gun.

"You could see them clear?" a detective asks McKenzie.

"Could see them clear," McKenzie replies.

Right before he hears the shots, McKenzie sees someone sitting in the backseat of the Camaro. Directly behind the driver's seat, immediately inside the open door of the car, just a few feet away from Trooper Black. A person with "long, light, light brown, sandy hair."

A woman.

"Sometimes things happen that you have no control over in life, and this was one of them. I was there in the car with my children, in the backseat, and it never occurred to me that I would ever be accused," Sunny told *20/20,* in 1992.

"I was a vegetarian, I wouldn't have killed a fly," she told the BBC in 2007.

"I was a peace and love vegetarian. Violence was anathema to my life," Sunny wrote.

· That last quote is from a book Sunny wrote about her case. I have it with me in my car. It's afternoon now and I am threading my way through a lost corner of tiny Dania Beach, Florida, a stitch of crabgrass just south of the Fort Lauderdale airport, looking for an address. Sunny's book is called *Stolen Time.* The front cover describes it as "the inspiring story of an innocent woman condemned to death." It quotes my *Miami Herald* story about Jesse's execution on page 490.

"A remarkable book," the *Daily Mail,* a British newspaper— circulation 1.16 million—calls it, according to a blurb on the front cover.

"An extraordinary and inspirational story," says the actor Susan Sarandon, in red ink on the back cover. Sarandon played Sunny in the movie version of *The Exonerated,* released in 2005. "Sunny Jacobs is a remarkable woman."

But people who knew Sunny Jacobs back in the day seem to have a different take.

Marianne, the Playboy Bunny, for one. Marianne knew Jesse before he and Sunny got together, and she knew them as a couple too. "I don't think any of this would ever have happened if it hadn't been for Sunny," Marianne told Jesse's lawyers. Marianne thought Sunny was "a complete sociopath," a weapons-obsessed rich girl with millionaire parents and a fascination with machine-gun-toting heiress Patty Hearst. Guns excited Sunny, Marianne said. Guns thrilled her. When I asked Marianne who she thought was responsible for the murders, Marianne did not hesitate.

"I think Sunny did it. I believe the truck drivers."

"The truck drivers?"

"Yes. The ones who saw Jesse bent over the police car during the shooting. I believe them."

A cold, controlling "princess" who was "into gun warfare." That's how Marianne described Sunny in the affidavit she gave Jesse's attorneys in 1989. "She thought she was Bonnie and Clyde. . . . That's why I'll never believe it was Jesse who shot those cops."

"Sunny was crazy," Jesse's mother, Kay Tafero, said in her statement. "Sunny was always the leader in that relationship—Jesse just went along with what Sunny wanted."

Kay and Marianne. The Welsh matron and the Playboy bombshell—they were friends. They went to church together and said novenas for Jesse and rode up together to death row. "She was a real lady," Marianne told me, about Kay. Wistfully.

This morning, after watching the newsreels on Peter's laptop, I continued my searches about Marianne and her friends. One thing I found was a report in the National Archives with a very dry title: *Organized Criminal Activities: Hearings before the Permanent Subcommittee on Investigations of the Committee on Governmental Affairs.* A U.S. Senate investigation into organized crime in South Florida—"loansharking, narcotics trafficking, arson, and murder"—in the 1960s and 1970s. The investigation included a long run of sworn testimony about a drug gang involved in "incredible violence," according to then-senator Sam Nunn. Marianne is mentioned by name in the transcript.

Murders. Extortions. A nightclub owner car-bombed over a bar tab. Men forced to dig their own graves in the Everglades. Men tied up in curtain cords and bedsheets, jammed into bathtubs, interrogated, and shot dead. The leader of the gang was a man named Ricky Cravero who, along with his high school friend Ronnie and their pals Stanley and Bobby and Billy the Kid, brought millions of dollars of cocaine and marijuana into South Florida. On Valentine's Day in 1974, a rivalry among Cravero's gang members ended in gunfire in the parking lot of the Pirate's Cove bar in North Miami Beach when Stanley—dressed up for a night out in a maroon slacks and sweater set—stepped out of his Lincoln Continental Mark IV to find his friends brandishing a sawed-off carbine and a .32 pistol with a silencer. "What is up, fellows?" Stanley asked. "This, Stanley," his friends replied, blasting him twenty-three times. "He sure looked funny," Cravero later said, laughing. The initial idea had been to kill Stanley in Billy's apartment, but they worried about blood getting on the velvet couches and shag carpet in the living room. And on the lion-skin rug in the bedroom. When police searched the call records for Stanley's home telephone, they found Jesse Tafero's name.

So now I'm wondering. How does a hippie peace-and-love vegetarian rich kid end up asleep in a beat-up Camaro with her two young children, a guy on parole with a gun, and a boyfriend on the call list of the most dangerous drug gangsters in South Florida?

Sonia Jacobs, also known as Sonia Leigh Linder, Sonia Lee Jacobs, Sonia Lee Jacobs Linder. Born in August 1947 to Herbert and Bella Jacobs, prosperous owners of a textile firm. Sunny grew up in a leafy Long Island suburb with her younger brother, Alan. In school, she was vice president of the student council, according to her book. In 1965, when she was in college, Sunny found out she was pregnant. She dropped out and got married, with a wedding reception at Tavern on the Green in Central Park. But the marriage didn't last, and by 1968 Sunny and her young son were in Miami, living in "a nice house" owned by Sunny's parents. Sunny "backed off from achievement," her mother later said, but doesn't "have a mean bone in her body." Interviewed by a court officer as part of a pre-sentence investigation after the murders, Sunny said that she only rarely drank alcohol and that while she occasionally smoked marijuana, she was "very anti-drugs." Her parents were convinced of her innocence. It was simply a matter of the "wrong time, wrong place, wrong people," her mother told the investigators.

In 1982, when Sunny was still in prison, her parents died in an airplane crash. New Orleans, Pan Am, takeoff, thunderstorm. "They cannot be dead. They will be found alive somewhere . . . my mommy and daddy," Sunny wrote in her book, about the moment she heard the news. "This is the saddest day of my life," she wrote to Jesse that afternoon. The value of Herb and Bella's estate in today's dollars was more than $4 million, including a payment from the airline's insurance company.

The old newsreels I watched this morning had footage of Sunny. On her way into the courtroom for her trial in 1976, shoulders back, gaze steady, chin up. Prim in a light blue suit, smoking a cigarette, handcuffed. Coming around a corner in the courthouse, she arches one eyebrow at the camera, halfway between a wink and a smile. Asked about Sunny, the mother of one of her ex-boyfriends said, "She thought she was God's gift to men."

That last statement is why I am now standing in front of a tumbledown apartment building just off Dixie Highway here in Dania Beach, in the rain.

In her book, *Stolen Time*, Sunny wrote about the life she was leading before she met Jesse. At the time, she wrote, she was in a "long-term, monogamous relationship" with her boyfriend John, "a laid-back kind of guy":

> We had a house in North Miami surrounded by tree nurseries. I called it the Ranch. It was a sweet old house with a stream running behind it and a family of ducks that would come to the door for their daily feed of dried corn. You could walk outside and collect your breakfast of oranges, grapefruits, bananas and coconuts fresh from the trees in the morning. It was a kind and gentle way of life.

One day, a buddy of John's dropped by for a visit and brought his friend Jesse. Sparks flew. "Jesse was the most fascinating human being I had ever met. And he was so beautiful to look at—the way he moved, the way he'd drape himself into a chair." Soon, Sunny and John were history and Sunny's young son, Eric, "was already calling Jesse 'Dad.'"

I have not been able to find John, but I'm pretty sure I have found his mother, because a woman named Marion Mulcahy—in this building I am now standing in front of—gave an affidavit to Jesse's attorneys in which she said her son John lived with Sunny in the early 1970s, and that John and Jesse were good friends. Marion's affidavit does not mention any fruit trees:

> John lived with Sonia Jacobs—we called her Sunny—for about two years. . . . Their whole life revolved around drugs. She was even more involved in them than he. . . . Sunny set her sights on Jesse and went after him full force. It was the same thing as with John—drugs, drugs, and more drugs. . . . All of this is so tragic. I mean, if it hadn't been for Sunny this never would have happened. She is a sick, evil person. She'll tell you anything you want to hear as long as it gets her what she wants.

In my detective work, I have always promised myself that if I ever have serious misgivings—a feeling, intuition, whatever— I will not knock on the door. I've only had to invoke it once—in North Carolina, at dusk, at the door of a shack down a gully, on a case where I had to find a guy and ask him if he'd raped his girl-friend. Today, my initial impression of this apartment building here in Dania Beach has been a similar feeling of *Oh shit*. But now I decide I'm just nervous. Because if Marion does not talk to me, I have no backup plan. I know who Sunny says she is now. But there's no one else to talk to about who Sunny Jacobs was that morning at the rest stop almost forty years ago.

The apartment building is a duplex, side by side, two doors facing the street. A cigarette burns unattended in an ashtray by the door on the right. I knock. No answer. I peek through the open window. No one around. I walk over to the other apartment. I'm about to knock there when a rough voice startles me from inside.

"What are you doing?" a man says. Big guy, barrel-chested, gray hair, gray beard. One of his eyes seems injured. Thick white flesh creeping over the iris. He is wearing a T-shirt with the word IRISH on it. He does not open the screen door. He does not look friendly.

"I'm sorry, is Marion here?"

"Who are you?" the guy in the IRISH T-shirt says.

"I witnessed Jesse Tafero's execution."

"You're asking about my mother," he says. "She's ill. She's not going to talk to you."

"Actually, I'm hoping to speak with John," I say. "Is he around?"

"My brother?" he says. "My *brother*?"

"Well, Sunny wrote about—"

"My brother John is dead," Irish says.

"Oh my God, I'm so sorry," I say. Instantly. "I didn't know. I'm really sorry."

"My brother was shot in the head," Irish says. Opening the screen door now and taking two steps toward me. He's large. "You're trying to find out the reason for what happened to Jesse and Sunny? There will never be a reason. Just like there will never be a reason for what happened to my brother. There could never be a reason for that, either."

"I'm not looking for a reason," I say. "I just want to know what happened."

"You will never know."

"I need to know," I tell him.

"Look, I could talk to you—I was around then, I knew them— but I'm not going to. Nobody from the old days will. People have put this to rest. Nobody wants to dig it all back up. For what. For you? No way. What you're doing is pointless and hurtful. You're going to have to figure out a way to just live with it."

"Yes, well, I've tried that. And obviously I've failed because here I am on your porch."

We stare at each other.

A moan from the shadows of the apartment. Frail, hollow.

"Be right there, Ma," he says, turning away.

The door slams behind him. He does not come back.

5

A Squealer, a Liar, and a Mute

I am shaking as I walk back across Irish's shitty lawn to my car.

What you're doing is pointless and hurtful. Nobody is going to talk to you.

Standing there on his porch with his damaged eye, its pupil diamond-shaped, glaring, fixed. With the sour smell of beer and the damp ash of burned-off cigarettes, and the rain.

I feel a stinging inside my rib cage and my throat, trapped, toxic. Like I have swallowed live hornets. A mixture of shame and fury.

But whatever, I think, as I slam the car into gear. This is not the first time I've been told to drop dead. It happens. Those two retired FBI guys in Dallas on that stock fraud case, back when I was just starting out. With their aviator sunglasses and Southern drawls, they'd straight-up called me a slut. *How do we know you won't go upstairs with the next guy who buys you a drink and tell him everything we've told you here?* I burst into tears right in front of them. *Pillow talk,* they'd mocked me. *She sure looks like a pillow talker to me.* That old grizzled cowboy roaring *No no no* as I asked his daughter about the heroin ring she'd been operating out of a San Luis Obispo surf shop. The secret lover of a murdered San Francisco tattoo artist, storming around his echoing loft as the night fell outside, accusing me of not caring about his pain. I had cared about his pain, actually. I just had no power to make it go away. My boss had warned me that getting yelled at came with the job. His advice: Don't take it personally.

But this is personal. That's the problem. All the times I've been yelled at before, it's been for the job. The boss, the client, the case. Now it feels like I've crossed a raw, exposed line. That guy Irish was yelling at *me*. The thing is, in my own life, I'm terrible at cocktail parties, terrible at chatting, terrible at knowing what to wear and what to do with my hair. It's only as a private detective that I can do this thing where I appear on your doorstep and you invite me inside. It's an alchemy I don't fully comprehend.

Usually people talk. I didn't understand why until my friend and fellow private eye Jacqueline asked me a question. Isn't there anything or anyone you'd talk about, if someone came to your door? I thought about it. The guy who robbed me at knifepoint outside the Metropolitan Museum of Art when I was in high school. Him. The guy who slapped me across the face on a Lexington Avenue bus after a tiny piece of paper I tossed out the window—I was in the seventh grade—accidentally bounced off his sister. Everyone frozen, staring, as he raised his hand high and slammed it down into my cheekbone. Him. The elderly janitor at the New York Society Library who lunged lips-first at me in that rickety cage of an elevator—absolutely, him too. The chapped old rat. Jacqueline nodded, and suddenly I got it. There is an incredible healing value to saying out loud what you know to be true to someone who is listening, who understands, and who might be able to help.

All of which makes me wonder now about this pal of Sunny's. Irish hadn't said thanks but no thanks. He'd told me to go straight to hell. Exactly as if he was afraid of something I might find out. But here's a fact I did not mention to Irish, back there on his front porch: You can patronize me, scold me, lie to my face, and I'll roll with it. But flat out telling me no? That word is a red cape in a bull-ring to me. Not sure why. Always been true.

In the morning, I call the Broward County State Attorney's Office.

If Irish is right that nobody is going to talk to me, then I am going to need to find every piece of paper there is on this case. I already have the case documents from the Broward County Circuit Court, but I'm sure those exploded old onionskin files are not the whole story. I want the records that the prosecutor gathered—the investigation papers, the trial files. Getting an answer from the State Attorney's Office, though, is turning out to be much more difficult than I'd thought. This feels like my tenth phone call over there. It should be so straightforward. Florida has an ironclad public records law. I remember that from my days here as a newspaper reporter. Ask for the files, get the files. Not this endless back-and-forth.

Is it because the prosecutor now is the same person who was the prosecutor then? It's incredible, but the current Broward County state attorney, Michael J. Satz, is the lawman who back in 1976 put Jesse and Sunny on trial for their lives, with soon-to-recant Walter Norman Rhodes Jr. as the star witness. When Satz tried the case, he was an assistant in the office, but days after Sunny was convicted, Satz announced that he was going to run for the top job. He was elected in a landslide and he's been in office ever since. Thirty-eight years, eleven months, and six days, as of today. He has not spoken publicly about the case in many years. I am going to have to get him, somehow, to talk to me.

As I listen to the office's phone ring and ring, I realize that another question has been forming in the back of my mind. The truck driver eyewitnesses at the rest stop did not tell the police that Jesse murdered those officers. According to the eyewitnesses, Jesse was pushed up against the cruiser when the shots rang out.

And yet Jesse Tafero was the person who went to the electric chair.

Is that why the State Attorney's Office is hiding the files?

"Hello?"

I am startled back into the present. The supervisor I've been calling at the State Attorney's Office has answered the phone herself this time. Super friendly, super apologetic about a plumbing emergency that she says has preoccupied her all week.

Yes, she has the files, she says. "You can come see them right now, if you want."

An hour later I am sitting at a table in a windowless library on the sixth floor of the Broward County courthouse. The library is lined floor-to-ceiling with law books, row upon row of black and red and gilt. Around me are a dozen boxes holding the prosecutor's files of *State v. Tafero*, stacked in tidy towers. These boxes are pristine. Well-tended manila folders, organized by subject, alphabetized. The files have some of the same documents as those shabby boxes over in the courthouse, but many more too—the entire case file from the Florida Highway Patrol, reports filed by the officers who rushed to the rest area after Trooper Black's 10-24, transcripts for both trials. The morning of February 20, 1976, is before me once more.

At the roadblock—twenty-three miles north of the highway rest area—blood has soaked into the orange-and-cream plaid upholstery of the bullet-riddled carjacked Cadillac. The Cadillac is still where it crashed, crumpled headfirst into a dirt-filled tractor-trailer truck.

A plainclothes police officer is leaving the scene, taking Sunny Jacobs and the children—the nine-year-old boy and the ten-month-old baby girl—over to the Delray Beach substation of the Palm Beach County Sheriff's Office. When they get there, Sunny and her children are separated. A clerk strip-searches Sunny, watches as Sunny uses the toilet and washes her hands and face, and then brings Sunny to an interrogation room. Two policemen and a tape recorder are waiting.

The officers are Captain Valjean Haley of the Palm Beach

County Sheriff's Office and Broward Sheriff's Office detective lieutenant Angelo Farinato. They read Sunny her rights, then get the interrogation off to a quick start. Haley informs Sunny that she is under arrest for first-degree murder. Sunny laughs. Farinato steps in.

DET. LT. FARINATO: Alright. Who was with you this morning?
SUNNY JACOBS: We were in the back seat, of the car.
[. . .]
DET. LT. FARINATO: Alright, where were you sitting in the car?
SUNNY JACOBS: In the back.
DET. LT. FARINATO: Alright, now who was—
SUNNY JACOBS: Through this whole thing I . . . I . . . I sat in the back of that car.

Who were the men in the Cadillac with her? The man in the blue shirt? The man in the tan pants, with the beard? Sunny does not know. She does not know their names or where they are from.

SUNNY JACOBS: I don't know. I don't know.

Sunny also does not know who fired the shots.

SUNNY JACOBS: I didn't see. I didn't see.

Asked directly, she says she herself did not shoot anyone or fire a gun that day. The officers remind her that she is under oath. She says she knows that. "I—I'd like to help but I'd like to help myself," she tells them.

Jesse Tafero, in a separate interrogation room at the Delray Beach substation, is not talking. The officers turn a tape recorder on and run through the Miranda warning questions, including "Do you understand that I am a police officer?" and "You have the right to remain silent. . . . Do you understand this?"

Tafero says just one thing: "I want an attorney."

With that, the questions stop. Tafero is taken to a hospital, where a nurse treats abrasions on his temple and finds a foil packet of cocaine in his sock. Jesse does talk briefly to the nurse. He tells her, "I have been on a bad trip."

Walter Rhodes is in the emergency room of Bethesda Memorial Hospital, waiting to be admitted to surgery. He is awake and in a great deal of pain, according to the hospital records. Walter's left leg has been shattered by the roadblock gunshot. His left knee is bleeding profusely and his left foot is cold and mottled with no pulse—early gangrene is setting in. He is surrounded by police officers as the doctors and nurses move him from room to room. He's been Mirandized two times already, once at 8:37 A.M.—he was unable to sign his rights card—and again at 9:43 A.M. He has not had pain medication yet, according to the notes on his hospital chart. At first Walter insists that he does not want to talk to anybody, but then he changes his mind. He tells Detective Fred Mascaro of the Palm Beach County Sheriff's Office that he "didn't do anything" and that he "wasn't the one that shot the trooper." Then Walter gets shots of Demerol, a painkiller, and Phenergan, a sedative, and after that he can't talk anymore.

The next day, after a long night on morphine, Walter gives another statement from his hospital bed, this time to Captain Valjean Haley. Walter is under oath, on tape. The statement is twenty-four typewritten pages long.

CAPT. HALEY: What is the only reason or what is the various reasons that you are making this statement?

WALTER RHODES: Because I feel like, I feel at ease with you, particularly I feel like I can talk to you, I don't feel like you are going to stab me because I believe, I just feel, at ease talking to you, you know, I would like to clear this up and you seem to be the one I want to talk to.

Then Walter tells Haley that he knows what happened. Sunny shot first from the back of the car, and then Jesse grabbed the gun and finished the officers off, Walter says.

CAPT. HALEY: Let me interrupt at this time, when the shot went off did you actually witness the shots?
WALTER RHODES: I actually witnessed the shots.

As Walter is giving his statement, a doctor pokes his head into the room and tells Walter that he is going to cut Walter's leg off.

Interesting, I think, as I put the folders back in their file boxes. Before coming in here today, I already knew that Walter had talked to the police and cut a deal to testify against Sunny and Jesse.

But I had not known that Sunny told the officers she didn't know the guys she was with in the Camaro, or that Jesse had not said one word at all.

A squealer, a liar, and a mute. Whom to believe?

It's the next documents, though, that rattle me.

In that wedding announcement in *The New York Times*, the one that took me by surprise at my breakfast table three years ago, the newspaper reported that Sunny and Jesse were in the car at the rest area with Walter Rhodes because "he was giving the couple a ride from Miami to the home of friends in West Palm Beach."

The Scotsman, a Scottish daily newspaper, reported in 2005: "Tafero's friend, Walter Rhodes, offered them a lift part of the way home. Jacobs didn't like him, but he was willing to drive them north."

Sunny Jacobs, to *The Scotsman*: "It was only a ride."

So the property receipts catch me off guard.

Officers who searched Jesse and Walter and Sunny and the crime scene and roadblock and the cars after the murders found two Smith & Wesson 9mm semiautomatic handguns, a Smith & Wesson .38 Special six-shot revolver, a North American Arms .22 short derringer, a Manuel Escodin Eibar .32 caliber revolver, a shoulder holster, a hatchet, and a bayonet. Those last two items were stashed in the backseat of the Camaro, behind the driver's seat, along with a denim purse holding baby pajamas and a jar of Beech-Nut baby food.

Drugs too. Amphetamines, cocaine, Quaaludes, marijuana, hashish, glutethimide—a hypnotic sedative that produces intense euphoria. Thorazine. Pentazocine. Cigarettes. Beer.

Jewelry: earrings, rings, necklaces, pendants, charms, loose gemstones.

Forty pieces of identification in other people's names, including birth certificates, driver's licenses, passports, adoption papers, voter registrations, Selective Service registrations, checking accounts, and library cards. A flesh-colored over-the-head rubber mask with a white wig attached.

And ammunition. So much ammunition. Bullets loaded in the weapons taken off Walter and Jesse at the roadblock, bullets loaded in the gun found in Sunny's purse. Bullets in cardboard boxes in the Cadillac at the roadblock and bullets in a black plastic ammo case at the crime scene, right there on the backseat of the Camaro, where Sunny and the kids were sitting.

"And not just the Cadillac and the Camaro. The apartment too," I tell Peter later, at dinner.

At the courthouse, I'd looked through a stack of case photographs from the archives. Eight-by-ten glossies of the crime scene and also pictures taken of Walter's apartment the evening after the murders, when his landlady let the police inside. I have copies of them here with me now.

Two thin and bare mattresses. A bullet on the floor next to a box of Pampers. A weight-lifting bench with a handwritten list on it of bills coming due. Rent, $165. Karate mementos. Cast-off clothes on the floor, on the couch, spilling out of suitcases. A black-light bulb, an empty container of L'eggs pantyhose, an eight-track tape for a Gregg shorthand course. Dirty coffee cups and cereal bowls and a baby bottle on the kitchen counter. The fridge door open, the fridge empty except for a tipped-over jar of baby food, a bowl, and a dirty yellow cloth.

"I'd say the apartment looks like a bomb hit it, but it actually looks messier than that," I say. I've put the photos on the table and we're studying them. "It looks like whoever was in that apartment was so busy doing whatever it was they were busy doing that they forgot to eat or sleep or clean up after themselves."

"Or pick their stray bullets up off the floor," Peter says, looking closely. And then he pushes a pile of news clips across the table. "You need to read these."

The Palm Beach Post, July 1974: A Miami man, described by a Dade County organized crime investigator as "the principal member of a major narcotics smuggling organization," yesterday was arrested in conjunction with a marijuana-laden boat which burned in Lake Worth two weeks ago. Richard Douglas Cravero was arrested with three other persons at the home of convicted stamp thief John Clarence Cook and charged with possession of marijuana with the intent to resell.

Fort Lauderdale News, June 1977: Two reputed minor members of the notorious Cravero gang have been indicted by the Broward County Grand Jury in connection with [a] brutal 1975 murder. . . . The body . . . was found floating in a western Broward rock pit . . . shot three times in the head and weighed down with rugs, concrete, and an anchor. . . . Cravero's gang, sometimes known as the Dixie Mafia, was heavily involved in South Florida drug traffic but it was their brutality which sparked their notoriety.

Boat-burning. Drug-smuggling. Car-bombing. Body-littering. The notorious Ricky Cravero was arrested in Marianne's home in 1974. He was arrested with Marianne in 1975. Ricky knew Marianne, and Marianne knew Jesse. But what does that prove? Nothing. Still, that apartment was a wreck. Bullets. Diapers. Jewelry. Guns, stolen passports, Quaaludes, cocaine. What did Sunny say? *It was only a ride.* She said Jesse was soft-spoken and gentle. "He was polite and well-mannered." That's what Sunny wrote about Jesse in her book. "He was the light and I had to follow the light." And Walter—Walter confessed.

As I look through the news stories and the photographs, I can feel myself starting to tremble. I try to steel myself against it: *Here it comes.* But it is stronger than I am, this undertow.

Fear. Real, visceral, immediate. The same fear I felt after I went to talk to Walter Rhodes. Not the first time I talked to him, in 1990, when he was in prison. The other time. When he was out of prison and on the run from the law.

6

The Fugitive

I t started with a show on the radio.

In October 2002, I was driving across the Bay Bridge into San Francisco when I heard the word "exonerated" together with the name "Jesse Tafero" coming out of the speakers of my car stereo. I turned the radio up. A play telling the true stories of six innocent people on death row was about to open in New York City, National Public Radio was reporting. *The Exonerated* was a documentary work, drawn entirely from court records, police reports, and interviews. "Every word in this thing is real," the play's director, Bob Balaban, told NPR.

REPORTER: Late one night in 1976, Sunny Jacobs and her common-law husband, Jesse Tafero, got a ride to a friend's house in Broward County, Florida. The driver got tired and pulled over to take a nap. On a routine patrol of the rest area, police ran a check on the driver and found he was on parole. Then, Sunny Jacobs says, the driver grabbed a gun and killed the two officers.

SUNNY JACOBS: After he shot the policemen, the man who had done it made us get in the police car with him, and he drove us off.

Sunny's voice coming through my car speakers was girlish, hesitant, sweet.

REPORTER: In 1992, two years after Jesse Tafero was executed, lawyers uncovered evidence clearing him and Sunny Jacobs.

The rest of my drive that day was a blur. I was heading into San Francisco to do interviews for a case about the ferries that ran out to Alcatraz, and I'd recently been spending quite a bit of time out on that prison island, listening to the wind whistle along the cold cellblocks as the gulls wheeled and keened overhead. That morning, though, I got a cup of coffee and took it down to the stone steps at the water's edge beside the old sailing ships of Fisherman's Wharf. I needed to think.

Up on Russian Hill, behind me, was the detective's mansion. Six years ago, I'd started my life as a private eye there. Since then I had worked as an investigator on some brutal cases, digging deep into crimes so violent that they'd stalked my dreams. A young woman kidnapped, raped, killed with a shovel, and buried in a shallow grave. An elderly drifter beaten to death in the marijuana hinterland up near the Oregon border. That case had hinged on the testimony of a young child. When I found him, by then grown up, he told me he wondered if maybe he had just dreamed the whole thing. Some of the murder cases I'd worked on for the detective, but after three years with his firm I'd taken a job as an investigator for the State of California, defending death row inmates. Now my friend Freya and I had our own detective agency, and just the past year we'd been down in Bakersfield talking to jurors who'd sent a serial killer to San Quentin State Prison. I'd seen death cases up close, I'd learned how complicated facts in those cases can be, how hard it is to overturn a conviction. How very rarely someone walks free, as

Sunny did, and how important that is when it happens. And all along the way, I'd tried not to think too hard about Jesse Tafero.

"I have to see this play," I told my new boyfriend that evening.

Peter and I had met exactly a year earlier, through a mutual friend. John was a buddy of mine from my newspaper days; for more than half a decade, he'd been telling me about this other friend of his and saying we should all get together sometime. It wasn't until October 2001, though, that brand-new world, that we all three finally made plans for a Saturday morning coffee. A totally routine thing, except that when I came around the corner of the coffee shop and saw the handsome man sitting at a table with my friend John, I thought: Oh hey, it's *you*. Just like that.

We were instantly friends. Peter grew up in Chicago; his dad worked in the steel mills and died when Peter was ten; Peter had spent years working as an actor and then in publishing; he'd written travel guides and directed plays; he loved theater and dancing and music and cooking and reading and gardening. Life, basically. Every thing, every day. A radiance. We met for drinks. We went out to dinner. We talked about our love lives. He was dating an emergency room nurse, I was dating an organic gardener. I thought Peter was smart and charming and funny. He had a lovely way of listening, free from comment, free from advice. He was warm and open and kind and honest. And he was gay. He'd dated women when he was young, but at the age of twenty-seven he'd come out and had identified as a gay man ever since—for almost twenty years. Which was fine. I'd always had gay friends and had dated women myself, so there was zero confusion about what was going on. Peter was my friend. My good friend. We were good friends who went out dancing. Who went out dancing pretty much every Saturday night. And one Saturday night, at the gay dance bar we always went to, something unexpected happened. We'd had a lot of tequila, I guess. We kissed.

"I don't see how this is going to work out," I told him, a few weeks later, on the telephone. Peter and I had seen each other constantly since that night at the dance bar, and every single time we saw each other was magic, but now I'd decided that no matter how good things seemed to be, our relationship was impossible—who had ever heard of such a thing?—and we should end it. Most of our friends were in shock, seeing the two of us together. There was no point in trying to invent something new when it would only lead to heartbreak. "It's too complicated," I told him, and hung up the phone.

About a half hour later, I heard a knock on the door. I opened it, and there was Peter, his collar turned up against the California winter rains. He took me in his arms, and he kissed me.

"This," he said, "is not complicated." And he kissed me again.

Now, six months later, we were on his porch in Oakland and I was going through the whole long story about Sunny and Jesse and Walter. And me. It had been a long time since I'd said it all out loud. I hesitated. I stumbled. I confided. Peter listened.

"The radio report said that lawyers uncovered evidence that cleared Jesse Tafero and Sunny Jacobs," I said. "*Cleared* them."

"Oh my God, you need to see this play," Peter said.

I was nervous as we took our seats at 45 Bleecker, the downtown theater in New York City where *The Exonerated* was playing. The stage was bare, just a row of music stands and stools. A hush fell over the audience as the actors came out and took their places. About ten minutes into the show, it was Sunny's turn to talk. The actress Anne Jackson—she'd played a doctor in *The Shining*—was Sunny this evening, feisty and fragile as the spotlight found her onstage. "In 1976, I was sentenced to death row, which for me wasn't a row at all, because I was the only woman in the country who had the sentence of death. So I suggested they put me in the same cell as my husband!" Sunny said, in the play. Laughter. A beat. "But let me start at the beginning." As one, the audience leaned forward to listen.

Ninety minutes later, the instant the play was over, I stood up and walked out. Peter rushed after me. New York City. Car horns, footsteps, headlights, cigarettes, snippets of conversation. I sat down hard on the curb outside the theater, my head spinning.

"I mean, Rhodes had just killed two policemen," Sunny said, in the play. That was it. No discussion. No evidence. That was the entire explanation. "I was a hippie, I'm one of those peace-and-love people, I'm a *vegetarian*! How could you possibly think I would kill someone?"

"But the guns in the car—those were Sunny's guns. She bought them," I told Peter, who'd come to sit next to me. I remembered that fact from the news stories I'd read.

"And she wasn't exonerated, actually," I added. Sunny's conviction had indeed been overturned on appeal, but not because the court had determined that she was blameless in the murders. In 1992, the appeals court ruled that the prosecution had improperly withheld the report of Walter's polygraph test from the defense, and also that statements Sunny made the morning of the murders had been admitted into evidence in violation of her constitutional rights. That's why the court reversed her conviction and ordered a new trial. Sunny had finally gotten out of prison on a special kind of plea called an Alford plea, which allowed her to claim innocence while admitting under oath that the state could prove certain incriminating facts against her. An Alford plea does have some important bells and whistles to it, but legally speaking it is a guilty plea. In the eyes of the law, Sunny wasn't innocent. She was a convicted felon.

I felt dizzy. Everything I'd learned over the past six years as an investigator was clanging around inside my head. You were supposed to look at all the facts. That was where the truth could be found. Not just the facts that fit whatever theory you were trying to prove. And anyway, Ted Bundy was a vegetarian. But that wasn't the only thing troubling me. Or even the main thing, if I was going to be honest with myself, which definitely now seemed overdue. It was the confession. Walter's confession.

SUNNY [*to audience*]: In 1979, Walter Rhodes wrote the following letter to a judge.

RHODES: I, Walter Norman Rhodes, hereby depose and say that I
am under no duress nor coercion to execute this affidavit. This
statement is made freely and voluntarily, and to purge myself
before my Creator. Briefly. On February 20, 1976, at approxi-
mately seven-fifteen A.M., I did, in fact, shoot to death two law-
enforcement officers with a nine-millimeter Browning pistol. I
state emphatically and unequivocally that my previous testimony against Jesse Tafero and Sonia Jacobs was *false* . . . I so
swear.

Of course I knew that Walter had confessed. Until seeing the
play, though, I had not known what Walter's confession had said.
What his exact words had been. "Before my Creator"—that
sounded just like the Walter Rhodes I interviewed in prison before
the execution. He'd been all into karma and fate and destiny and
souls. Walter had recanted this confession, along with all his other
ones. But to me those words rang true.

"Do you really think this is a good idea?" Peter said.

It was shortly after our trip to New York. We were moving in
together, we were engaged to be married, and now we were at the
front door of our house on the verge of a serious fight.

"It's a very good idea," I said, cramming a sweater into my suitcase. My plane was leaving in two hours. I wasn't used to reporting my whereabouts to anyone. Or getting permission to go.

After seeing *The Exonerated*, I decided that I needed to talk to
Walter Rhodes again. I needed to ask him if he "did, in fact, shoot
to death two law-enforcement officers," like his confession in the
play had said. I needed an answer, and I needed to hear it from
him. In the weeks since the play, I had not been sleeping. I'd felt
flashes of Q-Wing around the edges of my days. Smoke, flame. The
hollow buzzing. So I'd looked Walter up on the Florida Department
of Corrections website. But Walter was not in prison anymore. He
was not on parole, either.

"Walter Rhodes is a fugitive," Peter was saying. "He is on the run from the law."

That did happen to be true. According to the Florida Department of Corrections website, Walter was on the lam. And had been for the past nine years, ever since he was released from prison on parole—and disappeared.

"Walter knows me, I interviewed him," I said, zipping up my suitcase. A fugitive. Whatever. I was a private eye. I knew how to knock on a door. "It's going to be fine."

It had not been difficult to find Walter. Back in 1990, when I interviewed him at Avon Park Correctional Institution, he had told me he had a prison romance going with a woman who lived in New Mexico. Her name was Sara, and she called him Michael. A bit of computer research using Sara's first and last name in combination with "New Mexico" and the name "Michael" turned up a pair of likely people in a remote town near the Canadian border, in the high-desert heart of Washington where it seldom rains.

I flew up on a Saturday morning, first to Seattle and then in a small prop plane over the Cascades to Wenatchee. From there I headed north along the Columbia River gorge, a wild stretch of blue water and high dry cliffs. It was a far-flung part of the country, but I'd been along this road before—on a death penalty case, one with terrible crime scene photos of a woman bound hand and foot in a motel bathroom, violated and then beaten to death. I'd ended up driving for hours that night, unable to stop. The floodlit parking lots of the motels along the highway had seemed spectral to me. Today, though, I was on this road in daylight, and I felt okay.

Almost okay. The closer I got, the harder I tried to work out how it might go. Confronting a fugitive about murder. *Hi, Walter? So, I'm wondering, is there any chance that—* No. It's not like I could slide a question about the roadside slaying of two police officers into casual conversation. I was going to have to straight-up challenge him. *Did you kill them?* I definitely felt nervous about that.

With the river behind me, I turned west across a plain, climbing steadily. The afternoon sun cast long shadows across the tall grass. In dry streambeds, rocks shone like moonstones. My car was the only car on the road. I passed through a deserted town with houses of weathered wood and found the lake just beyond it, but then my sense of direction ran out just as the cellphone service did.

On my third pass along the south end of the lake, I saw a phone booth. The old-fashioned kind, right by the side of the road, out here in the middle of nowhere.

"I can't find them," I said, shouting down the line to Peter above the wind that hit me as soon as I stepped out of the car. "At this point I'm just driving around."

"Come home."

That was what I was afraid he'd say. I wanted to. I could hear voices in the background, the clink of drinks in glasses, shouts of laughter. A weekend night with our friends in San Francisco getting under way.

"You've done everything you can," Peter said. "If they don't want to be found, maybe you should just leave them be."

Just that instant a car pulled out onto the road from the trees beyond the phone booth. I peered over. There was a driveway hidden in that roadside thicket.

"Oh God," I said.

"What's going on?" Peter said.

"I've got to go," I said, already hanging up.

So here I was, easing my little gray rental car down a rocky dirt road, out of cellphone range, with the trees closing in around me. I was edging toward the home of a man who had pled guilty to two murders, pled guilty to kidnapping, served nearly two decades in prison, gotten out, gone on the lam, and tried his very best to disappear. It was almost five o'clock by the time I pulled up at the end of a driveway in front of a double-wide trailer underneath a stand of pines. There was a lake behind the trailer and on the opposite shore a steep wooded slope, cast in shadow. I stopped for a moment and listened. Nothing. Not a thing except for the ticking of the engine as it cooled. I remembered again the promise I'd made to myself when I began working as a private investigator. You can't un-knock on a door, but you don't have to let anyone know you're out there in the first place.

"You looking for the campground?" A woman's voice, from behind me. I recognized it from a phone conversation I'd had with her about Walter years earlier, when I was at *The Miami Herald*, right after the execution.

I took a deep breath.

"Actually, Sara," I said, turning around, "I'm looking for you."

A short, plump woman with graying hair, wearing a blue gardening shirt and khaki pants, she had appeared at the corner of the yard, standing near the house, arms folded across her chest. She did not look friendly. Not one tiny bit.

I'd have thought that the proprietress of a doomsday collective might be a little more chatty, just for marketing purposes, but no. I happened to know that in the years since we last spoke, Sara had been channeling messages from extraterrestrial beings called the Hosts of Heaven—*You are the sensory tip of a "finger" of your Oversoul, thrust into the "pudding" of your present space/time environment*—who had been telling her about the mother ships that would soon arrive to lift true believers to the Fourth Density. Walter had been helping out with the prophesies, under the name Lord Michael Andronicus. They had a website and a mailing list, more than six hundred hopeful souls waiting to be Harvested. *All is in hand. All is being prepared. You have suffered enough, beloveds. Soon you will be at the banquet.*

"I used to be a reporter for *The Miami Herald*," I told Sara now. "We talked on the phone a couple of times about Walter. Do you remember?"

"No."

"Well, I'm hoping to talk to Walter now—is he around?"

"Oh, he skipped a long time ago," Sara said, super casually. She started walking across the yard toward me, and when she reached me she kept going. I could see that I was being herded back to my car.

"I want to talk to him because I saw *The Exonerated*."

"Well, I don't know where he is. He just ran out and I haven't heard from him. For years."

She had brought me to a halt right outside the driver's-side door to my car, and was standing now between me and the house with a distinct *Okay! Bye!* expression on her face.

I was just about to get in and drive off—if he's not here, he's not here—when the door to the house opened and a man came out. He was heavier, his hair was longer and graying, and he had a salt-and-pepper beard, but otherwise, yes. There he was. Still very good-looking, with a wave of silver hair over chiseled features and intense dark eyes.

"Do you recognize me?" I asked Walter Rhodes.

"No."

"I talked to you in Avon Park."

He stared at me for what felt like a long time.

"Let's go inside," he said finally.

"The jig is up!" Sara cried out from behind us. She sounded angry. Or maybe afraid.

Inside, the trailer was tidy, a long rectangle with an office desk at one end and a bedroom at the other, kitchen and living area in the middle, a big couch against the far wall. Next to the couch a sliding glass door opened onto a deck. There were no electric lights on, just sun filtering in through the pine woods.

At Walter's direction I took a seat on the couch. Sara sat down next to me and Walter pulled a dining chair over and sat in front of me, almost knee to knee. They had boxed me in. Sara was discernibly tense and Walter seemed fierce. He was not friendly at all, I realized with dismay. He was also most definitely between me and the door. I'd have to clamber right over him to get out. It occurred to me that possibly Peter had been right. Dropping in unannounced on a fugitive in the middle of the woods in Nowhere, Washington, might not have been the brightest idea anybody ever had.

"Why are you here?" Walter asked.

I launched into an explanation: the execution, *The Exonerated*.

"But what I'm asking you is, why are you here? What are you getting at?" Walter said.

"Well, I saw the play, and they're pretty clear that they think you did it, and I thought I'd come here and ask you myself whether you'd changed your mind about what you told me, back in 1990. Because if you changed your mind about all that, I want to know."

I was about to say more, but Sara jumped in.

"In March 1981, the Christ materialized in my bedroom and put his hands on me," Sara began.

Uh-oh.

"I was a member of Christ's inner circle," she said, leaning toward me.

I nodded pleasantly. As one does.

"In 1987, Christ appeared to me again and told me to prepare my heart for 'the greater love that comes,' and a month later, I got a letter from this man right here. He was calling himself Walter Rhodes but I knew he was my twin soul from the higher density, and that his real name was—"

She faltered, and Walter put his hand on her back.

"His name was Lord Michael Andronicus," she continued.

"Walter Rhodes is dead to me," said Walter Rhodes.

I literally could not think of one single thing to say.

"Have you had anything to eat?" Walter asked Sara.

"No," Sara said tearfully.

"Well, why don't you do that, and Ellen and I will go for a walk."

A short lawn covered in pine needles led down to the lake. Across the water, a mountain ridge rose to the sky. The water was blue and black, clear at the shore but darker as it deepened, and it reflected the sky as a mirror. There was an aluminum rowboat up-

side down on the sandy beach, and Walter and I walked down to
that. Walter put his plaid overshirt on it and we sat down.

"You know, *The Exonerated* pretty much says flat out that you
killed those officers," I began. "Did you?"

"I did not murder those officers. No."

"I just need to know the truth," I said.

"That is the truth. I did not murder Trooper Black or Constable
Irwin."

"But you confessed."

"I really regret that."

"Yeah, well," I said, after a moment.

I dug a pack of cigarettes out of my pocket and offered him one,
but he didn't smoke, just as he didn't smoke thirteen years ago
when I interviewed him in prison. I lit one and smoked in silence,
thinking.

I believed him, absolutely.

Almost absolutely.

I did not know. It was hard to know. I felt like I knew Walter,
though. He knew about the murders, the blood monolith suddenly
in the center of my life again. We could speak the language of the
case—*Jesse, Sunny, the rest area, Trooper Black, Constable Irwin*—
without having to explain or define anything. What it meant.
That felt incredibly important to me.

He was watching me.

"See that ridge?" he asked me. "The one over across the lake?"

I looked where he was pointing. A steep stand of spruce, stepping up from the dark water.

"The UFOs are so beautiful when they land there."

But there's never any trace of them, Walter added. He hikes
over to see. Nothing.

I just nodded.

"Well, there's a lot about life we don't understand," I said, flick-
ing an ash off the end of my cigarette. Today, in particular, that
seemed true.

"We're energy, talking right now," Walter said. "I'm talking to
energy and so are you."

Next Walter took me on a little tour of the property, which was part of a campground, an old-school 1950s roughing-it kind of place. Just outside the door to the campground office was a pay phone, and as Walter and I passed it, I said I wanted to call my boyfriend.

I knew that if I did not call, Peter would worry, and if Peter got worried he might alert the police. He was not a sit-by-the-phone kind of person. He was a pick-up-the-phone-and-do-something guy. I liked that about him. It was just that it felt a little awkward right now, because possibly Walter suspected I was calling the cops myself.

Peter's phone rang just once before he picked up.

"You're with them right now?"

"It's fine," I whispered. "I'll call you later. I love you. Bye."

The sun had set by the time Walter and I got back to the house, and I told them it was time for me to go.

"Why don't you stay here?" Sara said.

"It would be great," Walter added.

This was crazy, obviously. To think about spending the night in this isolated house with an escaped convicted murderer and a woman who had Jesus on her own personal team. But I was curious. Maybe Walter's story was going to change, maybe he would tell me something new. Sometimes there's more between the last question and the door, and it might be worth hanging around to find out. Also, I was afraid of the long drive back to the airport, of those bleak roadside motels.

"Okay, thanks," I said.

I went outside to the campground pay phone to call Peter again. He didn't pick up, so I left him a message to tell him I was spending the night here with Walter and Sara. I didn't want to think of his reaction. It was almost dark, and as I walked back to the house the woods around me rustled, the sound of leaves and needles and branches and wind.

Dinner was beef with pine nuts in a tomato and zucchini broth, plus toast. Walter gave me a glass with "Let Go and Let God" on it and said water tasted better in it.

After dinner, a movie. *The Shawshank Redemption*. They could not believe I had never seen it.

We sat knee to knee to knee on the couch, Sara/me/Walter, bolt upright, each with our own lap blanket and glass of water. On-screen, prison cells, prison beatings, prison blackmail, prison rapes. A "very accurate" movie, Walter said approvingly. Their cat, Amador, was on my lap, purring, which they took as a good sign. Also good signs: I'm a Virgo, like Walter. I am from New York, like Sara. I have "good energy" and "good intuition," like Walter. There was a house empty next door, Walter said, maybe I should think about moving up there and spending more time with them.

After the movie, they gave me a fresh pile of blankets and pillows for the couch and switched off the lights. I went to sleep. I was dreaming about accidentally leading the cops to Walter when I was startled awake by a scream.

A choking, gurgling, strangly, coughing, howling, full-throttle scream.

I opened my eyes. It was dark.

Another scream, the same sound as the first, but higher pitched now. It was outside the windows just at the head of the couch. Getting closer.

That afternoon down at the rowboat, Walter had said something that fucking freaked me out. When he was released from prison, he'd said, he was a ball of rage, and he had made a list of everybody who'd ever crossed him. A list of people he wanted to hunt down and kill. He knew how to use the Internet, he told me. He was good at finding people.

Suddenly Walter and Sara burst screaming into the living room, in the dark.

"The other door, get the other door!" Sara shouted.

"You are a bad cat!" Walter shouted. To Amador, hissing on the porch.

I tried to fall back asleep, but no dice. The cat's air-raid-siren scream rattled inside my head, an echoing ricochet. I pulled the blankets over myself and slid down into the couch cushions, trying to hide. I could feel a darkness suddenly that was unlike anything I'd ever been near before. Empty, erasing, obliterating. Carnivorous. It was coming for me.

In the morning, I got up early and slipped out of the house. The woods had the cool of the night still on them as I walked down to the pay phone.

Peter picked up instantly. "My God, are you okay?"

"You are talking to the world's dumbest detective," I whispered into the phone. "I can't get into it right now. I'll be home soon."

Up at the house, Walter and Sara were cheery. Over a breakfast of ricotta omelets with blueberries, they mentioned an investigator named Walt LaGraves who had been very helpful to them; he'd shown up at Walter's parole hearing and vouched for Walter's release, they said. I made a mental note of the name, and I stepped outside to smoke a cigarette before hitting the road.

Walter joined me.

"You know, *The Shawshank Redemption*, it's accurate, but those were the old days. Prison is even worse than that now," he said.

Even in this sunshine, I could feel the fear from last night. Ice, inside my spine.

"I do not want to go back to prison," Walter said. He was looking at me closely. "But then I think, maybe going back to prison would be worth it if it would clear my name."

A pause.

"Why did you come here?"

"I need to know the truth about what happened," I said.

"The truth? What does the truth matter? The truth is just what the most people believe."

A couple of months after my trip to Washington, Peter and I went on our honeymoon. Just days earlier we'd been in San Francisco, in a bar filled with flowers and family and friends, holding hands while our friend John read our wedding vows and pronounced us—it was unbelievable—married. Now we were in the sea off the southern coast of Spain, clear waves breaking over us, aquamarine, dazzling in the light. The drums were starting again on the top of the cliff, and soon we would be toweling off, climbing the stairs, and heading to a club lounge in a tent overlooking the coast of Africa to sit and watch the night arrive.

"This is here all the time, this paradise," Peter said, with a wide sweep of his arm that took in—everything. The beach, the sand, the wind, the water, our wedding rings, the sunlight, me. "Now that I know about it, I'm always going to want to be here, always."

"You can't look at things that way." I laughed. "You have to look at it like you will always have it, just because we have ever been here at all."

Traveling with you in your heart. In your memory. In who you are. It's not just sorrow that carries forward. Joy does too.

"Don't you think?" I asked. I wanted it to be true.

We were just back from our honeymoon when the phone rang. Suitcases still in the front hall, mail stacked on the dining room table.

"It's Sara," Peter said, holding the phone out to me.

"Who?" But I felt a chill.

Peter and I had talked about my trip up to Washington State, of course. But not in detail. I didn't want to put him in peril by telling him too much—it can be dangerous to know what you know—and I also so regretted ever having gone there, the recklessness of that trip and how completely I had underestimated what I'd be getting into. Dropping in on an escaped convict, la-di-da. I just wanted to pretend the trip hadn't happened. "You were right," I'd told Peter, as soon as I got back. "I should never have gone."

"Sara?" I said now, into the phone.

"So, you turned us in," Sara said.

I felt myself freeze.

"Walter was arrested last week," Sara continued. For parole violation. For being a fugitive from the law. Sara and Walter had been on a quick trip to a local junkyard when they got pulled over and surrounded by armed policemen. Walter was back behind bars and facing a long term in state prison. Again.

"Are you happy now?" Sara asked me.

"Sara, I've been in Spain on my honeymoon. I have no idea what you're talking about."

"You haven't been on your honeymoon, Ellen. You've been with Sunny Jacobs. You've been doing this for her all along. I warned Walter about you but he didn't listen."

I glanced over at Peter, who was singing along to the radio as he sorted our mail on the dining room table. I thought of what Walter had said about his kill list of people who'd crossed him. I looked at the open front door of our little house, on its completely unprotected street in Berkeley, California, where nobody would ever call the cops on anyone "suspicious" lest they accidentally violate someone's civil rights.

After I got off the phone, I looked it up online. "FHP Captures Parolee Wanted Since '94 Using Computer Database Proficiency" was the headline of an article about Walter's arrest on the Florida Highway Patrol website. After seeing Walter's picture on the Florida's Most Wanted website, an FHP lieutenant ran some searches, found Walter at the same address I had, and notified the Washington State Police, who swooped in with weapons drawn.

Florida's Most Wanted. And me on the doorstep, so confident that my quest for the truth would protect me, like a magic shield.

A few months later, I came across Sara's new website, a compendium of documents from Walter's case. A "news/update" let her followers know that Lord Michael Andronicus was in prison, and stated as a fact that I had turned him in.

I was no match for these people, I could see that.

Walter's arrest coming so soon after my visit—it was a coincidence. That's all. True, I had been careful not to tip Walter and Sara off about just how easily I'd found them. I'd said it had been super hard work to track them down. I had not wanted to drive them further underground. Clearly, though, they did not believe in coincidences. Walter had probably already added my name to his kill list. He'd probably inked me in right at the top.

This was too much for me. I'd waded too far in and realized, much too late, that I had gotten in way over my head. And now I was getting out. Whatever happened, whoever was guilty, it wasn't my business. Working as a private detective had taught me to mask my own emotions—*be a mirror, be a blank slate*—and now I was going to use that job skill for my own benefit. In fact, I was going to take it one level deeper, and simply not feel anything about this at all. I was absolutely confident about my ability to carry that off. From here on, I promised myself, my policy was: I don't fucking care.

That December I wrote a short opinion piece for the *San Francisco Chronicle* about *The Exonerated*, the play that had spurred my rash trip in the first place, listing my intellectual concerns about the way it presented some of the facts of the case. Then I boxed up all my notes and court documents and drove over to the shredding plant. I put the two cassette tapes of my 1990 prison interview with Walter in the boxes too, but at the very last moment I pulled them out. Then I watched as every piece of paper I had about Walter and Jesse and Sunny got turned into dust.

7

Don't You Worry That
Someone Is Going to Kill You?

"What is that? Is that the wind?"

Peter and I are still at the dining room table in our rented Florida bungalow. The news clips about the Cravero gang are still in front of us. The police photos of Walter's apartment too. It's midnight now. I hear rustling. There is someone in the hedge. Or on the roof.

"That's the wind," Peter says.

The bungalow came furnished in midcentury modern décor, aqua and ivory. The floor is cold, bare, white. One whole wall of the living room is windows. Thin glass in aluminum frames. The curtains are sheer, billowing in the breeze. A person walking past could see right in. This house is exposed. How did I not notice that before?

For years after my visit to Walter in the woods, I startled awake in the night. *What is that noise, I think there's someone out there— quiet, be quiet, listen.* I'd lie there in the dark, my heart racing. Trying to reason with my fear. Failing. It was a corporeal alarm that defied the promise I'd made to myself to not feel anything, and resisted my best efforts to think it away. So I did the only thing I could do. I buried it.

Now it's back.

In the morning, I drive to Miami to look up Walter's criminal history.

In 1990, when I interviewed Walter in prison, I asked him about his past. He was on parole at the rest area that morning, and I wanted to know what for. "Was that armed robbery?" I asked. "Yeah," he said. But with a toy pistol, he told me. "That's the extent of me being a bad guy," he said. I pictured a plastic water gun. Back then, I believed him. But today I need to know: Did Walter Rhodes have a motive to murder two officers that morning?

Interstate 95 is jammed all the way down. The highway is paved out to the horizon, cars rushing and veering, sunlight bouncing off chrome. It takes me an hour and a half to go thirty miles. In 1976, when Trooper Black pulled into the rest area to begin his daily rounds—waking people up, moving them along—this road wasn't even finished yet.

At the rest area, Trooper Black and Constable Irwin step out of Black's Florida Highway Patrol cruiser into the dawn mist. It was a chilly night that just passed, and Black is checking to make sure everyone in the rest area is okay. To his left, traffic on the new interstate highway is light, three mostly empty lanes in each direction separated by a wide grassy median. As Irwin hangs back to observe, Black walks over to a green two-door Camaro. It's dented, this car, rusted, front bumper twisted, headlights held on with electrical tape. Two men are up front, in bucket seats. Asleep. A wisp of a woman in the back with two children. They're asleep too. Black leans in to look more closely. A blue denim diaper bag is behind the driver's seat. Baby food, baby pajamas. But a gun, down at the driver's feet.

To the south, a truck pulls into the rest area. A Food Fair driver, on his morning coffee break.

Black has the gun from the Camaro now. He's woken the driver up, taken his license, and he's back at the cruiser requesting a criminal history check on one Walter Rhodes.

DISPATCHER: The middle name on Rhodes was Raymond?

TROOPER BLACK: It's Walter Norman Rhodes Jr.

DISPATCHER: Walter Norman Rhodes, 9-2-50, does have a past, also possibly on probation.

TROOPER BLACK: Check Rhodes on his probation again. He was the one that was in possession of the weapon.

It's against the law in Florida for a convicted felon to possess a gun. Punishment: up to fifteen years in prison.

Now Black is walking back over to the Camaro. Walter has gotten out of the Camaro and Black orders him up to the front of the patrol car. Next Black stands at the open door of the Camaro and talks to Jesse, who has moved over from the passenger's side and is now sitting in the driver's seat, and to Sunny, in the back. He's asking them for their identification. Black spends some minutes there, bent over so he can get a good look inside the car. Then he backs out, straightens up, walks to the cruiser—and radios in again. He wants some advice.

TROOPER BLACK: OK. We got a car stopped up here at the rest area, woke them up, two white males, white female in the back with two infants, uh, recovered a weapon from under the driver seat. I believe he's on parole. Uh, the male passenger in the front seat has no identification, he's given me three different home residence addresses. The woman in the backseat claims to be his wife. She won't give us any identification at all. They had a locked, uh, expensive looking attaché case up under the front seat. It's locked by a combination lock. Uh, they hesitated, fiddled around with it, they both denied, denied ownership of it. 10-43?

DISPATCHER: 10-23 KIM 776.

TROOPER BLACK: We've run everything—given everything to the station we could finally put our hands on.

But then Black calls out:

TROOPER BLACK: *10-24 Lauderdale.*

"When the report came back on the police radio that Walter Rhodes actually was on parole at that point, the shots rang out," Sunny told NPR in 2003.

At the Miami courthouse, the clerk tells me Walter's case file from his armed robbery conviction is in the archives, so I will not be able to see it today. The file for Jesse's prior, however, is right at hand.

In *Stolen Time*, Sunny mentions Jesse's criminal record. "He had been in prison for seven years for robbery," is how Sunny described it. "He was so wounded. It was just awful to think of how much he'd suffered, being put in prison at such a young age."

This case file, though, on a blurry microfilm reel I'm reading at the clerk's front counter, says it was not just robbery that sent young Jesse away.

In 1967, according to Case 67-4835, Jesse Tafero—then age twenty—and a friend broke into an apartment, ransacked it, and sexually assaulted two young women at gunpoint, I'm reading now. They stripped, hog-tied, blindfolded, slapped, and dragged their victims; stole jewelry, money, silver, furs, a radio, and underwear; and when a neighbor tried to come to the rescue, they shot him and jumped off a balcony to get away. The victims were an Avon lady and a go-go dancer, and they lived on an island called North Bay Village, out in the middle of Biscayne Bay.

In 1967, North Bay Village—between Miami Beach and the mainland—had a lot going on. There were ten bombings, including the blast on John Clarence Cook's boat, docked just across the water in Miami. "Open vice" flourished within the city borders, aided by a "deplorable lack of effective law enforcement," a Florida Senate investigation reported. Anthony "Little Pussy" Russo, reportedly a top capo in the Genovese crime family, was among the village's winter residents, dividing his time between a home there and his grand jury appearances up north, where his red corpuscles suffered in the cold weather, news reports said. Frank Sinatra hung out on the island at a nightclub called Jilly's South. That's where the young go-go dancer in Jesse's case worked. Next door to Jilly's South, Dean Martin owned Dino's. Nearby was A Place for Steak, notorious for a mob hit on Halloween night in 1967, when Anthony "Big Tony" Esperti whacked Tommy "the Enforcer" Altamura in the lounge. Five shots to the head. Actress Eva Gabor kept a plush condo on the island, and one night Ms. Gabor was tied up, pistol-whipped, and robbed of a twenty-five-thousand-dollar diamond solitaire. She named as her assailant the same debonair Miami stunt diver who, a few years earlier, had made a big splash by stealing the 563.35-carat Star of India sapphire from the American Museum of Natural History in New York City. The diver's name was Jack Murphy. A sun-and-fun beach boy—and a buddy of John Clarence Cook.

On March 4, 1967, the go-go dancer got home from her shift at Jilly's South at about half past six in the morning. As she opened her front door, she heard a voice say "Hey, you." A man was standing inside the door, nude, with a nylon stocking over his head, holding a gun. The nude man put the gun in her face, told her not to scream, and told her this wasn't a joke. He forced her into the bedroom, forced her to lie down on the floor, tied her hands and feet, and then called someone named "Jessie" on the telephone and told him to come over.

Jesse Tafero said it wasn't him. But both women picked Jesse out of a lineup, and, as the jury heard during the trial, Jesse lived with his parents just ten minutes away over the causeway bridge. Mr. and Mrs. Tafero testified that Jesse had been at home that morning, but Jesse's mother later phoned the Florida Department of Corrections to swear that the nude man had pointed a gun at Jesse and forced her son to commit the crimes. And while defense counsel did try to impugn the victims during the trial, the prosecutor wasn't having it. "This is America, I thought," prosecutor Edward Carhart told the jury. "I didn't know we had reached a stage in this country where because someone dances for a living that they are sick in their mind and deserve whatever they get and should be beaten and raped at will."

Both victims took the stand to tell the jury what happened. First up was the young dancer, who testified that Jesse came into the apartment dressed in a gold jacket and wraparound sunglasses, put a gun to her head, and "told me not to resist and not to put up any fight."

By Mr. Carhart:
Q: Did you put up any fight?
A: I put up a little until he got serious with the gun.

Jesse "started to have sex" with the young woman but she "started shaking and crying and I begged him to stop" and he slapped her in the face and told her that "since I am such a lousy lay, that I would be better giving him head," she testified. He grabbed her head and she "started pushing him and crying and carrying on, and I got very, very sick at that time" and Jesse hit her again and she fell and he dragged her naked and bound across the floor.

Her roommate testified about Jesse too. She told the jury that she was tied to her bed and could hear Jesse assaulting her friend in the living room, and then Jesse came and found her.

By Mr. Carhart:
Q: What happened in the bedroom?
A: And Jessie sat on the bed and he said, "I want you to take care of me."
Q: What happened then?
A: And he forced me to suck him.

"Oh God, I remember that case!" Edward Carhart, the retired prosecutor, says. I've found him at home in South Miami, in the afternoon. He's an elegant old man in a wheelchair now, vibrant, sparkling. He's being generous to me with his time.

Carhart didn't think that case would ever go to trial, he tells me. The reason? The young dancer that Jesse sexually assaulted was rumored to be the girlfriend of Tommy "the Enforcer" Altamura, the bigwig Mafia loan shark. It was Altamura who finally ended the attack that morning. Because of Altamura, Carhart was convinced that Jesse was doomed. "I felt for sure Tommy Altamura would gather his wits about him and go kill them." But instead Altamura was shot in the head at A Place for Steak on Halloween, just before Jesse's trial was due to start. It was one of Miami's most notorious mob executions.

That is what I'm having trouble understanding, I tell Carhart now. Why would anyone break into the apartment of a known mobster's girlfriend? Was it part of some larger plot against Altamura and his crew? What was Jesse Tafero involved in?

Carhart is looking at me with amusement. None of the above, he tells me, when I finally finish my list of possibilities. They broke into the wrong apartment, is what happened. It was all a big mistake.

See, the lounge at the Gold Dust used to be a mobster hangout, Carhart says. A Place for Steak, Jilly's South, they all were. A loose group of people who all kept the same hours and met at the same clubs. A group that was just starting to get into cocaine. These guys weren't the polished pros who took over the cocaine trade a couple of years later; they weren't the cartels, the savvy and sophisticated kingpins that made Miami flashy during the *Vice* years. These were more your liquor-store robbers, your breaking-and-entering burglars, a bunch of high school friends who'd stumbled into a high-stakes, high-profit gig. What they lacked in brains they more than made up for in bravado.

"One of the hallmarks with this group was they'd kill you out in the Everglades and then they'd blow up your body," Carhart says.

Jesse was on the edges of the group; the leader was drug dealer Ricky Cravero, Carhart tells me. People were afraid of Cravero, with good reason. One time, Cravero and his friends were partying and talking a little too much and they noticed that one of the girls in the room was getting up to leave. They thought she was going to rat them out, so they ran after her and caught her at the elevator and stomped her. There was that Valentine's Day when they shot their friend Stanley Harris twenty-three times in a parking lot. They'd planned to lure him to a shag-carpeted crash pad and kill him there, but that plan got fucked up when they accidentally snorted all the cocaine they had set aside for bait and the night dissolved into a huge screaming match that only calmed down when someone got out a machine gun. In the parking lot, after they shot Stanley and he lay bleeding on the pavement, Ricky Cravero kicked him in the face. And then there was the afternoon Cravero's gang killed a witness who was due to testify against them in court. That murder happened in Burdines, the fancy department store. Something to do with an escalator.

The break-in by Jesse and his friend was cocaine-fueled, Carhart says now. No doubt about it. Normal home-invasion robbers do not get naked and spend eleven hours torturing their victims. And when Tommy "the Enforcer" Altamura showed up and tried to break the door down, there was a gunfight, Altamura was shot in the leg, and Jesse and his friend jumped off a second-floor balcony to make their escape. Police found the apartment torn apart and the two women naked, bleeding, bruised, and sobbing.

"This was a particularly vicious, vicious group," Carhart says.

I leave Edward Carhart's house and walk out into the warm afternoon feeling stunned. The Gold Dust—that was Marianne's place. Stanley Harris, the Cravero associate who was shot to death— Harris's home phone records showed Jesse's number. I'm finding it all a bit difficult to reconcile: pallid Jesse with his dark eyes in the electric chair; the shy, polite, chino-clad Jesse that Marianne remembers; the tragically innocent Jesse of all the recent news stories and *The Exonerated;* the sexual sadist Jesse of the court testimony; the gangland Jesse of Carhart's description. In the past, when I've thought about Jesse Tafero, I thought he was (a) possibly innocent; (b) guilty but in a wrong-place/wrong-time kind of way; or (c) Clyde. Not real-life Clyde Barrow, but Clyde the charming outlaw as played by Warren Beatty. For twenty-five years, I've assumed that the murders were a devastating spur-of-the-moment heartbreak. A cataclysmic catastrophe, not a calculated act.

But: drug using, drug dealing, home-invasion robbery, rapes, car bombings, witness stompings, escalator murders. A car full of guns and bullets and cocaine and amphetamines. Stolen passports, a rubber mask, a hatchet.

"Well, when certain people come together, you know, certain things happen. With us it was a bad combination," Walter Rhodes told me, when I interviewed him in prison. "It's like when atoms come together."

Or split apart. Maybe it was dark and deliberate, like that.

Sunny also had a criminal history on the morning of the murders, according to the Miami courthouse case files. She was arrested in Miami in November 1968 and charged with prostitution; in December 1970 with possession of marijuana and amphetamines and contributing to the delinquency of a minor—her son, Eric, then age four; in November 1971 with forgery; and in July 1974 with violating South Carolina's gun laws, possessing marijuana and LSD, and possessing with the intent to distribute amphetamines and barbiturates.

On the South Carolina case, Sunny was arrested with an individual who gave his name as Antonio Martes. A copy of the North Myrtle Beach Police Department mugshot of Antonio Martes is in the court records, and the photograph is of Jesse Tafero, who by 1974 had been paroled from his rape and home-invasion robbery conviction, had absconded from parole, and was living life on the run, with Sunny at his side. "I didn't understand it, but I was going to help him," Sunny wrote in her book, about the day Jesse told her he was going to jump parole. South Carolina police found two rifles in their van during the traffic stop, and a loaded .25 caliber automatic handgun in Sunny's purse. She and Jesse didn't stick around for the trial. The courts tried Sunny Jacobs and Antonio Martes in absentia in September 1974 and found them guilty of the drugs and weapons charges. By early 1976, Jesse had added the names Nevel Carmack and Tony Caruso to his alias list. On the morning of February 20, 1976, when Trooper Black and Constable Irwin happened across the Camaro in the rest area, Jesse had been a fugitive on the run for more than two years. Both Jesse and Sunny refused to give Black any identification or even tell him their names, but if they had, FHP dispatch could have let Trooper Black know about the active warrant out for Jesse's arrest.

On Sunny's 1970 criminal case, the one where she was charged with possession of marijuana and amphetamines and with contributing to the delinquency of a minor, she had a codefendant named William DiCrosta.

"Billy," according to his ex-wife, who at this moment is standing on her front doorstep in Fort Lauderdale, looking at me from under a fringe of blond bangs. Her blue eyes are wary and tired, and it hasn't helped that I've just accidentally smashed a clay pot her sister gave her. Billy is now deceased, she says, but in his heyday he played for the St. Louis Cardinals. A good-looking hotshot with a gambling problem, she says.

A story instantly starts to spin in my head about Sunny and some glamorous god of a ballplayer smoking weed back in the day. But when I get back to our bungalow and look it up, I find it was not that. It was a lot more serious.

In December 1970, DiCrosta and Sunny were arrested after Sunny was caught on a wiretap negotiating the purchase of a pound of cocaine. In taped conversations with a man by the name of Ivan Hertzendorf, who was under investigation by the Organized Crime Bureau of the Dade County police, Sunny also discussed buying twenty pounds of marijuana and five hundred hits of LSD. On the wiretapped calls, Sunny told Hertzendorf that she'd given her customers a taste of the cocaine and was waiting for further instructions, and then six days later negotiated a purchase price of six thousand dollars for the full pound. Three days after that, and based on the wiretapped calls, police executed a search warrant and arrested DiCrosta and Sunny. Hertzendorf was later convicted on ten counts of narcotics violations. Sunny was described as a "go-between for other customers" and "capable of dealing large quantities of narcotics in a relatively short period of time," according to the court records.

In that 1970 arrest, Sunny had a good lawyer. She was, after all, the daughter of well-to-do textile manufacturers, and the lawyer took her case as a favor to her parents, he later told investigators. She pled to a single charge of possession, with adjudication of guilt withheld, and was sentenced to probation. Her attorney, Harold Rosen, later became mayor of Miami Beach. And on the day in February 1976 when Sunny was arrested for the murders of Trooper Black and Constable Irwin, her parents talked to another very well-known, high-profile criminal defense attorney about handling her case. Foremost among that attorney's other clients: Ricky Cravero.

"I was representing primarily professional criminals, rather than amateurs," the attorney, Bill Moran, tells me when I reach him by telephone a few days later. "Ricky was a psychopath. Ricky was a dangerous man, period. You don't meet a lot of people like that. Ricky Cravero was one of these human beings that if you got involved in a physical altercation with him, the only option you had, other than dying or being beaten to a pulp, was to kill him."

And it wasn't just Ricky. "It was that whole group of lunatics," Moran said. "It was like a progressively more disturbing, psychotically violent series of episodes fueled by cocaine abuse. They would just feed on each other's psychosis. And of course the drugs."

Moran—who would later count among his clients Colombia's murderous Cali cartel, "source of most of the world's cocaine," according to *The New York Times*, and who in 1998 was convicted of conspiracy to launder money in connection with his work for the cartel—recalls talking on the phone to Sunny's parents that day in 1976 and then going and trying to find Sunny at the Broward County jail. The jailers claimed they had no idea where Sunny was, Moran says. It was a cat-and-mouse thing. "They were telling me, 'We don't know where the person is that we have in custody.'"

But Moran didn't end up working on the case. At the time, his clients were coming into his office and dumping garbage bags full of cash onto his desk, he says. "Blinding amounts of money. The money was beyond belief." He wasn't inclined to take a pay cut to represent a client facing charges of the first-degree murder of two police officers. He remembers explaining his fees to Sunny's parents "in that context," and recalls that they said they understood, but nothing happened after that.

In her book, Sunny wrote that Moran came to find her at the jail after getting a call from her old boyfriend John, who was also Jesse's good friend. Sunny wrote that at the jail Moran told her, "I am, shall we say, the family attorney." I ask him now about this.

"It wasn't a *family*, in the first place," Moran snaps. He has clearly taken "the family" to mean the mob. "As a general thing, I just don't need to hear about that shit," he says. "They were a group of associated people who engaged in joint criminal conduct." And Sunny Jacobs and Jesse Tafero "were just peripheral figures."

But as he tells me this, he's pronouncing Jesse's last name with the emphasis on the first syllable, not the second. Not *Ta-FER-o*, as everyone in the present day does. *TAF-ero*, which is how the Tafero family themselves said it. How people who knew Jesse in 1976 say it.

"Okay?" Moran says. And hangs up.

The court in Miami has finally produced Walter's case files from the archives, and I take a seat in a spare cubicle to review the convictions he was on parole for that morning in 1976.

When I interviewed Walter in 1990, he explained his prior record to me like this:

ME: When you were in before—before this all happened—that was for armed robbery?

WALTER: Yeah. I used a toy pistol and threw down some people and stole their car. I was stupid, and I was a kid.

ME: You used a toy pistol? Where was this?

WALTER: Miami. Homestead. The guy had his paycheck in his wallet and I gave it back to him.

ME: You used a toy pistol, and—what?

WALTER: I used a toy pistol and I stole the guy's car. That was one armed robbery. The other armed robbery was, I used that same toy pistol and I robbed a couple of two hundred and something dollars.

A *toy* pistol. I asked him twice. He said it three times.

The court file, though—just as in Jesse's and Sunny's cases—tells a different story.

In January 1969, when he was eighteen years old, Walter used a ".25 caliber automatic pistol" to carjack a young grocery store clerk in the parking lot of the Dadeland Mall. That pistol is a Saturday night special. A classic stickup gun. Wielding the gun, Walter got into the clerk's 1958 Corvette and demanded his wallet. "Are you going to kill me?" the clerk asked. "Not right now," Walter replied. The clerk jumped out of the Corvette and Walter took off in the car "at a high rate of speed." Walter drove the Corvette to Tijuana, Mexico, and then to San Francisco, ditched it, stole another car, picked up a hitchhiker, and drove back to Miami. There Walter and the hitchhiker invaded the home of an elderly couple who had once rented Walter a room, tied the couple to chairs with electrical cords, ransacked the house, and at gunpoint stole two hundred dollars. The file describes Walter as a "vagrant." Walter was charged with armed robbery in both cases. "Your honor, the only thing I have to say is that I am guilty, and I have got to pay," he told the judge. Walter was sentenced to fifteen years and in late 1969 he entered Florida State Prison. There he was soon to meet Jesse, sent up two years earlier for his breaking-and-entering, attempted-rape, and crime-against-nature convictions.

So, inside that Camaro at the rest area that morning were an armed robber on parole, a fugitive rapist with some very dangerous friends, and the fugitive's gun-owning, gun-toting girlfriend, who apparently knew her way around a cocaine deal. It wasn't just Walter Rhodes who had a motive to kill Trooper Black. All three of them did.

In January 1974, Walter was paroled from Florida State Prison, and in December 1975, he met with his parole officer in Fort Lauderdale to discuss a special request. Walter had been working as a pest exterminator, but now he told his parole officer that he didn't like the "dangerous chemicals" involved and requested permission to change his profession. The probation officer wrote: "He related that he would be looking for a new position, perhaps in an Escort Service." Elsewhere in the files, the name of the company itself.

I drive west from the Miami-Dade courthouse, past bodegas and warehouses and trash-littered sidewalks flashing with broken glass. I find the junkyard just as the clock pushes five, its metal gate rumbling shut as I pull up, stacks of rusted metal everywhere. I park and dash up a ramp that runs along the side of the junkyard office building to a doorway at the top. The person I'm looking for here might have been, I'm guessing, Walter Rhodes's boss.

The doorway opens into a warehouse. In its center is a big wood desk. There is a crowd of young men and women standing around the desk, and sitting at it, in an old office chair that tilts back, is Mark. He's got white hair and is wearing tortoiseshell sunglasses with dark green lenses. He does not take them off.

"Never heard of him," Mark says, when I mention Walter Rhodes.

"Your name is on the corporate records for the business he was working for," I say.

"Never heard of it," Mark says, when I tell him the company's name.

"It was an escort service."

"And I ran it?" Mark says skeptically. He's getting ready to throw me out, I can tell, and all these nice young people are going to help him.

"You and a guy named Peter Blucher," I add quickly.

I have mentioned a magic phrase. Mark laughs uproariously and claps his hands together.

"Peter Blucher! I knew Peter Blucher. I lent Peter Blucher money to start a gay escort service!" Mark says. He pauses and looks at me anew. "Why do you want to talk to me about this?"

I explain the electric chair malfunction. I say that I hadn't known much about any of these guys, and now I was finding out that Walter Rhodes was a for-real armed robber and Sunny may have been involved in cocaine dealing and Jesse maybe wasn't such a nice person either. That I seemed to have wandered into a darker, stranger world than I'd expected.

"Yeah, they're the mob, they all kill each other, going around in a circle," Mark says. "What other names have you come across?"

"Ricky Cravero." The cocaine mobster arrested with Marianne.

"That rings a bell. Who else?"

"Stanley Harris? The guy who was murdered on Valentine's Day?"

"Oh, yeah, okay, I know that name."

"Jack Murphy?" I say, taking a guess. The jewel bandit who was friends with Marianne's husband, and who allegedly pistol-whipped Eva Gabor.

"Oh, I know Murph, we used to surf with him, he was cool. But all we knew about was the Star of India sapphire."

We've moved outside. Mark has pulled the huge metal gates closed behind us.

"Aren't you worried that someone is going to take a dislike to what you're doing?" Mark asks me now. His junkyard looms like a ghost ship behind us. "You shouldn't fool around with this. You seem like a nice girl—nice lady, sorry—I don't mean to be sexist, it's not that, but you should stop and do something else. Don't you worry that someone is going to kill you?"

8

So Much Blood

"I never even saw the junkman's eyes," I tell Peter at dinner that night, at a fish restaurant on the beach. Men in bone-flecked rubber overalls walk past our table carrying buckets and tackle. "'Don't you worry that someone is going to kill you?' He said that with his dark glasses on."

I mean, come on. Yes. That is the answer. Yes, I worry. I'm not a fucking robot. Go home, I tell myself. Get on with your life. Quit asking questions that make people wonder about you being dead. It is exactly this worry that stopped me cold after my visit to Walter Rhodes in the woods twelve years ago. And now I've come down here to Fort Lauderdale expecting to spend a few quick weeks with some dusty old court documents and instead I've tripped into this cocaine backstory of terrorized go-go dancers and the Star of India and a murderous narcotics mob.

"But you know," I tell Peter, "as soon as the junkman said that, my fear disappeared." *Don't push me, pal.* My basic reaction since forever. Something I learned growing up in New York City. It's an asset until it's a liability. "He was standing right next to me and looking through his dark sunglasses at me with his arms crossed over his chest. So I smiled and gave him my business card and told him to please feel free to keep in touch."

Peter and I sit for a while, watching the water. I almost believe what I've just told him. My pep talk to myself. The night is warm, humid, a salt brace from the sea spray and a twinkle of stars. To the south, we can see the lights of freighters heading out to sea.

I do feel upset, though. Mad at myself. I want this to be easier. Weeks of wrangling with the Broward County State Attorney's Office to see the case files—it should have taken just one call. I keep asking for an interview with the prosecutor, Michael Satz, and I keep getting told no. Satz is a legend in this county. He's famously ascetic, tough-minded, intense. I think he should talk to me. I cannot get him to agree.

As I was leaving the junkyard today, a car ran a red light and almost hit me. Sailed across the intersection right toward me, everything freeze-framing as I hit the brakes, spinning, gasping. The driver turning to look at me, windows down, wind in his hair, slo-mo, then turning away, speeding on, gone. I wouldn't even be here right now if I'd been just a little farther across. I'd be dead. Maybe it's the murders, but I feel that a lot now. The fine, fine line between an ordinary day and catastrophe.

"I found the town where Sunny is," Peter says, casually.

Every news story about Sunny in recent years has said she lives in Ireland. But none of them have given any clues as to where. It's a nation of 4.678 million people. Thirty-two thousand square miles.

"She lives in a tiny Gaelic-speaking village in a far western part of the country," Peter says. "Casla. She's raising money to open a center for exonerated inmates. She's got a charitable foundation in New York." He slides a printout from her website across the table.

No street address. No telephone. That's tricky. I need to talk to her, obviously. It's hard to foresee how this one's going to go. But still. Now at least it seems possible to try.

The next morning, I take the crime scene photos I found at the State Attorney's Office and spread them out on the dining room table. In an hour I am going over to the courthouse to view the physical evidence in the case. I know now that everyone in the Camaro had a motive to commit the murders. But who had the means? That's crucial. That's what I need to find out next. And the physical evidence that I'm going to see today—those objects were there at the rest area. That very day. Time travel. I am taking a step closer, in toward the instant when the shots rang out.

In the crime scene photographs, the Camaro is parked tight along the curb at the rest area, its headlights pointing north, next to a patch of grass. It's a two-door car. The passenger-side door is on the right, next to the grass. That door is closed. The driver's-side door, on the left, faces the pavement and is wide open.

To the north of the open driver's-side door, toward the car's headlights, Black's Stetson is on the ground. Next to the Stetson, a pistol. The pistol almost touches the Camaro's front tire. There is no blood north of the door.

South of the door, blood runs underneath the car, glistening all the way to the curb. Where the open door meets the body of the Camaro, directly under the driver's seat, the blood is thick, and red, and deep.

Shards of glass are scattered on the car's running board and into the backseat, which is plainly visible through the wide-open door. Glass is scattered in the blood below the door, along with a foil packet of cocaine, two bullets, and a set of police handcuffs, shining silver on the ground.

Room 407, the Broward County courthouse. I've been buzzed in through a locked metal door past armed guards and am sitting at a table beneath a bank of closed-circuit television cameras. Next to me: a big cardboard box. It's the physical evidence from the Jesse Tafero and Sunny Jacobs trials in 1976.

Dave, the evidence chief, has gone off somewhere with my driver's license. A couple of weeks ago, I met Dave and filled out a public records request to see this box of evidence. Just now, Dave has explained the protocol here. It's very simple: I am not allowed to touch anything. Now Dave is back, pulling on a pair of blue surgical gloves.

"Ready?"

When crime scene investigators examined Trooper Black's cruiser, they found it had been damaged by gunfire during the murders. There was a crack in its windshield, a dent in the front door on the passenger side, and a rip in the metal window trim just above that. And there was a bullet hole clear through the cruiser's windshield post on its passenger side, the side that had been parked alongside the Camaro.

Dave is holding the windshield post now. "Do you want to stand up and take a closer look?"

It's long and thin, this post, made of shiny silver metal and about the size and shape of a yardstick. It ran along the passenger edge of the windshield, from the hood to the roof. The bullet hole is about in the middle and it pierces the post clear through, in one side and out the other. At the point of entry, the bullet hole is round; at the exit, it is U-shaped, bursting upward and outward, its edges like petals that have been pushed apart.

Dave puts a photograph on the table—a picture of Black's cruiser. In this photo, the windshield post is still on the cruiser, the bullet hole is visible, and there is a metal rod sticking out of it, showing the trajectory of the bullet. When it smashed through the windshield post, the bullet was traveling forward, upward, and from the right. The rod looks like it points directly to where the Camaro would have been.

The shots appeared to come out of the back of the car. That is what the truck driver eyewitness Pierce Hyman said.

Through this whole thing I . . . I . . . I sat in the back of that car. That's what Sunny Jacobs told police.

"Okay, thanks," I tell Dave.

Now I'm looking at photographs of the Camaro's interior. In the front passenger wheel well, a jean jacket is crumpled in a heap next to the center console, by the gearshift. On top of the jean jacket is a bronze-colored metal cylinder about an inch long, hollow with a flat cap. Another of these cylinders is in the center of the ribbed floor mat in the front passenger wheel well. Shell casings, ejected from a gun while it was being fired.

Next Dave holds a wrinkled piece of paper. It's a handwritten sales receipt, white with blue ink, made out to Sunny at the address of her family's textile business in North Carolina. The receipt is for two Smith & Wesson Model 39 9mm semiautomatic handguns, serial numbers A187854 and A234895.

Serial A187854 was the gun Trooper Black saw at Walter's feet, inside the Camaro. Black picked up A187854 and took it back to his patrol car. After radioing in the serial number, Black put A187854 on the front seat of his police cruiser. Walter was later arrested at the roadblock with A187854 stuffed down his pants. The other 9mm, A234895, was the gun Jesse was arrested with.

There were other guns in the Camaro too. There was a Smith & Wesson .38 Special revolver in Sunny's purse, a .32 revolver in an attaché case hidden under the front seat, and a short-barrel .22 pistol that ended up on the ground next to the Camaro's front tire, by Black's Stetson hat.

All the guns were in good working order, but only one matched the casings found on the jean jacket and floor mat in the wheel well of the Camaro. That same gun also matched metal jackets recovered from the bodies of Phillip Black and Donald Irwin. So only one of the five weapons in the Camaro could be linked to the murders. That gun was A234895. At the roadblock, Jesse was arrested with A234895 strapped to his hip.

Now Dave is holding up a small gray rectangular box. Two thin wires snake out of it. Dave puts this box on the table along with a glossy pamphlet titled "Read This Before You Attempt to Use Your Taser." Then he puts down two more of the boxes, exactly the same except that at the end of their wires is something that looks like a cigarette butt with a fishhook sticking out of it.

"What on earth are those?"

Taser cartridges.

I look closely. Each cartridge has two darts, made up of "barbed contacts and conducting wires which are projected to target by a small propellant," according to the glossy pamphlet. Each time the Taser is fired, it shoots the darts out and if they both land on the target—or one on the target and the other on a grounding element—they deliver 50,000 volts of electricity. That's enough to "achieve incapacitation," the pamphlet says, and "unlike a gun, you don't have to be a great marksman to use the Taser." These cartridges were found in the attaché case that Black mentioned in his second-to-last radio call. When police recovered the attaché case at the roadblock, there was a Taser in there too. The Taser is under seal, in the vault.

"Wait a minute," I say, going back to the photographs. A photo of the police cruiser. Rear window on the side that had faced the Camaro. Something is stuck in the weather stripping. Something that looks like a dark cigarette butt with a white tip. Yes. That could be one of these Taser darts.

So it seems there were two weapons involved in the murders of Black and Irwin. Not just the gun Jesse was arrested with. A Taser too. I make a note.

The last item is a set of glass vials. Small glass test tubes, elastic-banded together in a plastic box. Swabs. Gunshot residue evidence. I stare hard at them, because these fragile vials are key to two things that are really starting to bother me.

Both truck drivers saw Jesse being restrained against the cruiser as the shots rang out. Up against the cruiser with his hands held behind his back. But that is not what Walter said. Walter testified that Sunny shot first from the back of the Camaro, and that Jesse broke free, grabbed the gun from Sunny, and finished the officers off.

Which leads to the second thing.

The morning of the murders, Jesse and Sunny and Walter all had their hands swabbed for gunshot residue. Trooper Black and Constable Irwin were swabbed too, posthumously—they both tested negative for the indicative chemicals of gunshot residue. Even little Eric, the nine-year-old boy sitting next to his mother in the backseat, had his hands tested.

Five days after the murders, test results came back from the Florida Department of Criminal Law Enforcement.

Two of the swabs tested "consistent with the subject having handled an unclean or recently discharged weapon." Those were Sunny and Eric.

One of the swabs tested "consistent with the subject having handled an unclean or recently discharged weapon, or possibly discharging a weapon." Jesse Tafero.

And one swab tested "consistent with the subject having discharged a weapon." That swab was of the hands of Walter Norman Rhodes Jr.

9

=

The Missing Pixels

Not even a year after Jesse Tafero was sentenced to death, Walter Rhodes began to confess.

In March 1977, two prison inmates came forward to say Walter confessed to the murders to them while in line at a prison amputee clinic.

In 1979, Walter confessed again, this time in writing. Three new inmates witnessed Walter writing the confession out, typing it up, and sending it to Sunny's lawyer.

In early 1982, Walter wrote out another confession and mailed it, unsolicited, to a newspaper reporter in Jacksonville, Florida.

And in September 1982, Walter gave his final confession, this time to an attorney representing Jesse Tafero. That statement, on tape and under oath, was forty-five pages long.

"I just turned around—I lied about that. I said that I stayed there with my hands up. And I just fired from that position where I said Tafero fired from. So, that is another lie there."

From 1977 to 1982, Walter confessed three times under oath to murdering Trooper Black and Constable Irwin. Then, under oath, Walter recanted every one of those confessions. Demonstrably, Walter Rhodes has lied under oath—either when he confessed or when he recanted. Walter was the State of Florida's star witness. And Walter was the one with gunshot residue on his hands.

In 2003, up there in that isolated trailer in the far north woods of Washington State, Walter Rhodes told me about an investigator who had worked on his case. Walter said the investigator sat with him, talked to him, understood him, believed in him. "It's the hardest thing about being a fugitive," Walter said. "That man believed in me, and I let him down."

Now, more than a decade later, I'm standing in front of a stilt house out on the water at the end of one of the smaller Florida keys. It's hot here, and empty. Tangled mangroves in a white-green sea beneath a pale violet sky. I'm down here because I need to talk to the investigator. His name is Walt LaGraves.

Because I don't get it. Three people, three motives, five guns, and a Taser. Walter was a felon on parole with a weapon, Jesse was a fugitive, Sunny was living with Jesse on the run. The eyewitnesses saw shots come from the backseat of the car, where Sunny was sitting; Jesse was arrested with the murder weapon strapped to his waist; and Walter had the dirty hands. Everything I learn leads to something more I don't know. I'm not sure how to go forward. I have no way back.

From the reverent way Walter talked about LaGraves, I assumed LaGraves was working for Walter's attorney in the service of Walter's defense. But I've just learned from the files at the State Attorney's Office that actually LaGraves worked for the prosecution. He investigated the case before the trials in 1976 and then kept on for the next decade and a half, looking into every one of Walter's confessions and obtaining all of Walter's recantations. For ten years, I've been told, LaGraves worked on this case every single day. He was the prosecution's chief investigator. And yet Walter seems to have believed that LaGraves was on Team Rhodes too.

That's impressive. Playing both sides is an investigator's dream game, and winning takes nerve and skill. So if he will talk, La-Graves can help me understand this case—facts, strategies, and Walter Rhodes too. I am certain of that.

"Hello!"

A big bear of a man with his arm in a sling and an Ernest Hemingway beard is hollering at me from the top of the stairs to his deck, here in the Keys. An American flag floats next to him, snapping in the salty breeze.

Historically, law enforcement officers and lady private detectives don't always get along so well. They think we're dilettantes, is why. "Divorced women are ruining the PI profession," a retired FBI agent once told me. I'm not divorced, if that was his point. But now here is Walt LaGraves, extending his hand. "Welcome!" he says, as I reach the top of the steps. It's encouraging. Although maybe he's being Officer Friendly just so he can find out what I'm up to. There's that possibility. A sharp listener can learn more from your questions than you do from any replies, that's for sure.

Inside, white shutters are closed against the noonday glare. LaGraves takes a seat at the head of the dining room table as his wife, Carol, arrives with cold drinks. Rush Limbaugh brand "Two If by Tea" iced tea.

"I hope you're not a liberal," LaGraves says.

I glance over at him. He might be teasing me, but he's definitely not joking.

The iced tea glass sweats in front of me as I launch into my explanation of what I'm doing. As I go along, it occurs to me, belatedly, exactly whose dining table I'm sitting at right now. This man helped put Jesse Tafero in the electric chair.

"I mean, there are all these newspaper articles about Jesse Tafero saying he was a good dad," I continue, stumbling.

"You don't take your children on drug deals and have your nine-year-old son act as a lookout," Carol interrupts. As it turns out, Carol worked as secretary to Michael Satz, the state attorney. "Tafero was anything but a good dad."

LaGraves jumps in. "He was a down-on-his-heels, evil, little angry man. A hard, cruel human being."

"A sociopath, that's what I thought," Carol adds.

"And Sonia was a cold, hard bitch," LaGraves says. "Rhodes, now, he was a fascinating guy, but you wouldn't want him to date your sister."

"Have you met Walter?" Carol asks me.

"I interviewed him before I witnessed the execution, in 1990."

"What did you think of him?" Carol says.

"Well, I was twenty-six, and he was the first prison inmate I'd ever—"

They both burst out laughing.

"I personally believe that they were heavy narcotics users," Walt says, when he and Carol collect themselves. "These are not big-time criminals. Scum-sucking bottom-feeders, all of them."

I am writing this down when Carol adds something out of the blue.

"My thing is the Taser," Carol says.

"Sonia deploying the Taser started the whole mess," LaGraves agrees.

The Taser. After I saw those gray cartridges in Room 407, I'd gone back and read through Walter's confessions. No mention of a Taser. Then I'd read through the initial statements given by the truck drivers and by Jesse, Sunny, and Walter. Nobody mentioned a Taser there either. Walter was specifically asked about a Taser in the statement he gave officers the day after the murders, and Walter said no, he did not see a Taser used.

"This?" I ask LaGraves.

I've come here with my stack of evidence photos from the State Attorney's Office. I slide the first one across the table now. It's the one of the rear window on the passenger side of Black's cruiser, with the object that looks like a cigarette butt lodged in the weather stripping. LaGraves and Carol look at it. Yes, that is a Taser dart, they confirm. Absolute proof that a Taser was fired, they say.

But I thought the two officers were killed with gunshots, I say.

Picture the rest area, LaGraves says. It's just past seven o'clock in the morning. Trooper Black is in his cruiser, pulling up alongside the Camaro, parking, getting out. Black walks over to the Camaro. What does he see? A gun on the floorboard at Walter's feet. Black leans in, gets hold of the gun, takes it out of the car.

"That started the whole affair," LaGraves is saying.

Black orders Walter out of the car. Walter gets out. Then Black orders Jesse out.

"We believe Tafero exploded out of the car," he says. Black and Irwin try to subdue him, pushing Jesse up against the passenger-side door of the police car. Sunny is in the backseat of the Camaro, just inside the open door of the car, watching as Jesse and the officers start to struggle.

"That's when Sonia fired the Taser," LaGraves says. "This whole thing probably started when Sonia fired the Taser at one of the officers."

But ballistics tests were useless when it came to the Taser. The weapon left no identifying marks on the darts it fired. The Taser dart in the cruiser window proved that a Taser had been involved, that's all. No link to the specific Taser at the crime scene. No clue about who fired it.

Another photograph. It's 1976, and LaGraves is sitting in the backseat of the green Camaro, holding a gun. A234895, the murder weapon.

LaGraves picks up the photograph and looks at it.

"God, I was young," he says.

After the murders, two bullet casings from A234895 were found inside the Camaro near the front passenger seat, one on a jean jacket, the other in the wheel well. The prosecution needed to understand how those casings got there, so LaGraves climbed into the Camaro with a ballistics expert, he's saying now. "We took the Camaro down to the FHP lot on State Road 84 in Fort Lauderdale, and parked the Camaro and Trooper Black's cruiser side by side to as best we could reconstruct the relative positions based on testimony."

Specifically, they were testing whether firing the gun from the backseat—where Sunny was sitting—would have landed those two bullet casings up front like that.

LaGraves and the ballistics expert fired the murder weapon about fifty times inside the Camaro, according to the ballistics report that was attached to this photograph in the state attorney's files. Of those shots, just four bullet casings landed up front, and only with the gun held sideways, lying flat. They did not fire the gun outside the car to see if the casings bounced in. The report did not make a whole lot of sense to me, which is why I want to ask LaGraves about the ballistics test now.

"What did you find out?" I ask him.

"I don't think we could prove to the exclusion of every reasonable doubt that Sonia fired from the backseat," he says. "I don't think we could do that. But there's a whole lot of circumstantial evidence, and in a civil trial we could prove it."

I glance down at my notebook to hide my surprise. This is the state attorney's chief investigator speaking. A civil trial? They sent Sunny Jacobs to *death row*.

"Did you talk to Angie?" Carol asks. Meaning Angelo Farinato, the detective who said Sunny confessed to him.

Farinato's handwritten notes were in the files at the State Attorney's Office. Farinato interrogated Sunny immediately after the murders, and later that same day he drove Sunny down to the Broward County jail, just the two of them in the car. Along the way, Farinato wrote, Sunny confessed. His notes use "Tony" as the name for Jesse. It was the name Sunny gave to police when they asked her who Jesse was.

Statement from Sonia in Vehicle 20 Feb 76

On returning from PBSO Sonia stated that she fired one shot from vehicle and heard someone outside the vehicle state give me a gun give me a gun, at which time she threw the gun out

& did not know [*sic*] picked it up. She believes that Tony had fired the fatal shots that killed FHP Trooper & Canadian police officer.

Sunny vehemently denied confessing to Farinato. But Farinato's statement was admitted as evidence at her trial and was upheld by the courts, including on Sunny's final appeal, the one that resulted in her release from prison in 1992. That ruling, though, included a footnote that stopped just short of calling Farinato a liar. The court wrote: "The credibility of the statement to Farinato is not unassailable. Farinato insisted that Jacobs referred to Irwin as 'the Canadian,' although there is no evidence in the record indicating how she could have known he was Canadian at that point in time."

In October 1990, five months after Jesse Tafero's execution, Farinato was the subject of a complaint filed with the Broward County sheriff, alleging that Farinato had ordered deputies in another case to falsify an official police report. Farinato was indicted on one count of official misconduct, a felony, and in June 1991 his case went to trial. The jury acquitted him. But after the jury's verdict, the internal affairs division of the Broward County Sheriff's Office conducted its own investigation into Farinato's conduct and in July 1991 issued a report that sustained misconduct allegations against him. Among the investigation's findings was that Farinato had violated the Broward County Sheriff's Office policy that "employees will not make false statements in any communication, verbal or written, concerning official matters" and brought "discredit to himself" and to the sheriff's office as well. Shortly after the investigation, Farinato retired.

Last week, before coming down here to the Keys, I drove to Angelo Farinato's house, out near the sugarcane fields. I talked to him in his front yard, through a shiny wire fence. Farinato told me that the state had been lucky to get a conviction in the case, and that the shell casings inside the Camaro were crucial to the conviction.

Those casings meant that shots had to have been fired inside the car, and Sunny had a gun in her purse, Farinato said.

Also, the two truckers saw the shots coming from the back of the car, he added.

"Well, you're an important part of the case too," I told him. "You're the one who got Sunny Jacobs to confess."

He looked blank. Then he corrected me.

"No, Valjean Haley got the confession."

"Haley did?"

"Yes. Haley got her to admit that she was in the back of the car."

He held my gaze for a long moment. A wiry man with ice-blue eyes, dressed all in white. In his hand was a metal wand he had been using to pinch pine cones one by one up off his perfect crew-cut lawn.

"I did talk to Detective Farinato," I tell Carol now.

"Did he remember getting Sonia's confession?" Carol says, crunching up and winking both of her eyes hard on the word *confession*.

"No," I say, looking from her over to LaGraves. "Actually, he did not remember that."

LaGraves and Carol both burst out laughing again.

I feel upset now. Okay, fine, this is all a joke. I feel foolish too, with my typed-up study notes and my list of questions. All of which LaGraves is brushing right off.

Bullet trajectories? Meaningless, according to LaGraves. "You can't depend at all on the path of a projectile through the body." The gunshot residue tests? "Oh, Rhodes was *covered* in gunshot residue." The bullet blast through the Cadillac door, the one that blew into Rhodes's left leg, sprayed gunshot residue everywhere, plus the officers at the roadblock stood right over him with shotguns aimed at his body. So those tests were meaningless too, La-

Graves says. In fact, the state's own expert testified on the witness stand that the test was unreliable. What about Tafero's possible connection to this guy Ricky Cravero, the violent cocaine over-lord? *Meaningless*, I write down, in my notebook, as LaGraves replies. These cases are complex, they're messy, and maybe if I were a trained police detective with a badge and a gun instead of a Girl Scout waltzing in with my pie-in-the-sky questions and unrealistic factual expectations, then I wouldn't be insisting on answers nobody is going to be able to provide. That could be the message I'm getting.

"So why did you believe Walter Rhodes?" I ask LaGraves. Because that's really the reason I'm here.

LaGraves nods. He's been expecting this.

After Jesse, Sunny, and Walter were indicted, Walter's court-appointed attorney said Walter might be interested in a plea in exchange for his testimony. Michael Satz, the chief homicide guy in the office, asked LaGraves to visit Walter in jail along with Walter's attorney and size Walter up.

Walter had just had his leg amputated and "he was terrified," LaGraves says. "A deer in the headlights. And he started telling his story."

As Walter talked, LaGraves took note of Walter's body language, his inflection, his choice of words, and his emotions. "He was strongly indicating to me that he was telling the truth," LaGraves says. "Or at least that he absolutely believed he was telling the truth."

"I'm sorry?" I say. I'm not sure I've heard that last part correctly.

"I was convinced Rhodes was telling us what he believed to be the truth," LaGraves repeats.

So, no ballistics, no trajectories, no gunshot residue that could conclusively show who murdered Trooper Black and Constable Irwin. Just the testimony of Walter Rhodes, who later confessed multiple times to murdering the two officers, and who had that positive gunshot residue test, apparently from being leaked on by shotguns at the roadblock. Walter Rhodes believed what Walter

Rhodes was saying, which does not seem like the same thing as LaGraves believing it himself.

"Okay," I say. "What is the proof that Jesse Tafero was even involved?"

"There was no single item—there never is, there almost never is—the single item that is the golden nugget," LaGraves says.

"I'm sorry?" I say, again.

For almost twenty-five years, I have wondered if Walter told me the truth the day I interviewed him in prison in 1990. And for all those years, I have assumed that whether Walter told me the truth or not, there must have been evidence that backed up his trial testimony. Not bullshit evidence, direct physical evidence. Hard facts. I have simply taken it for granted that the state would not have relied on just one man's word to send two people to death row, especially after that man began confessing to the crime himself. There must have been more evidence than that, I've told myself. But now the prosecution's chief investigator is telling me the case against Jesse Tafero was all basically, what, circumstantial?

"I don't see it as a single instant. I rarely see it as a single instant," LaGraves is saying. "It's like a film loop. You look at each frame, you put it all together, and what do you get? To quote a Disney movie, bibbidi-bobbidi-boo."

He and Carol look at each other and laugh again.

"Look, Rhodes had given up," LaGraves says. "When Black radioed in, Rhodes gave him his real name, his real date of birth. He had his hands in the air, you got me. It was over, for him."

"Walter Rhodes was telling a story that was completely reasonable and Jesse Tafero, you can tell from the outset, he was a mean, evil person," Carol adds.

But there are people who believe that Jesse Tafero was innocent, I'm thinking. Staring at my notes while I try to figure out my next question. Jesse's friend Marianne, for example. Marianne was in touch with Jesse all the time he was on death row. Marianne told

me Jesse was innocent, just before she handed me the letters Jesse
sent her. Some of which turned out to be pretty steamy.

March 17, 1988
I've really been in love with you for so many years. . . . You're
everything I desire in a woman. . . . You're soft loving and sen-
sual, you're strong willful and smart, you're all the things I
find most pleasing and desirable. . . .

The letters were a surprise to me, actually. Because the official
story of Jesse and Sunny, as told in newspapers and on television
and onstage in *The Exonerated*, is that Jesse and Sunny were madly
in love—with each other. "You're my woman, as close as my
breath," Jesse writes to Sunny, in the play. "Hand and glove, you
know?" The night I saw the play, the woman sitting next to me
reached for her Kleenex when she heard that line.

If I hadn't read Jesse's letters to Marianne, I might not have
searched for more information about her. But I had read the
letters—*you've never really tasted all my love*—so I did. The first
thing I found was that story about Marianne and her husband and
his blown-up boat. Next I found stories saying John Clarence Cook
was a jewel thief. Then I found news reports linking John Clarence
Cook to Jack Murphy, the beach boy and jewel thief. And then I
found a transcript of Jack Murphy testifying to the Florida Parole
Commission about Jesse Tafero. By the time of his testimony, Jack
Murphy was a famous man, a dazzling celebrity bad boy turned
devout Christian prison evangelist. Bringing his full star power to
bear, Jack Murphy told the commission that he personally knew
Jesse Tafero was an innocent man.

"What about Jack Murphy?" I ask LaGraves now.

Jack Murphy: high diver, smooth talker, cat burglar. Legend.

In 1964, Jack Murphy and a friend scaled a fence surrounding
the American Museum of Natural History in New York City, Spider-
Manned up the façade to the fourth floor, slipped through a window

into the Hall of Gems, and stole the Star of India sapphire, a gray-blue stone with white blazes on both sides, one of the largest cabochon sapphires in the world. They also stole the flawless DeLong Star Ruby, the yellow Eagle Diamond, and a smash-and-grab bagful of other rare jewels. Outside again, Murphy coolly hailed a taxicab to get away. "One of the greatest jewel burglaries in history," the newswires said. It didn't take long for police to arrest Murphy, but the debonair, talkative, insouciant thief was an instant hit with the press. "Murph the Surf," the newspapers called him, detailing his days as a cabana boy, a surfer, and a stunt diver who had wowed crowds on Miami Beach. Nora Ephron, then a cub reporter, was among the writers who covered the story. "Murphy was, in a sort of pop-art way, the true twentieth-century man," Ephron wrote:

> He might have been invented as the hero of an ABC television series. *Surf Side Suspect*, or some such thing: tall, blond beach boy tends cabanas and leaps from high diving boards by day and, police insist, robs by night.

In 2011 this famous beach boy jewel thief appeared before the Florida Parole Commission. The hearing was not on Jesse Tafero's case, but Murphy brought Jesse up all on his own. Murphy told the commission: "I've been working with the largest prison ministry in the entire world for the last twenty-four years. I've been in over 2,500 prisons . . . and I've met many, many people that all say, 'I'm innocent, I'm innocent,' and I just, I don't even bother with it. But I was there with Pitts and Lee," Murphy said, referring to Freddie Pitts and Wilbert Lee, who spent nine years on death row before being pardoned, perhaps the most notorious wrongful conviction case in Florida's history. And, Murphy added, "I saw Jesse Tafero die in the electric chair, who was innocent, because I know the man who killed the officer."

"Jack Murphy?" LaGraves is saying now. "Jack Murphy and I go way back."

Jack Murphy was the first case LaGraves investigated for the Broward State Attorney's Office, he tells me. It wasn't a far-out cat-burglar jewel heist. It was a vicious double murder.

In 1968, Jack Murphy and a man named Jack Griffith were charged with killing two young women and tossing their bodies into a shallow backwater near Miami called Whiskey Creek. At the time, Murphy was a big part of the North Bay Village scene, LaGraves says. The Jilly's/go-go dancing/Frank Sinatra scene. The victims were two "swinging young secretaries" who stole half a million dollars' worth of securities from the brokerage house where they worked and ended up in a dispute with the two Jacks about the loot, according to news accounts of the trial. That's when Murphy and Griffith invited the women on a boat ride. "They gutted them, sliced their bellies, and then tossed them overboard," LaGraves says. "They ripped the wires out of the boat and used the wires to tie concrete blocks to them."

Carol interrupts. "Well, and wasn't one of them giving him a blow job when they killed her?"

LaGraves looks at her, and then at me.

"Yes," he says, like this was not an absolutely necessary detail to be discussing.

Both Jacks were convicted of murder, and in 1969 they both went to prison—Murphy sentenced to life plus twenty years.

Fast-forward to 1977, one year after Jesse's trial. Two prison inmates came forward to say they had heard Walter Rhodes at a prison amputee clinic confessing to the murders of Trooper Black and Constable Irwin. LaGraves investigated, and interviewed the inmates on tape. The two inmates swore to LaGraves that Walter had indeed confessed, and one inmate gave a very detailed statement about Walter's confession. LaGraves asked him if anyone had helped him prepare that statement. The inmate said yes. Jack Murphy.

"But why would Jack Murphy get involved in Jesse Tafero's case?" I ask LaGraves.

Because Jack Murphy loves the limelight, LaGraves replies.

The Whiskey Creek murders cast a pall over Murph's image,

but not for long. Murph found God behind bars, served seventeen years, and in 1986 was released amid front-page fanfare from prison. Murph announced his reentry to society with a press conference in a chapel, standing at a pulpit lit with seven candles and proclaiming the Lord as the "master of my life." In 2014 a *Vanity Fair* story titled "The 50th Anniversary of New York's Most Sensational Jewel Heist" celebrated Jack Roland Murphy as a beach boy, a playboy, a compelling prison evangelist, and fascinatingly intelligent outlaw—a truly original man.

"Jack Murphy is a really bad guy," LaGraves tells me. "But he's a bad guy with a lot of class."

To Jesse and Sunny, though, Murphy was a beacon of hope. In her book, Sunny wrote: "Jack Murphy, better known as Murph the Surf, was the chaplain's clerk, a born-again ex-jewel thief who had done a lot of time and was well respected as a 'stand-up' guy."

When those two inmates told Jack Murphy that Walter had confessed to the murders, Sunny wrote, "he advised them to do the right thing. They went to the authorities."

But the courts let the death sentences stand.

There was a case LaGraves worked on years ago, he's telling me now. Two girls whose car broke down. Two guys came by, said, We'll give you a ride to a gas station so you can call for help. The girls were like, No, that's okay, we'll stay here. But the guys kept on and finally one of the girls said, Fine, sure, okay, I'll go. Her friend stayed with the car. The guys did not take the girl to a gas station. They took her down to an abandoned house on the beach and they raped her and beat her until she died.

LaGraves has seen a couple of executions, and they didn't bother him at all. Just one less evil person in the world walking around to worry about.

"There truly is evil," LaGraves says. "Evil does exist."

I want to agree with him, because it seems so easy. That clear-cut delineation. The thing is, I was totally in favor of the death penalty until I witnessed Jesse Tafero's execution. Then I was totally against it. And then the daughter of a friend was murdered and I realized that I might be a novice, actually, about grief. About its requirements, what it asks of you, what it takes. But evil? I think if you go with that explanation, you're heading toward vengeance, not justice. It's justice that interests me.

"I just thought they'd have more proof," I tell Peter at dinner. About Walter Rhodes, in particular. *"I believed he believed what he was saying*—what does that even mean?"

Around us the restaurant is filled with partying Canadians toasting the moon as it rises over the water. I watch them glumly. I need to talk to prosecutor Michael Satz, clearly. But his office is not returning my calls. And LaGraves told me that even if Satz does agree to an interview, I am not going to enjoy the experience. He and Carol laughed about that too.

"LaGraves called it quixotic, what I'm doing," I tell Peter. "I had to look it up. Do you know what *quixotic* means? Extremely idealistic. Unrealistic and impractical. So he doesn't think it's possible. Why would it be quixotic, to want to know exactly who killed whom that morning?"

I realize, with a burst of panic, that I did not ask LaGraves a crucial question. So right there in the middle of dinner, I rush downstairs onto the beach and out onto a dock, shouting into my phone.

"Why don't the testimonies of Rhodes and the truck drivers match?" I ask LaGraves.

"Why? I don't know why."

"Okay, let me rephrase that. What was the effect on your case of the testimonies not matching?"

"You know those paintings, what are they called, that are made of little dots," LaGraves says.

"Pointillist?"

"Yes, pointillist. It's like that. Or pixels. Just because a few pixels are missing doesn't mean you can't see the whole picture."

We hang up, and I walk out to the end of the dock, the sea indigo around me with the night. I think over what LaGraves has just said. Pixels: *Rhodes, hands in air, truck drivers, shots from backseat, Taser dart, Tafero with murder weapon.* Maybe they've never really known for sure. I can't help but think that now. Maybe they simply ballparked it and got a jury to convict. Then when the star witness recanted his trial testimony and confessed to the murders himself, their trusted investigator got him on tape, taking it back. And too bad about that unsightly electric chair malfunction, but shit happens. The End.

You know what? No. That is just not good enough for me.

The next morning, on the way back up the Keys to Fort Lauderdale, Peter and I pull over at a fishing pier, a white concrete span over the aquamarine sea. We walk out. At the end of the pier, there is a gap—the sea, far below—and then, out in the open water, a remnant of the old overseas highway, the road that was here before the new one came through. The old road is a strip of two-lane blacktop with a thin yellow stripe down the middle and rusted metal railings on each side. It's an island now, with weeds and trees growing up through its pavement and dust blowing off into the clear blue below. It looks like the past, this road that goes nowhere, that you have to leap over a gap to get to and from which you cannot easily return, a span from here to there in midair, crumbling down, so stunningly desolate—and lovely. So entirely in ruins.

10

Fifteen Miles, Seventeen Minutes

The summer after I first started working as a private detective, I found myself in a courtroom, testifying under oath about the way Jesse Tafero died.

"It was actually pretty intense," I'm saying now, on the shaded patio of a sports bar in Coconut Creek, Florida. I'm with John Sutton, the lawyer who defended Jesse Tafero at trial in 1976. It's a few days after my visit with Walt LaGraves in the Keys.

It was 1997, I'm telling Sutton. Seven years after Jesse's execution. I came home one day to find a letter on my doorstep from an attorney in Florida saying that the electric chair had malfunctioned again. Flames, smoke. The witnesses heard gurgling. The next inmate up for electrocution was suing the state, saying that the chair was cruel and unusual punishment. But his attorney was having trouble finding anyone to testify about what it looks like when a man catches fire on the state's dime. I read the letter in the backyard of the house I was living in then, an old cottage in San Francisco. Fruit trees woven into a canopy overhead, blossoms in the springtime, then bitter fruit. I thought of what Sister Helen Prejean told me outside the prison that morning: *Bear wit-*

ness. So I went to Jacksonville and in a courtroom there I testified about Jesse Tafero's death.

Q: When the electricity was turned on, were you able to hear that or how did you know it was turned on?
A: I knew—I could hear it. It was sort of a large sound, a humming sound, but also I saw Tafero kind of jump backwards in his chair and flames and smoke rose from the—underneath his headpiece.

After the hearing, the court ruled that the electric chair worked just fine. Then two years later the chair malfunctioned again. Blood, this time. Dripping from underneath the hood covering the condemned man's face. Another lawsuit. I testified in that hearing too. One piece of evidence introduced: the leather strap that had been used to gag the condemned inmate. Tied so tight into his jaw that it had twisted his face into a deep-red bloody knot. *Does this look like the strap that was used over Mr. Tafero's mouth?* the attorney asked me. Holding it up in his hand. Coming closer. I felt the room fall away. Once again, after the hearing, the Florida Supreme Court ruled that the chair was good to go, but this time Justice Leander Shaw, in dissent, uploaded photographs of the blood-soaked dead man in the electric chair to the court's website, where anyone could see them. In the uproar that followed, the Florida legislature quickly passed a law allowing for lethal injection instead.

After that second court ruling, I resigned from the detective's firm, left the office in his mansion behind me, and went to work for a California state agency that defends death row inmates. I personally worked *for* condemned killers. That might have been what Walt and Carol were poking around at, with the Rush Limbaugh iced tea. Fair enough. But I only lasted six months. It was too wrenching. Because of the clients, yes. The doom of their impending executions. But because of their crimes too. Their vicious, violent, heartless, shocking crimes. I'd thought the electric chair hearings had given me a fiery determination to fight for equitable treatment under the law, but I was wrong. All they'd done was make everything about the death penalty too much to bear. For those six months, I went to work each day and investigated the excesses of human cruelty, and then I mostly went home and sat by myself. Every so often I'd go out on a bad date, or rather someone would go out on a bad date with me. My fault. I was living in a world where very terrible things happened, but I could not talk about it, so I had nothing whatsoever to say.

And then one day Freya called me to ask if I wanted to start a detective business with her. Not too long after that, I met Peter. Slowly, I began to find my way back.

Back here.

I've got a bad habit of staring at the ceiling when I think. I'm doing it now, here on the sports bar patio. I snap out of it to find Jesse Tafero's trial attorney taking a sip of his iced tea, watching me.

"Well, I can tell that you're not going to like what I have to say." Sutton laughs. He has a soft voice, white hair, a freshly pressed white shirt, faded blue jeans, lively brown eyes. A big square of white gauze is taped to his forehead. I don't ask.

"What are you going to say?" I ask him.

"Jesse Tafero was a killer," Sutton tells me. Almost cheerfully. "He was a stone-cold killer." Pause. "And Sunny? She sure wasn't much to look at. I mean, how good in bed can someone be?"

Sutton kicks back in his chair and laughs again.

"Those two were so into Bonnie and Clyde," he says. "They were fascinated by Bonnie and Clyde. They *lived* that movie."

He drops his voice to a stage whisper. "Didn't they watch it all the way to the end?"

I have found Sutton unexpectedly. Jesse's primary attorney, Robert Staley McCain, died in 2002, but in reading the transcript for Jesse's trial I noticed a quick reference to a young lawyer who was working with McCain on the case. At the time, John Sutton was fresh out of law school, a member of the Florida Bar for just one year. Now Sutton is telling me that getting the court appointment to represent Jesse was going to be a wonderful thing for him and McCain. That's what they thought at the time. "We were going to be in the paper every single day, and that's advertising you could never purchase."

But that's not how it worked out. The problem, Sutton says, was Jesse Tafero.

"The first time I met Jesse, he said to me, 'If I wasn't chained and handcuffed to a table and I thought I could get away with it, I'd kill you right now.' Jesse was a bad guy—he was really a bad guy. That guy was scary as hell."

There was never any question of Jesse testifying, Sutton is saying. "We couldn't put Jesse on the stand, for Christ's sake. He would have lied so much. He was not a smart man. He wasn't one of the brilliant ones, he was one of the ballsy ones. They'd have eaten him alive."

Jesse did not testify at his own trial in May 1976. But after he was convicted and sentenced to death, he testified for Sunny at her trial that July. And on the witness stand, under oath, Jesse Tafero told the jury that he had personally witnessed the murders of Phillip Black and Donald Irwin. His was a new version of events, one not offered at his own trial or in police reports. Jesse testified that while Constable Irwin was holding him down on the police cruiser, Jesse saw Walter Rhodes standing at the front of the Camaro with a pistol in his hand.

ATTORNEY: What did he do with it, if anything?
TAFERO: I saw a flash come from the muzzle of the pistol; and shortly, you know—this all happened in just a seconds period— I was being pushed back and forth on the hood of the car by the man that was holding me. [. . .]
ATTORNEY: Did you eventually get up off the hood?
TAFERO: Yes, sir, after the shots had stopped. During the last cou-

ple of shots, the last couple of seconds, the man that was holding me went sort of tight, and then he just wasn't there
anymore.

On cross-examination, prosecutor Michael Satz asked Jesse to
demonstrate exactly how Walter was holding the gun.

SATZ: According to you, how was Rhodes holding that gun? Stand
    up and show us.
(*Witness indicated.*)
SATZ: Down by his private parts?
TAFERO: Yes, sir.

With Jesse's testimony, I now have three possible scenarios to
consider for the murders of Trooper Black and Constable Irwin.
Scenario number one is the state's case, which relied on Walter's
testimony to convince two juries that Sunny fired the first shots
from the backseat of the Camaro and then Jesse grabbed the gun
from her outside the car and continued firing. Scenario two was
presented on television, on *20/20* in 1992 and in the made-for-TV
docudrama *In the Blink of an Eye* in 1996. It contends that Walter
Rhodes shot the officers from a position behind the Camaro, putting the bullet hole through the police car's windshield post. But
now there's this new-to-me scenario, from Sunny's trial, that Walter shot both officers from a position at the front of the Camaro.
Eyewitness testimony from Jesse Tafero himself, spoken under
oath in open court.

It's confusing. But something even more basic is troubling me
now.

You know the moment in a TV courtroom drama where the
prosecution rests and the defense counsel rises to present the defendant's side of the case to the jury? That did not happen at Jesse's trial. McCain and Sutton presented no evidence on Jesse's
behalf. No testimony, no witnesses, no physical evidence. Nothing.
Not one word. In a capital murder trial. Zero. Then, after the jury

convicted Jesse, Bob McCain—instead of presenting mitigating evidence for the court to consider to spare Jesse's life—dressed himself in black as the Angel of Death, stood up in open court, and denounced the entire proceeding:

> I will be very brief here today, in that I have consulted with Jessie [sic] Tafero and he feels very strongly that he did not receive a fair trial. He feels very strongly that this verdict was not fair, and he feels that to participate in the sentencing argument in any way, would be a charade. He will not beg for his life, nor mercy.

Three years later, Bob McCain was convicted of conspiring to sell more than one hundred pounds of marijuana and of attempting to bribe a witness in a federal drug case. He was sentenced to serve twelve years in prison and was disbarred.

"What about Bob?" I ask Sutton now, on the patio. The lunch crowd has thinned out and it's just the two of us left. "Was he using cocaine during the trial?"

"He was certainly into it during the trial," Sutton says. "It was a circus."

But why didn't you and McCain put up a defense? I ask.

Sutton leans forward. There's something he needs me to understand.

Jesse refused to talk about what had happened at the rest area, Sutton says. Even under the attorney-client privilege, Jesse wouldn't say anything. And Jesse would not say one word against Sunny.

"Jesse was under her spell. As a woman, you've got to be smart to get a man like him under your control. She didn't think they'd get caught, and she thought that if they did get caught, they'd go out in a blaze of glory. That's why it became such a disaster at the rest area—Sunny saw that cop getting too close to her man, so she was like, 'I've got to kill him.'" Sutton pauses. "Women murderers are actually very rare. A woman who kills two strangers? Very, very rare."

Sutton looks at me. "But in reality, we just didn't have much of a defense. That's the reason. We put on no defense because *we had no defense.*"

The instant I introduce myself to Bob McCain's widow, however, she tells me something entirely different.

"Jesse Tafero?" Michele McCain says. "Jesse Tafero was innocent."

I'm standing at her front door over on Florida's Gulf Coast. In addition to being married to Bob McCain, Michele was his secretary, and she helped him during Jesse's trial. She's vibrant, gray-haired, dressed in a T-shirt and jeans. A long scar, blood-dark, fresh, runs across the left side of her throat. I don't ask. A German shepherd bounces behind her, all teeth and nose and ears.

"Did Jesse tell you what happened?" I ask as we sit down in her living room.

"Jesse said he didn't do it. He said it was Walter that did it. He kept proclaiming, 'I didn't do it, I couldn't have done it.'"

The key, she says, was the autopsy photographs.

Nobody's told me about autopsy photographs, I say.

Oh yes, Michele says. After the murders, the officers were taken to the morgue. There, examiners inserted metal rods into the officers' wounds—through their bodies, from entry to exit—to show the angles of the bullets, and took pictures. Michele saw the photos herself.

"The angle of the bullets came straight down." She takes a pillow and demonstrates, holding her hand up above the pillow, directly perpendicular to it. "That meant somebody tall had to be standing and shooting them. It was the angle of the bullets, that downward angle."

Jesse was bent over the hood of the cruiser, so no way could he have done it, and Sunny was sitting in the car, so no way could she have done it, and therefore the only person who could have shot the officers from that downward angle was Walter, Michele says.

"Walter is six feet tall, isn't he?" she asks.

"I think he is," I say, remembering.

Michele only met Jesse Tafero once, but she talked to him on the phone many times. He was courteous but all business. When she saw him—in the courtroom, at his sentencing—the thing that struck her was his eyes.

"His eyes were cold. They were very, very cold," she says.

As she says it, I see him again. He's looking at me from the chair.

Locked in. One, two, three, four, five, six. Then his stare moves on.

Michele is still talking.

"It scared me, his eyes were that cold," she is saying. "But that doesn't mean he killed them."

As I drive down Interstate 95 back to our bungalow, I tally it up.

John Sutton, partner of Tafero's trial attorney: Jesse Tafero was guilty.

Michele McCain, widow of Tafero's trial attorney: Jesse Tafero was innocent.

All the bullet casings and metal jackets recovered from the crime scene and the slain officers that could be ballistically matched came from one gun: A234895.

Jesse was arrested with that gun strapped to his waist. Sunny was sitting in the backseat of the car, where the eyewitnesses saw the shots coming from. Walter was the one who tested positive for having fired a gun.

Taser dart in the patrol car window.

Bullet hole in the patrol car's metal windshield post. Trajectory: back to front, low to high.

Jesse: *I saw Walter Rhodes in front of the Camaro. . . . I saw him with a pistol in his hand. . . . I saw a flash come from the muzzle of the pistol.*

Sunny: *I didn't see, I didn't see.*

Walter: *I actually witnessed the shots. When the gun first went off Sonia was the one holding the gun. . . . I believe then Jesse pulled the gun from her and shot him one more time and then he shot the other cop twice.*

I turn off the interstate toward our bungalow. Every day, I drive past the spot where the rest area was. Long gone now, taken over by the road. As I pass it, I glance over, as always. Wondering.

When I first figured out where the rest area had been, I was surprised. So I timed the drive from the rest area back to Walter's apartment in Fort Lauderdale to be sure. Fifteen miles, seventeen minutes.

That's what hits me now.

Walter's apartment was pretty crappy. True. But it did have four walls and a roof.

Yet they spent the night just minutes away on the side of an interstate highway. Three adults and two young children in a small and rusty Camaro.

Why were they in that Camaro?

11

Everything. It Was All Gone.

"The Camaro," I tell Peter, walking into the house and straight past him to the back bedroom, where my files have been taking up more and more space.

Forest green, two-door, bashed up. In police photos, the Camaro's paint is rusting, its hood and trunk don't close, its bumpers are twisted, half its front grille is missing—one running light askew like a boxer's blacked-out eye—and its side-view mirrors are totally gone.

"Check out this car." I'm holding the photos. Peter has followed me in here and is leaning against the doorframe. "This piece-of-shit car is the *key*."

"You look tired," I add, noticing.

For more than two months now, Peter and I have been talking only about the murders. Michigan seems like distant memory—the hush as snow falls, red cardinals in the icy woods, the warmth of hearth and candlelight on a cold clear night. Here in the sunshine, every conversation ends up at the rest area in 1976. At breakfast, at dinner. On walks to the grocery store. At the beach, on the couch, at night in bed. Peter is a great listener. He's my best friend. He's a private detective with a decade of experience too.

Detective work is not just search and retrieval. An algorithm can do that. Detective work is finding something you didn't know you were looking for. Pattern recognition with unknown unknowns. Freya's approach was blazingly exact. I hopscotch. That was a great combination, but we still sometimes got stumped. Over the years, we hired a lot of different people to work with us—a lawyer, a construction worker, a bartender, a journalist, a librarian, a brilliant medical student—and they were all great in different ways, but I came to believe that the capacity for detective work has much more to do with how a person experiences the world than with anything it is possible to teach, aside from *Do not fuck up.* Peter had worked as an actor, a director, a waiter, an editor, and a writer, but it was just luck that, as Freya and I discovered when we asked him to help us out, he was a natural detective as well. A client needed early drafts of an artwork for a copyright dispute, but the artist had died. Peter tracked down the person who had inherited the artist's computer, and she handed over not just one or two early drafts of the artwork but the computer's entire hard drive. Handsome and charming, right there on the doorstep. Peter's main strength, though, is honesty. Transparency. It's an odd asset for a private eye, but it works. Because good news or bad, he just wants to know what's really going on. He'll tell you, too.

Later, when we're on our way back home to Michigan, on the first night we spend driving north, in the safety and solidity of our friends' house in Savannah—no rattling windows, no curtains billowing in the wind off the sea—Peter will tell me that he was so lonely here in Florida that he wondered if he even still existed. That he worried about me. About us. That he feared I might be disappearing into these murders, never to find my way back. That he locked himself into the bathroom one evening and wept.

Right now, though, it's eleven o'clock at night and we're both exhausted. I am scrambling through my file boxes for the transcript of my prison interview with Walter Rhodes and for my collection of news interviews with Sunny. Peter, shadows under his eyes, is studying a blurry xeroxed picture of the crime scene and the car.

"Here, read these too," I say, handing him more papers from my files.

According to Sunny, she and Jesse and the kids were in the Camaro because her "old clunker" of a car broke down and "we were just kind of stuck." That's what she told *20/20*, back in 1992. And so, the show reported, "for two hundred dollars, Walter Rhodes agreed to drive Jesse and his family north, to West Palm Beach. At three A.M., the Camaro pulled into the rest area."

But when I interviewed Walter in 1990, he had a whole different explanation.

According to Walter, they were in the Camaro in the rest area because Jesse and Sunny were paying him to drive them around to do drug deals. He said they'd been riding around earlier in his red Ford Fairlane, all three adults plus the two kids, dealing drugs, and some "gangsters" had chased them, so they dropped by a friend's house and borrowed the Camaro to throw the gangsters off the trail.

ME: Where was the car? Where was this that you swapped cars?
RHODES: This was at some guy's house named Steve Addis.

A new path has appeared. Sunny says they were simply catching a ride from a friend up to West Palm Beach. Walter says they were driving around to deal drugs.

"I finally have a litmus test," I tell Peter.

It all comes back to the Camaro. Who is telling the truth about that, Walter or Sunny?

One quick online search later, I find that Steve Addis is real.

But Steve Addis is dead.

South on Interstate 95, then a turn onto Sans Souci Boulevard. *No worries*, in French. A four-story apartment building from the 1970s, peach stucco and coral pebbledash, shaded by palm trees.

Peter found this address last night after I gave up and fell asleep on the couch. At the building intercom, the directory is broken, so I take a guess and punch in the apartment number.

"Taliaferro?" a voice says. It's a terrible connection, buzzy. "Never heard of him."

"Tafero," I shout.

"Jesse Tafero?"

"Did Jesse Tafero borrow your brother's car?"

"*My* car," the voice says. "Not my brother's car. My car."

Then he adds, "I can't hear you." And hangs up.

I call back.

"It's not like I am going to talk to you, honey."

"I witnessed Jesse's execution," I shout. Louder.

There is a pause.

The voice says: "I'll be right down."

The man who appears at the entrance to the building is tall and skinny in acid-washed jeans and iridescent mirrored sunglasses. I hand him a photo of the Camaro taken at the rest area crime scene. Gene Addis—he's fifty-seven, the youngest Addis brother—stares at it. "That's my car," he says. He points to a light dusty line on the inside of the left front tire and says something about the axle coming undone and that the tires rode differently after that. He says he wasn't there that night, he was out of state, visiting with Miss Teenage Kansas. "When I came back, my car was gone."

"Did you ever see it again?"

"Nope," he says, and invites me inside.

At the elevators, I hesitate. Gene seems nervous, which is making me nervous. I'm getting into a tiny elevator and going up to an apartment with a total stranger. Usually I'm outside on the doorstep when I first meet someone, not locked in a small box with them. In the elevator, Gene is telling me about his brother—not Steve, who loaned Walter the Camaro that night, but one of his other brothers—and he seems upset. He'd started talking about this other brother in the lobby and he seems incredulous and hurt about him. We get out on the fifth floor and start down the hallway. Gene is still talking a mile a minute about his asshole brother. Who happens to be Mickey Rourke. That is correct. The Hollywood actor.

Those magazine interviews Mickey gives, saying mean things about their dad? Never happened, according to Gene. Their dad was a police officer and tough, yes, but he never crossed any lines, and if there's one thing that Gene cannot stand, it's a liar, and do I want to know something else? Gene and Mickey haven't spoken in eighteen years, since the night Gene was in Club Deuce in Miami Beach drinking and Mickey refused to be introduced to his friends. Still, "Mickey is not alone. I love him to death. He's creating his own wilderness." But if Gene ever catches him . . .

Actually, it's not what I'm here for, and I am concentrating pretty hard on figuring out if walking down this long hallway is a good idea. So when Gene opens his apartment door and introduces me to his best friend, Adam—"We've been friends since we were six years old, we're not gay" is what he says—I am relieved. Adam is a tidy, rosy-cheeked, non-nervous guy in a polo shirt and khaki shorts.

"Adam, she has a picture of the Camaro."

I hand Adam the photograph.

"Oh, yeah, look at that tire. Remember how on the highway the whole thing used to shake like it was coming apart?"

They both laugh.

"Where were you then, Kansas?" Adam says.

They both laugh again.

"When I got back, all my stuff was gone," Gene says, suddenly serious. All of the swords and coins he had collected. His knives. "Everything. It was all gone."

Four days after the murders, two federal narcotics agents visited Walter Rhodes in the hospital room where he was recovering from the amputation of his left leg. Walter told the agents that on the days immediately preceding the murders, he drove Jesse and Sunny around so they could buy and sell cocaine, marijuana, hashish, and Quaaludes. Walter claimed that among the people Jesse and Sunny bought cocaine from were a man named John and his mother. John and his mom had "pounds" of cocaine, Walter said. "Bags of coke" that they were weighing out on a machine. Steve Addis had a weighing machine too, Walter alleged. Whenever Jesse "would get a whole lot of coke, he'd either go to John's or Steve's to weigh it up." The night before the murders, Walter said, they went to Steve Addis's house, traded drugs for an ammunition clip and a knife, sold four grams of cocaine to some guys across the street, and swapped Walter's red Ford Fairlane for the Camaro. Then they took off in the Camaro toward the rest area.

After the murders, police descended on the Addis household. Their father was a Miami Beach policeman, and the Teflon-coated bullets that had taken the lives of Trooper Black and Constable Irwin had come from a box in the attaché case marked "National Police Supply Company."

But Steve Addis told the investigating officers he had no idea what they were talking about. Shown a mugshot of Walter, Steve Addis admitted that he had seen Walter before, but when shown booking photographs of Jesse and Sunny and asked "Do you know either one of these individuals by their correct name or by a nickname?" Steve Addis replied, "No, sir, I don't."

Now Gene Addis is smoking a doobie and letting the memories of old times flow over him. We're in the living room, facing the palm fronds of Sans Souci through an open balcony door. The apartment is full of faded pictures of Miami Beach from the 1960s and 1970s. No neon lights, no glitter. Just Gene and Adam and their friends, squinting into the camera, in bathing suits, on deserted sidewalks in front of the old Art Deco hotels, partying up on the peeling rooftops, legs dangling off the roof edges, sea and sky and sun.

It's been a long afternoon. Six hours, rounding into evening now. Every time I've asked a direct question, I've gotten "no" or "yes" or "I don't know" as an answer. But I'm hearing a ton of stories. When Gene was little, his father married Mickey's mother, and that made for a lot of kids under one roof. House rules: triple bunk beds, speak only if you are spoken to. Gene's father was six foot three, 260 pounds, and twice a day he made his children line up in a row for an inspection, like in the military. Imperfections were punished with bare-ass whippings. But they had the run of the beach. Long afternoons crabbing off the jetties, blue crabs, stone crabs, tackle football games in the shallow water. There was no love, is the thing, Gene tells me. It would've been okay if there had been love. "If my elbows touched the table, I got a backhand literally into the wall."

Later, Gene and his friends worked as pool boys at the Eden Roc, hanging out on their lunch breaks in the shade underneath the high diving board. He had a trick where he lay motionless on the bottom of the pool, scaring the tourists. He's proud to say he can take a punch. He drank vodka one time until blood ran out his nose. Gene has scars on his forearm, on his collarbone, his elbow, his shins. He thinks I'm pretty. He thinks I look like his mom, whom he loved and who died.

There was one afternoon, after his mother died. Gene was fifteen. He was living with his dad and stepmother then in Miami Beach; the neighborhood is priced in the multimillions now, but back then, in the early 1970s, a policeman could buy in. His brother Steve had an apartment with friends nearby, and Gene went over to say hello. He knocked on the screen door, but nobody answered, and so he went around the side and peeked in the window. "I didn't know that you don't do that to drug dealers," Gene says. At the window was the business end of a shotgun, pointed directly at his head.

His brother Steve was rough, Gene says now, as if the memory is shaking loose. Steve was one tough dude. A bad guy. A real bad guy. Steve was a biker. An Outlaw. When Gene was in sixth grade, Steve punched him into a glass door—split his upper lip almost right off his face—after Gene found Steve's weed by accident. Nobody told Steve what to do. Steve and his friends, that whole group—they were robbers.

"Don't tell her that," Adam says, from his chair.

"It doesn't matter, they're all dead."

"I already know about the robberies," I bluff, from the couch. I do, kind of. Jesse's name was on a police memo from 1974 about a robbery ring.

"That's what they were—robbers and drug dealers," Gene says. "And nobody messed with them."

Jesse was a friend of Steve's, Gene says. That's why Steve lent him the Camaro—because if you were Steve's friend, you were golden.

"And Sunny used to date John Mulcahy, which is how we knew her," Adam adds.

I look up from my notebook.

"You guys knew John?" I ask. Thinking of his brother Irish, the big guy who slammed the door on me when I asked to talk to their mother about her affidavit. Marion Mulcahy swore that on the night before the murders, Jesse and Sunny and Walter were in her house, visiting with her son John. Thinking too of what Walter told the DEA agents, that Sunny and Jesse bought cocaine and hash from a drug dealer who lived with his mother. *His name's John and his mother is, like, in it just as much as he.* That's what Walter said. Which might explain why Irish shut me down.

I look at Gene now. "I tried to talk to John's brother about all this, but he said no."

"Yeah, he'd never talk to you," Gene says. "He's a punk."

But yes, they were friends with John. And yes, Steve Addis was a robber and a drug dealer and he most definitely knew Jesse and Sunny too, Gene confirms.

"It's almost like a pack of dogs when you're dealing with these types of people. If you walk into a room full of alpha dogs, you always take a look at the one you do not want to touch," Gene says.

In this group, the alpha dogs were Joe Rourke—the actor's brother—and John, Sunny's ex and Jesse's close friend.

"And then you got the people who are willing to do the really stupid shit and that's where you get Jesse and his cohort," Gene continues. "There were certain ones that were willing to go over certain lines. John, Jesse, my brother Steve. You just knew—no words needed to be spoken."

"You just had a sixth sense to be careful," Adam says. "To watch your back."

After the murders, after the police came by and asked how the Camaro ended up as a prime piece of evidence in the roadside slaying of two officers, Gene tried to ask his brother Steve about it, but "he just shut down on it." There was no going there, so Gene didn't. Then everybody took off out of state for a while to wait until it all blew over.

"To be honest with you, I believe the right people were executed, from what I've seen in my life," Gene says. "I don't believe in the death penalty, though. I believe if you put someone in a cell for the rest of your life, that's the worst thing you could do."

"Living with that grief for all eternity," Adam says.

"Guilt, Adam," Gene says. "Not grief, guilt."

"Guilt, grief," Adam says.

"Never touching a woman again," Gene says.

"Never being with a good friend," Adam says.

"Never touching a woman again," Gene says.

"To be lonely but never being alone," Adam says.

Out at my car, in the dark—it's night now—I check my phone.

Where *are* you? Peter has texted, about eight hundred billion times.

The instant I get back to our bungalow, Peter hands me an envelope.

It's addressed to me in my own handwriting, with block capital letters stamped in red ink across the top: MAILED FROM A STATE CORRECTIONAL INSTITUTION. I'd sent Walter Rhodes a letter over a month ago, with a self-addressed stamped envelope. I had begun to wonder if he was going to write back.

"Dear Ellen," the letter begins, in Walter's meticulous script. "I knew there was a major catalyst on the way, but had no idea it would come from you."

———

12

The Personification of Death, If I Chose

This is what a haunting feels like.

A dark hum that starts as a shudder and turns into a tidal-wave single-note drone, hollowing out the bones of my spine.

"We had both felt you were the catalyst that resulted in my arrest," Walter's letter says. He's talking about my visit to his house in the north woods, twelve years ago. A stab-flash, ice-cold. Fear. "I was a wanted fugitive. It may be you had no choice. . . . If you did it, I forgive you."

He forgives me. Walter Rhodes forgives me.

A TNT python, coiled inside my chest.

And now the sensation of falling backwards, of spinning down. Darkness. This is so fucking stupid. I don't want to feel this. I can't help it. When I was a child, I read *The Lord of the Rings*, but only until I got to the Ringwraiths, merciless cloaked horsemen with glowing hypnotic eyes. They scared me so much I had to stop. Those horsemen are coming for me now.

"Even after all these years, I can still hear that cat screaming," I'm saying to Peter. We are driving west across Florida so I can meet a friend of Walter's. That is what the letter has instructed me to do. Walter has written an autobiography. This friend has it. I need it. The buzzing has started again. Resonant, consuming, from the death chamber that morning. I cannot hear myself think. I have blocked Walter Rhodes out of my life for more than a decade. Deliberately. Assiduously. And now he's back. Because I invited him back. Because I am not going to be able to solve this mystery without talking to him again.

Walter and Sunny and Jesse did borrow a car that night. They borrowed that Camaro from a drug dealer who was the son of a police officer, just like Walter said. Which means that the story Sunny has been telling all these years—*it was only a ride*—is incomplete, at best. And it means that whatever else Walter Rhodes may be, he's not one hundred percent pure liar. He told me the truth about how he and Sunny and Jesse came to be in that Camaro. A credibility point in his favor. But does that mean he told me the truth about the murders of Trooper Black and Constable Irwin?

"At some point, you do have to make peace with yourself," I said to Walter Rhodes, in that prison conference room the week before Jesse Tafero's execution. Now here I am, a quarter century later, taking my own advice. Driving across Florida in the hopes of getting hundreds of memoir pages written by a man who has spent half of his life behind bars for murder. A "magnum opus," as Walter called it in his letter. I'm interested in what it will tell me about Walter. But maybe I need it in order to understand my own life too. *You have to be tough with yourself, and what you know, and how you screwed up too.* That is what Donn Pearce told me. Admitting I never have known much—not anywhere near enough—about Walter Rhodes is a start.

"What's that around your neck?"

It's ten o'clock the next morning, and I'm sitting at a kitchen table with a man who calls himself Z. We're in his airy condominium near the Gulf of Mexico. At Z's elbow is a thick stack of loose-leaf pages. I recognize Walter's handwriting. His beautiful copperplate script.

"This?" I say, raising my fingers to my throat. "I think it's a smoky quartz."

"I love quartz."

Z is the friend that Walter Rhodes's letter instructed me to call. "I believe you are a god(dess)send at this point in my life because of the many things you don't know," Walter's letter said.

I have to be honest. I'm nervous. "I am walking into my own darkness here," I told Peter this morning as I left our beachside motel. Aside from Walter's wife up there in the Washington woods and Walt LaGraves, the law-enforcement investigator in the Keys, I've never met anyone who knows Walter Rhodes, and I've had no idea what to expect. But Z has turned out to be a super-mellow guy in a cream guayabera, a marketing executive in his sixties with a gentle inquisitive vibe.

"Very powerful!" Z's wife says, from the doorway. She's talking about smoky quartz too. She is toned and barefoot in yoga tights, with a mane of dark curls and huge amber eyes. A professional astrologer and a seller of water deionizers, she tells me.

"So how do you two know Walter?" I say.

"We met through an online message board devoted to Ra," Z says.

I must look blank.

The Law of One, Z explains. A series of channelings received by a Kentucky librarian and her partner, a college engineering professor–turned–commercial airline pilot, from a sixth-density social memory complex—an "extraterrestrial missionary"—who landed on earth eleven thousand years ago "with the objective of helping Earthman with his mental evolution," according to the Ra website. Ra speaks in English, answers questions, and provides guidance to the higher realms as well as factual information about our own planet, including the revelation that the United States has 573 psychotronic particle-beam spacecraft that are made in

Mexico, used "in many cases" to change the weather, and hidden in bases on the moon, beneath the sea, and in the skies.

When Z first encountered Walter on that Ra message board, Z had no clue that Walter was a fugitive from a murder conviction. That piece of news came as a shock. But, Z adds, there is no way Walter Rhodes is a killer.

"I've met him," Z says. "I can tell."

That is so exactly what I once thought that I pause for a moment, watching Z. It is comforting to believe there is a rhyme and a reason to this world—and to other people—that you can discern simply by trusting yourself. But your gut instinct isn't always right. Sooner or later, I have come to find out, everyone gets fooled.

For the next two and a half hours, Z slowly reads aloud to me from Wikipedia entries about Jesse and Sunny that he's printed out and highlighted in neon yellow. After Z reads each page, he hands it to me and watches to make sure I read it too. I pay full attention and take careful, respectful notes. "It will be up to his discretion whether he shares the M.O. with you," Walter's letter had said, about Z.

Finally Z says yes, I can have a copy of Walter's magnum opus.

There is a tight traffic jam on the road off St. Pete Beach, a crush of construction equipment and elderly drivers. Peter is at the wheel now as we make our way to the copy shop. I hold Walter's manuscript on my lap.

"Jesus fucking Christ," I say, when Peter takes what I think is a wrong turn. We are heading across a tangle of stupid streets next to the beach instead of the way that I—having been here exactly never before in my whole life—think we should be going.

"The Google Maps lady can go fuck herself," I inform Peter. "I could get down on my hands and knees and *crawl* faster than this," I tell him. I am shaking. So, so anxious and angry. I feel like I'm going out of my mind.

I flip through the sheaf—it is 452 pages long—and stop at random: *There was no question in my mind I would have little trouble becoming the personification of death if I chose to do so.*

I slap the pages back together and stare out the window.

At Z's condo, as I was taking my leave, I'd noticed a piece of paper on his kitchen table. Written on the paper was my full name—including my married last name—and the address of our house on its little country lane in Michigan. Neither of which I've given Z—or Walter Rhodes.

That night, back in Fort Lauderdale, I sit down with my copy of Walter's autobiography.

"I was rather stupid or mentally defective," Walter writes, by way of introduction.

Walter Norman Rhodes Jr. Born in Alabama in September 1950 to Walter Senior, a sheet metal worker, and Joan, a housewife, Walter grew up in Maryland as the eldest of six.

From the age of eleven, Walter was in trouble with the law. Shoplifting, housebreaking, auto theft, joyriding, larceny, and forgery. Twice as a juvenile, Walter was committed to the Maryland Training School for Boys, at fifteen he dropped out of high school, and at sixteen he stole a car and won a ticket to the Maryland House of Corrections. Walter served half his sentence, was released on parole, and fled. A warrant was issued for his arrest. Two armed robberies later, at the age of nineteen, he arrived at Florida State Prison. He'd been behind bars before, but this was the big time. A negative vortex of murderers and rapists and assorted "psychic vampires." He was young and he was afraid.

Walter got a pentagram tattoo on his hand and started wearing an upside-down crucifix. He called up demons. He studied black magic. He studied white magic. He tamed a rat snake and carried it in his shirt pocket. One night he woke in his cell to a tiny high-pitched sound. Looking over, he saw a spider gripping a fly. "The fly was screaming!" Shortly after that, he was at a drinking fountain about to take a sip of water when a vision flashed into his head. The fountain was next to a dayroom with a television, and as Walter watched, the vision he'd just seen in his own mind was broadcast to all on the TV. He had picked up a television commercial "*before* it was transmitted to the screen!"

This is the man whose testimony put Jesse Tafero in the electric chair, I write in my notebook. *This is the man I believed.*

Walter dropped acid at Florida State Prison. He started meditating. He had visions that he was merging into gold flames that appeared on his cell wall. He got into fights. He saw a guy get stabbed in the neck and killed. He saw guys get hit with pipes and hit with hammers and set on fire. And every so often, he ran into Jesse—in the carpentry shop, where Jesse borrowed a piece of wood from him; in the bathroom, where Jesse was hitching up his belt and promising to kick some dude's ass; in the electronics shop, where Jesse seemed to be in a blank trance. Walter felt that Jesse was different, and powerful, with a dangerous aura. One night Walter dreamed that he and Jesse shared a past life in which they were "Orientals. Probably Japanese." And Walter and Jesse both practiced "this mysterious art called karate." All the "baddest motherfuckers" in the prison system did, a select, sadistic group of deadly individuals determined to win and hold power at all costs. The stars. Jesse was very good at and very committed to karate. Walter practiced hard too. Punches, strikes, kicks, breaking each other's forearms and shin bones with mop handles, breaking their own knuckles by punching concrete walls. "Crazy egotistic insanity," Walter writes.

During those first years at Florida State Prison, his 1969-to-1974 stint for armed robbery, Walter and Jesse had some friends in common. One of whom was Jack Murphy.

Murph the Surf, the guy who stole the Star of India sapphire from the American Museum of Natural History, who was sent up to FSP for the bathing-suit murders on Whiskey Creek, and who later told the Florida Parole Commission that not only was Jesse Tafero innocent, but "I know the man who killed the officer."

"Murphy was a very likeable guy, and extremely intelligent," Walter writes. "I knew him very well."

In 1974, Walter was paroled and went home to Maryland. He got married and in late 1975 he and his wife drove back down to Florida. As they were traveling late one night on a dark country road, a huge red glowing sphere the size of a small house zoomed up behind their car. The car engine quit, and Walter jumped out to get a better look.

The sphere was floating like a soap bubble on the side of the road, luminous and fiery and perfectly round, Walter's memoir says. The sphere seemed to be a vehicle, but it was not a machine, and within its round fiery luminousness there was an intelligence, an entity, who was looking right at Walter. Electrical sensations started running along Walter's spine, and he could feel his hair standing on end. In a way that was neither pleasant nor unpleasant, Walter felt chills.

This was not the first UFO he had seen. As a teenager behind bars for stealing cars, he had yelled "Take me with you" out the window at lights zigzagging across the sky. And later, out in the Everglades, he would see a giant spacecraft landing in the middle of a dark highway. But encountering this burning, floating sphere was, Walter writes, the most significant event of his entire life—mystical, magical, supernatural. He knew that whatever it was, it was not from Earth. Walter felt awe. He was "thunderstruck. Amazed. Excited. And transfixed."

By February 1976, Walter—still on parole—and his wife were living in the garden apartment in Fort Lauderdale. One of the conditions of his parole was that he not set foot in Dade County, but Walter asked if he could please be allowed to go down to Miami. His parole officer told him no, but Walter went anyway, to big jams of Florida State Prison alumni out in the Everglades. "I'm talking about Party," Walter writes—drugs and alcohol in a huge house with a great stereo, Jacuzzis, a sauna and a gymnasium, plus trail bikes, horses, and a trained attack dog. Walter snorted so much cocaine out there that he felt like "Superman and Einstein and Casanova all rolled into one" and ended one night face-up on the floor, unable to move.

It was at one of these parties that Walter bumped into Jesse, who was out of prison too and on the run. That night, everyone got completely fucked up on weed, booze, and coke. A couple of days later, Walter's wife found Walter in bed with another woman, they argued, he slapped her, and she split. Later the same day, Jesse called Walter and asked for a favor. Could Jesse pay Walter to drive him around? Walter said yes, jumped in his "bad ass, heat-seeking" red Ford Fairlane, and drove down to Miami to meet Jesse for a few drinks.

Walter was excited. He and Jesse had both done time behind bars and they knew the same people from prison and they were both into karate—all of that felt like a bond. Plus, Jesse was better than Walter at karate, and to Walter, that seemed auspicious, career-wise. A chance to get ahead in life.

After drinks, Walter drove Jesse and Sunny and the kids back to his apartment. Walter put a favorite record by his man Joe Walsh on the stereo and fired up some weed. Right there in Walter's living room, Jesse pulled a few slow-motion karate moves, and Walter noted with appreciation Jesse's precise and excellent technique. Very much like Walter's own technique, Walter thought.

Soon, Walter writes, he and Jesse were on the same wavelength. A unit, a team. Partners, "vibrating in resonance" along the warrior path. Being around Jesse Tafero made Walter feel superior. Arrogant. And definitely up for some action. He turned to Jesse and said as much right out loud:

"To the death!"

13

The Closest Thing to a God in Prison

That night I stay up late reading Walter's memoir.

Walter Rhodes received TV transmissions in his head and saw UFOs. He dreamed he was beamed up onto a starship in a tube of pure white light. He spent nights out in the ocean in a speedboat, floating above the sunken city of Atlantis, watching strange lights in the sky while his drug-running buddy killed eels by crushing their heads. That was weird, Walter wrote. Walter's wife was a CIA agent, or so Walter suspected. Two of his girlfriends turned tricks in massage parlors and gave him fistfuls of cash. A mafia guy hooked him up with his apartment. He had his future predicted at a séance. And he was a literal sex magnet, attracting and tapping hot chicks like he was "God's personal gift" to womankind.

Walter Rhodes is also the only person who saw Jesse Tafero shoot the officers.

Walter's testimony, plus Jesse being arrested with the murder weapon strapped to his hip, were—as far as I've been able to tell—what sent Jesse to death row. I've got my notebook in front of me now and I'm charting it out. All the other facts point either to Walter—his confessions, the gunshot residue on his hands—or to

Sunny: the metal windshield post, the truck driver eyewitnesses, the bullet casings in the car. I am planning on trying to talk to Walter again, if he'll put me on his prison visitor list, and to Sunny, if I can find her in Ireland. But today I need to talk to a friend of Jesse Tafero's named Art, I decide, as dawn starts to gleam along the edges of the windows. Because in 1989, Art gave an affidavit to Jesse's attorney that squarely blamed the murders on Sunny and Sunny alone.

"Jesse and Sunny? I introduced them to each other," Art says, at his front door a few hours later. His apartment is just down the road from where the Cadillac crashed that morning. "Sure. Come in."

Art is a retired United States Air Force mechanic, dressed this rainy Sunday afternoon in a T-shirt and shorts, barefoot, with a shock of silver hair. His voice is low and slow, like Karo syrup poured on a bass guitar. I'm grateful for that. He sounds so mellow that he's calming me down, and I need it—I am running on fumes now. It's not simply my long night with Walter's memories and Walter's voice in my head. My time in Florida is almost up. I've been here just shy of three months. An entire winter. In a week, I have to head home.

In addition to the Air Force, Art also worked as a substitute teacher, as a bus driver for disabled schoolchildren, and as president of the local food co-op, he's telling me as we sit down together on his couch. Oh, and he was in the drug business too. Art is entirely matter-of-fact about this. He mentions the .38 handgun and the shotgun he used to have with such laid-back casualness that I find myself thinking, Oh, hey, sure, that's just two guns. A totally reasonable number.

Art knew Jesse his whole life, he says. They met as children in grammar school in Miami and were close friends from then on. Art knew Jesse's mom, Kay. "A sweet lady." Jesse's dad was "stricter." And Art knew Sunny, from the old North Miami flea market, a skating rink near the co-op on Dixie Highway. Sunny sewed yoga pants to sell, that was her thing. "She was really friendly, and she got to be in our group because of her sewing ability," Art says. In 1973, after Jesse was paroled from prison on his robbery and attempted-rape convictions, Art arranged for Jesse and Sunny to meet. "I thought they might hit it off." Also, Jesse needed a place to stay. "So Jesse stayed with Sunny one night and they got sexually involved and then he was just living there." At the time, Jesse was going by the name Tony Caruso, and dealing drugs.

But Jesse was not a successful drug dealer, according to Art. "Jesse had access to drugs from a lot of different people. From Ricky Cravero. From me. Jesse's problem was that he had no buyers."

Drug dealing is a social business, Art explains. You have to sit down with people, do the drugs with them, hang out. And that's why people didn't want to buy drugs from Jesse. It was his personality. "Jesse was a wild man," Art says. It turned people off.

What Art has just told me matches what I read in Walter's memoir last night. On one deal, Walter wrote, Jesse tried to entice a balking cocaine customer with a sample snort and a threat of bodily harm: " 'I'll pistol whip you and take all your money motherfucker!' "

That had not seemed like tip-top pharmaceutical salesmanship to me, but then again, it's not like I know the etiquette of the 1970s cocaine marketplace. So it's helpful to hear what Art has to say.

But Art does not believe that Jesse murdered the officers.

"Write this down," he tells me, looking at my notebook. "Write down that one of Jesse's best friends says Jesse never pulled the trigger."

Before Jesse met Sunny, Art says, "to my knowledge I don't think he ever had money to buy a gun. Jesse didn't know anything about guns. Sunny did. Sunny—even though she denies all of this—Sunny knew guns. We were all in the drug business in one way or another. Some of the guys we knew were very dangerous people. She tries to play herself off as an innocent bystander, but she was as active in everything going on as Jesse was."

That is exactly what I'm here to talk to him about. I hand Art his affidavit from 1989:

> Some time after the shootings, I met Sunny's brother, Alan, at a party. We were all talking about what had happened, sharing what we had heard about it. I remember that Alan laughed, and said that he knew what really happened. He said that Sunny had told him that she was the one who actually fired the shots from the backseat of the car. He said that to a group of people. I'll never forget it.

"Yeah, I remember this," Art says now, reading it over.

I watch him from my end of the couch. He looks a little hesitant, I think. Holding the statement carefully, like it might bite him.

Now Art is handing the statement back to me. When Jesse's attorneys first approached him for the statement, Art says, he didn't know what to do. So he told them he'd agree to give the affidavit only after hearing from Jesse himself that this was what Jesse wanted. Art worked out a code, something Art told the attorney to ask Jesse, something only Jesse would know. When it came back correct, that's when Art felt like it was okay to sign.

Jesse blamed Sunny for the murders, Art says. "He thought she killed the cops."

Sunny, I think. Not Walter. Interesting.

I'm about to say goodbye when Art asks, apropos of nothing, "Have you heard of Jack Murphy?"

Murph the Surf. Beach boy, Star of India, Whiskey Creek. "A really bad guy," investigator LaGraves called him, "but a bad guy with a lot of class." Just this morning I read in Walter's memoir that Walter was in a band with Jack Murphy in prison. Murph the Surf played the violin and was "exceptionally good."

"Yes, I have heard of Jack Murphy," I say to Art.

"Have you heard of Jack Griffith?" Art asks next.

Murph's codefendant in the Whiskey Creek killings. Yes, I've heard of him too.

Well, the two Jacks were high-rise cat burglars, Art says. They were real quiet about it, but they were working together. And in addition to burglary with Murph, Griffith was also into karate. Art knows this because he and Griffith studied at the same dojo in North Miami. Which is how Art happens to know that Griffith taught Jesse karate in prison. "Jack Griffith the cat burglar taught Jesse Tafero the martial arts."

This is fascinating for a whole bunch of different reasons, none of which I mention right now to Art. All of which have to do with Walter's confessions. Walter Rhodes's confessions are at the heart of Jesse's and Sunny's claims of innocence. They've troubled me for half my life. *Before my Creator.* Why would Walter confess like that, using those words, unless he had in fact committed the murders?

I asked Walter myself about his confessions. In 1990, when I interviewed him in prison, and in 2003, up there in the woods. Both times he claimed that he confessed because friends of Jesse Tafero's pressured him behind bars. They were going to kill him if he didn't sign the statements, he claimed. But that seemed to me like a flimsy explanation. If it was even true.

"Did they come and visit you?" I'd asked Walter, in 1990. "What kind of friends were these? How come Jesse Tafero would have friends coming for you?"

So what Art has so casually mentioned about the two Jacks might be important.

In her book, Sunny writes that Jesse had a *sensei,* a teacher, who was his "mentor and protector" in the tough Florida prison system. This sensei, she wrote, was the man who taught Jesse karate. She doesn't give a name for the sensei, but Art has just accidentally told me who he was. Jack Griffith. Jesse's teacher. His mentor. His protector. And a legendary badass revered by the inmates of the Florida Department of Corrections as the fiercest, most mysterious motherfucker of all, according to none other than Walter Rhodes.

Jack Griffith was "the closest thing to a God in prison," Walter wrote in his M.O.

In 1979, Walter confessed again. This time, Walter signed the confession himself. It's the confession quoted in *The Exonerated*. In addition to Walter's signature, that confession bears the signature of three other inmates, attesting to it. Investigator LaGraves put those inmates under oath and interrogated them. One of the inmates told LaGraves that there was a contract out on Walter, to force him to sign or else. A price tag on Walter's head. LaGraves asked: How much was the price tag? Answer: Thirty to forty thousand, "more if we can get it over with." LaGraves: "Okay, who'd you hear that from?" Answer: Jack Griffith.

The same Jack Griffith who was Jesse's sensei and friend and protector. The same Jack Griffith who cat burgled with Jack Murphy. And it was Murph who brought Walter's first confession to light in 1977, sparking hope in the hearts of Jesse and Sunny.

I have a picture of the two Jacks together at Florida State Prison, a Polaroid dated January 28, 1977—two weeks before Walter's first confession. I found it online, on a genealogical website. In the photo, Jack Murphy has his arm around Jack Griffith, and Griffith has his hand on Murph's knee. Convicted murderers. Cat burglars. Karate buddies. Friends.

It seems these two Jacks fully believed Walter was guilty. Not Jesse. And not Sunny.

That, or there is more to this story.

The night before the murders, Jesse was at Art's house, Art is telling me now. Art was living then in a place he'd rented from an antiques dealer, a big house deep in a mango orchard, only moonlight to see by at night. The house was full of antique furniture—and marijuana. A huge stash hidden upstairs.

That night, Art heard a car pulling into the yard. A commotion. Voices, shouting. Art ran outside, into the orchard. Jesse was standing there in the shadows, holding a gun. A man was on his knees on the ground in front of Jesse, cowering. Art recognized the guy—he was a mutual friend of theirs. Jesse was pointing his gun directly at the friend's head. I'll get it for you tomorrow, the guy was pleading. He owes me money, Jesse told Art. He added, "Art, I got no place to stay."

"So I had to come out in the garden with my own gun and say, 'Take it off my property, I have a hundred and fifty pounds of pot in this house,'" Art says. "And I took a fifty-dollar bill out of my wallet and I gave the money to Jesse. I told him to use the money to get a room."

Art's next question is clearly something that he has been carrying for forty years: "So I don't know why they were in that rest area. Why didn't they just go to a hotel?"

Because they were being chased around by four goons in a Lincoln Continental. Because the goons had figured out where Walter lived. Because there was a strange car in the parking lot of Walter's apartment building, so they went to Steve Addis to borrow his green Camaro. Because at Steve Addis's house, Walter saw the Lincoln Continental again, with the same four guys in it. Circling the block, slowly. Because they'd spent days driving around doing drugs and Walter, for one, was "not in my right mind," according to his own M.O. That's why Walter decided they had to sleep in the rest area.

Joe Rourke, brother of Mickey and stepbrother of Steve Addis, saw Walter that night. Rourke testified in a deposition that Walter was "so paranoid" that he "was sitting outside waiting for a car to come by that he thought was following him." Rourke added: "I thought he was kind of nutty myself."

And Jesse, according to his psychiatrist, was suffering from "delirium" and "delusional thinking" in the early morning hours of February 20, 1976, brought on by "having taken drugs indiscriminately on a daily basis from morning until night for several months prior to the crime" and possibly having been slipped a dose of LSD the previous evening at the home of John Mulcahy. "Perceptual disturbances, misinterpretations, illusions, hallucinations, and persecutory delusions," the psychiatrist wrote. "Paranoid ideation, overall paranoia about being constantly followed and watched, inability to carry on a conversation, limited contact with reality, hyperalertness," plus sleep deprivation, nutritional deprivation, and a "drug-induced inability to think, reason, assess or recognize reality."

Or, as Jesse told a nurse after his arrest: "I have been on a bad trip."

Trooper Black, pulling up alongside the Camaro, stopping his cruiser, stepping out. His wife and child are at home, having breakfast, getting dressed. Constable Irwin in his white T-shirt. This is the last day of his Florida vacation. As Constable Irwin hangs back, Trooper Black walks through the morning mist over to the Camaro, and looks in the driver's-side door. A gun, down at the driver's feet.

"The reality," Walter wrote, "is that I am somewhat responsible for our being at that rest area. . . . Was this destiny? I don't believe in accidents. Karma/catalyst. FATE."

14

Naw, He Ain't Shot Him

The truck driver is in his seventies now. Robert McKenzie, the only living independent eyewitness to the murder of Trooper Phillip Black and Constable Donald Irwin. It has taken me these three winter months to find him. His address in the old court records led to an abandoned building underneath a half-dead tree in a Miami neighborhood of shuttered stores, men in wheelchairs begging on highway exit ramps, and falling-down houses on trash-filled lots. There wasn't even anyone there to ask where McKenzie might have gone. Now I'm at a tidy brick house off a red dirt road in south Georgia and Robert McKenzie is standing in the doorway to his kitchen, dressed in a blue pajama set with a sleep mask pushed up on his forehead, telling me to go away.

I'm trying to explain. All of it—chaos, confusion, truth, lies. Last night I read more of Walter Rhodes's magnum opus. Walter admires some killers and thinks other killers "need a good killing." It's not just guns that kill—words kill too. He himself feels good around killers. Always has. Comfortable. More powerful. He wonders: "Does this mean I'm a killer?" Crows hop through the pines in the yard behind me, their calls sharp like needles. It's morning on the last Sunday before I have to go home.

The other truck driver died twenty years ago, I tell Robert McKenzie. Please, you are the only person who can help me, I say.

"I'm sleeping," he pleads. "Can you come back later?"

In investigation, later means never.

"I'm so sorry," I say. "No."

On February 20, 1976, Robert McKenzie was thirty-two years old and working for Food Fair, a Miami company. He started his shift that morning at five o'clock, and at ten minutes past seven he pulled into the rest area for his coffee break. That's what he told the detective who interviewed him, days before the start of Jesse's trial.

"Did you see anything that was unusual?" the officer asked McKenzie.

"Yes," McKenzie replied.

Like Pierce Hyman, the other truck driver, McKenzie saw the Camaro and the cruiser at the north end of the rest area, parked side by side. McKenzie saw Trooper Black standing at the open door of the Camaro, talking to Jesse Tafero, who was sitting in the driver's seat. He saw Walter Rhodes, in a blue shirt, standing at the front of the cars. Then he saw Black lean down and start talking to someone in the backseat of the Camaro. A woman.

At that point, McKenzie put his big rig in gear and started to pull out, watching the Camaro in his side mirrors as he headed toward the highway on-ramp. Trooper Black, standing up, reaching toward Jesse to frisk him, reaching toward Jesse's front pocket, Jesse jumping back.

Black and Jesse struggle. Constable Irwin steps in to help.

That's when Walter, in his blue shirt, moves from the front of the cars to the back, McKenzie told police:

> 'Bout that time, the other guy, with the blue on, the blue shirt on, he walked behind the car, behind the car on the other side, he walked behind, in the back.

Suddenly: Gunshots. Both officers fall to the ground. "They dropped instantly. Instantly."

McKenzie's testimony that Walter was behind the Camaro as the shots rang out was not what truck driver Hyman saw. Hyman saw Walter standing in front of the cars during the shooting. The discrepancy between the two eyewitnesses was not hugely controversial at trial. But in the years since, McKenzie's testimony has become a crucial piece of evidence in the case. The reason?

That slender strip of metal I saw in Room 407.

The metal ran along the edge of the front windshield on the passenger side of Trooper Black's cruiser. When forensics examined the cruiser after the murder, they saw that a bullet hole had been shot clear through this windshield post. The bullet entered the metal strip low and exited high, and it entered from the right—that is, from the direction of the Camaro. Whoever shot that bullet did so from a point lower than, to the right of, and to the rear of the front windshield of Trooper Black's car. At trial, the state argued that the bullet hole was physical proof that Sunny Jacobs fired from the backseat of the Camaro. But the *20/20* broadcast—and, later, *In the Blink of an Eye*, the ABC Sunday Night Movie—argued that Robert McKenzie's testimony showed Walter Rhodes to be the true killer. In an interview with filmmaker Micki Dickoff—a childhood friend of Sunny's, and the director of *Blink*—*20/20* reported:

REPORTER TOM JARRIEL: The key to the murder mystery: Could Walter Rhodes have been at the rear of the Camaro when the fatal shots rang out? Micki Dickoff believes she found the answer to that question when she re-created the crime scene. There were only two eyewitnesses, truck drivers parked 150 feet behind the Camaro and the police car. One of them, she discovered, told a very different story than Walter Rhodes.

DICKOFF: That truck driver, without a shadow of a doubt, saw the "man in blue"—Rhodes was wearing blue—move from the front of the Camaro around the passenger side to the back of the Camaro. Absolutely, positively.

JARRIEL: According to this driver, Rhodes walked from the front of the Camaro to the rear, putting him in position to have fired the fatal shots.

"I am so sorry to bother you," I tell McKenzie now, in his garage. "But I witnessed the execution of the guy who was convicted in that case, and I'm trying to figure it out."

"Naw," McKenzie says. "He ain't shot him."

A pause.

"He got electrocuted?" McKenzie asks.

I nod.

McKenzie shakes his head. "I don't think that guy did that. Let me tell you, I don't think he did it."

Pause.

"That lady in that car got to have shot him. She was talking to the officer and then bang bang bang, and they fell. It had to be her. It was from the car."

There is a car right in front of Robert McKenzie and me right now. It's a blue four-door sedan in McKenzie's garage, where we are talking. McKenzie is standing alongside the passenger side of the car, about where the handle is on the front door. Now McKenzie steps sideways, faces the backseat of the car. That's how the officer was standing, he says, looking at me. Real close up, like this, talking to someone in the backseat. The car's door was open and the lady that the officer was talking to was sitting right behind the driver's seat, right inside the open door, he says.

"I didn't realize Trooper Black was standing that close to the backseat of the Camaro," I say.

McKenzie nods and looks at me with a puzzled expression. "How were the officers shot?"

"I don't know the answer to that," I confess.

That is one of the most important things in this whole case, and I do not know it yet. I've read the autopsy reports but I don't understand the medical terms. I have not been able to reach the doctor who was the medical examiner on the case. I asked investigator LaGraves when I was down in the Keys, but he told me there's no way to determine from the wounds to the officers the position from which the shots were fired. Michele McCain, widow of Jesse's lead trial attorney, said the shots were fired directly down into the officers, and that there are autopsy photographs showing exactly that. I have not been able to find those photographs. The medical examiner testified at trial, of course, and I have read the trial transcript, but the questions from prosecutor Michael Satz are along the lines of "Was it like this?" and "Was it like that?" without any kind of physical detail. Black was shot four times: in the arm, in the head, in the neck, and in the shoulder. Irwin was shot twice, in the head and in the shoulder. But what path did the bullets travel as they passed through the officers' bodies, taking their lives along with them?

"Would you mind drawing what you saw for me?" I ask McKenzie, putting my notebook on top of the car. He takes my pen and sketches it out.

"It had to have come from there," McKenzie says, pointing to the Camaro in his drawing. "The lady had to have shot them, because that's when they fall. I saw it, bam bam bam, it had to have come from the car."

McKenzie heard about the murders on the radio all that day, and the next days as well. He didn't tell anyone what he'd seen. But the other truck driver who was there told the police that there had been a Food Fair truck at the rest stop, and the police came to the warehouse and told everyone that if they didn't tell the truth they'd all go to jail. "I ain't never been in jail," McKenzie said. "A friend who had been there told me to tell the truth."

"Did the police put words in your mouth?"

"They ain't told me nothing," McKenzie said.

"What about the state attorney? Did he tell you what to say?"

"They just told me to tell the truth. They didn't tell me what to say, how to say, nothing."

He was scared, McKenzie says. He didn't want to go to court. He didn't want to testify. And he's never talked about it since. A television program called him one time, but he said no.

"I can't get it off my mind—it's bothering me all the time, I ain't never seen somebody get killed before. I'm telling you, it's something else—I'm seventy-one years old, and I still remember that day. It's been a long time. And I ain't talk to nobody about this. I wish I could get it out of my head."

He falls silent, and I watch him for a moment. He looks tired, and so sad.

"I'm so sorry," I tell him. For being here, demanding answers, bringing it all back. Me, the intrusion. Appearing on the doorstep, past in hand, knowing full well how it feels to have one morning of your life come back around again and again, present tense. I do not want to cause anybody pain. I do believe in truth. I'm not sure how those add up right now.

"I am so sorry," I say again.

Robert McKenzie nods. He's going to go inside and take a shower and have some breakfast, he tells me. Then he's going to mow the lawn to help himself forget.

15

A Very Uneasy Feeling

It's typewritten and faded, this report. A copy, not the original. Titled "Narrative" and dated February 20, 1976–March 5, 1976, it is a day-by-day account of events in the immediate aftermath of the murders, as observed by a social worker. I am at the State Attorney's Office in Fort Lauderdale, at the start of my last three days in Florida. I'm back in the office library, being allowed to retype the report into my computer but not to make a copy. The report is about another person in the backseat of the car that morning. Sunny's son. Little nine-year-old Eric.

When the Cadillac came to a stop at the roadblock, police found an attaché case that contained, among other items, six Polaroid snapshots. Three were images of young Eric with a gun. In two of the photos he is on horseback, pointing a handgun into the air. In the third, Eric is sitting on a flowered futon couch next to Jesse Tafero. Eric is wearing a sweatshirt and a pair of plaid slacks; Jesse is bare-chested, with feathered necklaces draped around his neck. They are both smiling. Jesse is holding a handgun, pointing it almost directly at the camera. Eric is holding a machine gun. A real one.

Police believed, based on trucker Hyman's written statement, that at least some of the gunshots that killed Black and Irwin came from the backseat of the Camaro. They'd already begun interrogating Sunny. Now, seeing the photographs, together with some statements the child was reported to have made after the murders, they were considering Eric as a suspect too.

"Extremely disturbing," the police captain said of the evidence. "Very incriminating information," the social worker wrote.

The social worker's report has an old-fashioned look about it. The typing skitters and trips on the page, and it's packed with small details—impressions, snippets of conversations. It feels contemporaneous, spontaneous, something the social worker wrote as she went along to document what was going on:

2/20/76
"Eric" and "Tina" were the two minors who were found to be with the three adults who are being charged with the murder of two policemen in Deerfield Beach. . . . Among the three adults was a white female who is allegedly the children's mother. Her identity has been undetermined at this time. "Eric" allegedly nine years old . . . was in the back seat of the car when the Canadian officer was killed. Also in the back seat of the car were his alleged mother and baby sister "Tina," ten months old, date of birth unknown. According to reports, it has been alleged that the Canadian officer was killed from the back seat of the car, thusly leaving as suspects "Eric" and his alleged mother.

At the police station after the murders, police tested Eric's hands for gunshot residue and fingerprinted him. While they were fingerprinting him, Sunny was taken out of her cell to be transferred to the Broward County jail. On her way past Eric, the social worker reported, Sunny "leaned over and said to the child, 'Eric, shut up!' "

Sunny, too, wrote about seeing Eric at the jail after the murders. In her book, *Stolen Time*, Sunny wrote that as she was being led through a jail hallway, she saw Eric. He cried out *"Mommy!"* and she told him, "You don't have to talk to these people. Tell them you want a lawyer."

Eric obeyed his mother, according to the social worker's notes. In the days that followed, Eric claimed to not remember his last name, where he lived, where he went to school, "or anything that would lead us to his true identity." Eric's grandparents hired a lawyer for him—a veteran criminal defense attorney who had recently represented two associates of Ricky Cravero in the Stanley Harris murder trial—and Eric handed out the lawyer's business card when anyone asked him a question. The social worker reported that Eric was "a very innocent and lovable child" but that he also "radiates a very uneasy feeling to those who communicate with him when he 'cannot remember' the facts surrounding his and his family's identities." She described Eric as "brainwashed."

On February 24, 1976, the social worker wrote that "the tests they took on Friday to see if Eric had fired a gun had come back positive and that Broward County was going to charge Eric with 1st Degree Murder today."

But that did not happen. And on February 24, Walter Rhodes provided a new statement to police. From his hospital bed, where he was recovering from the amputation of his left leg, Walter wrote that he now thought that perhaps a Taser had been used during the murders. Sunny, sitting in the backseat, "may have had the Taser in one hand—Pistol in the other," he wrote. It was the first time Walter had linked a Taser to the crimes; he'd previously told police, under oath, that he'd not seen a Taser used.

By February 26, 1976, almost a week after the murders, Eric still was not talking. Anytime he was asked about the shooting, or his family, or himself, he displayed "a tremendous amount of fear," his social worker wrote. So the psychiatrist treating Eric asked the social worker to "get in touch with the judge to get authorization to use drugs on Eric to see if the boy would talk." According to the social worker, Eric overheard that conversation and "went into hysterics," saying, *"My mother made me do it, my mother made me do it."*

•

When I visited investigator LaGraves weeks before on the Keys, I'd asked about Eric.

"Could he have fired the Taser?"

"I don't recall ever considering it," LaGraves said.

But then LaGraves kicked back in his chair, nodding his head a little bit, thinking. It's such an investigator thing to do, seeing if the puzzle pieces fit together a different way.

"He may well have," LaGraves said, after mulling it over. "The boy was of the age and size that he could have fired a Taser, at Black and maybe the Canadian, or both."

I mentioned that I had read a police laboratory report that said Eric had tested positive for gunshot residue.

"He could very easily have tested positive," LaGraves said. A Taser has a "mini-cartridge that projects the darts out," and when fired that could produce a positive gunshot residue test, he said. Also, "Eric was in the confined area where we believe that Sonia fired a handgun," which would have gotten residue on him as well. "Or he could have fired a gun. It's possible that he could have. It would be easy to construct a scenario where Eric was the one who kicked everything into high gear—substitute Eric for Sonia."

But if you substitute Eric for Sonia, I think, as I write that down, the state's entire case against Jesse and Sunny is based on a false premise. It's no longer a double murder planned and carried out by two street-smart lovers trying to avoid arrest. It's a tragedy triggered by a terrified little boy. The theory of the crime is wrong. If you substitute Eric for Sonia, a fabrication, a fiction, a *lie* put two people on death row. That matters. It matters to me.

I'd asked Fred Mascaro too. Mascaro was the Palm Beach County detective who spent a week in 1976 with Eric and the social worker while Eric was in police custody. He's mentioned by name in the social worker's report. When I stopped by to talk with Mascaro a few weeks ago, he was still on the job, still specializing these forty years later in criminal cases involving children. Mascaro told me that at the police station on the morning of the murders, Eric was in a panic.

"He was very meek and very scared," Mascaro said. "He was *very* scared."

"Sure, it must have been very upsetting," I said, imagining.

No, Mascaro corrects me. Eric was scared of his mother. "Before she left, she turned to him and told him not to say anything."

Could it have been Eric who fired first?

"Well, he had gunpowder on his hands, so they wanted to charge him too," Mascaro said. But Mascaro didn't think it happened that way. The shots that killed Black and Irwin were too on target for Mascaro to believe a child had committed the murders all by himself.

"He might have stuck the gun out the window and shot one time," Mascaro said.

Paul Weber, too, had mentioned Eric, when I talked to him. Weber was the deputy sheriff who helped fingerprint Jesse at the station house that morning, and who kept an eye on Sunny after she was first taken into custody. Weber remembers Sunny as cold, "very unemotional," and completely entranced by Jesse. "She was the type of woman who was so involved with blind love for him that she would do anything for him—that's the impression I got. I remember that because of the casual way she wanted to know what was going on. She wasn't traumatized. She just sat there with her legs crossed, smoking a cigarette."

At the substation that morning, the officers wondered at Eric's behavior too, Weber said.

"There was the suggestion that possibly the boy fired the Taser which immobilized Trooper Black, because the boy knew how to fire a weapon," Weber told me. "There was discussion among the investigators because of the fact that they saw these pictures, and the boy had such a defiant, arrogant attitude, that maybe he had some involvement in the case."

I didn't ask Marianne about Eric when I visited her at the start of all this, almost three months ago. She brought him up all on her own. We'd just sat down in the ornate chairs on either side of her fireplace, sunlight bathing her in a radiant glow. Marianne herself thought Sunny did the shooting. But "Jesse, not directly, said it was the boy."

"Eric?" I said. Surprised. "How did you hear that?"

"Kay told me," Marianne said. Jesse's mom.

My mother made me do it.

I stare at those six words on the old report now, a knot of anxiety in my stomach.

The small boy in the backseat, that nine-year-old child—he needs to be on my witness list too.

16

Grace

"Oh! You found me," Grace Black says, as she opens her front door.

It is my second-to-final day in Florida, and I've come to her doorstep only as a last resort. Grace is the widow of Phillip Black, the Florida Highway Patrol trooper murdered on the morning of February 20, 1976. Before showing up here today, I wrote her a letter. No response. I spoke to her briefly on the telephone to ask if she might talk. She said she'd consider it but did not call back. I wrote and called Constable Irwin's family too. No response from them either. Last month I stopped by the address given for Trooper Black on the police reports from the day of his murder and spoke to their son, Christian, who still lives there. Christian was extremely nice, but he'd been a very young child when his father died. He lent me a photograph album of his dad. In one photo, handsome, clean-cut Trooper Black is standing in the sunshine, smiling and holding a license plate the State of Florida had issued to promote safe driving. ARRIVE ALIVE, the plate says.

"I'm so sorry, but I wanted to introduce myself to you, and make sure you had this back," I say, handing Grace the photo album that her son lent me. We are in the front courtyard of her waterside condominium; it's sun-splashed and neatly swept, tidy, bright.

"This isn't a good time," Grace says, firmly. Small, slender, blond hair and blue eyes, Doris Day–pretty in a pink-and-gray Hawaiian shirt, blue capri pants, blue sandals, and sheer pink lipstick. She holds the photo album up against herself like a shield.

"Yes, of course," I say. I offer my deepest condolences. "If you ever do feel that you want to talk to me—or if you have any questions about what I'm working on—please call me, anytime."

She takes my card. She pauses, and asks me to wait a moment. She disappears into her house for a few minutes. Then she comes back to the door and invites me in.

Inside, the living room has a cathedral ceiling. Waves of light play across it, reflected from a canal just beyond the sliding glass doors. Grace remarried in the years after the murders, and her husband, frail, sits in an easy chair, recovering from a recent illness. He and I say hello, and then Grace shows me to her dining table and brings us both glasses of peach iced tea.

"I witnessed Jesse Tafero's execution," I begin.

"You told me that on the phone, yes." Her eyes are on mine. Steady, still.

"There's been—as I'm sure you know—quite a bit of discussion since then about his case, and whether he and Sonia Jacobs were guilty. What I've been working on is to try to find out what—what really happened that morning."

I can't bring myself to say it. *Murder.* Not here.

Phillip A. Black was born in Wheaton, Illinois, in March 1936, the youngest of three children. The family moved to Florida when he was three or four years old because his sister had asthma. His father and mother both died young of cancer, and after his dad died, Phil Black joined the Marines. Black went through boot camp and was posted to Camp Pendleton, near San Diego, where he was a member of a specialized unit made up of paratroopers and scuba divers. As part of his training, he learned to jump out of airplanes, deep-sea scuba dive, and survive in cold water. He was a Marine's Marine, Grace says. "Lean and mean," was what he used to joke.

Grace was from Canada, working at the San Clemente Inn, near Camp Pendleton. Phil Black's sister was friends with one of the other women who worked at the inn—that's how Phil and Grace met.

Not long afterwards, Phil injured his back parachuting and had to hang up his Marine uniform. He and Grace moved back to Florida in 1966, settling in Hialeah. Phil found a job as a salvage diver, but the money from diving came in only when there was work. A neighbor at the end of the street was a Florida Highway Patrol trooper and he encouraged Phil to join the force. So Phil signed up. His first assignment was in the Florida Keys.

"How did you like living there?" I ask Grace.

"Well, there's a lot to do if you like to drink and fish," she says, with a smile.

When their son, Christian, was born a few years later, Phil was so excited, Grace says. "My husband was the greatest father. He was just a really, really great father. He couldn't wait for his little baby to be out walking so he could take him everywhere."

In the summer of 1975, the Blacks went on vacation to Canada. While there, they happened across a terrible traffic accident. Phil Black got out to talk to the officer in charge, and at the end of the conversation, he invited the officer to look him up if he was ever in Florida. That next winter, the winter of 1976, the Canadian officer, Don Irwin, gave the Blacks a call. Don and his wife, Barbara, wanted to take them up on their offer. Could they come spend a week?

Sure thing, Phil Black said. The Blacks set up a camper in their backyard as a guest room, and Black got permission for Irwin to come with him on a couple of ride-alongs. Friday, February 20, 1976, was the last one, on the last day of the Irwins' Florida vacation.

"It was about eight in the morning," Grace says. "I was getting ready to go to work and to take my son to school when the phone rang. It was my pastor calling. Just as I was saying 'Hello, Pastor, how are you,' there was a knock on the door. My husband had sometimes called me late at night when he was on the night shift, and I always said, 'Oh, honey, you scared me when I heard the phone ring,' and he always told me, 'No, Grace, you don't have to worry about the phone. If anything happens to me, they'll come to your door.' I asked my pastor to hold on a moment, and I went and opened the door. A trooper was on the doorstep, and he said, 'Mrs. Black, I need to take you to the hospital.' Barbara Irwin was standing next to me, and I said, 'That's Mrs. Irwin, what about her?' And the trooper said, 'She needs to come too.'"

We sit for a moment, in silence.

"I've read that Sonia Linder has said that she was in the wrong place at the wrong time," Grace says, using the name that Sunny Jacobs was known by at the time of the trial. Grace is looking directly at me now. "But that is not true. Phil Black and Don Irwin were in the wrong place at the wrong time, to encounter them. Not the other way around."

When Sunny's conviction was overturned, Grace says, "It was tough, it was very tough. I thought they should have locked her up and thrown away the key." The casings that police found in the Camaro—those are what convinced Grace Black that a gun was fired in the car. The truck driver eyewitnesses too.

About the constitutional claims that resulted in the reversal of the conviction, Grace says, "I guess if you look long enough, you'll find something." But the plea deal that let Sunny Jacobs out of prison was a guilty plea, which was the whole point, she says. "Hers was not an exoneration. It was a plea bargain for time served."

The problem with retrying the case in 1992 was all the time that had passed, Grace says. Walter Rhodes had recanted, the truck drivers could not be found, and Leonard Levinson, the man whose Cadillac they carjacked, had died. "A lot of the people who had known a lot of the facts were not available for the second trial," Grace says, and so the prosecutor "recommended that this was the way to go. The plea deal—which was why we went for it—was she would still be guilty, time served."

But then Sunny went on television. "I don't know how you can put a positive spin on criminal behavior, but people tend to believe stories when they've seen them on TV," Grace says. "You get confused about who's good and who's bad."

Phil Black was a gentleman, Grace tells me. He had chivalrous manners and he was a devoted father. When he looked into the Camaro and saw a woman sitting with her little baby, he would not have seen her as a threat. "That's what tricked my husband," Grace Black says. Grace believes shots came out of the back of that car, where Sonia Jacobs was sitting. "I never once felt that she was innocent."

And what about Eric? There's a document in the State Attorney's Office's files that mentions that they were going to charge Eric with murder, I tell her.

That is one of the things she has wondered about, Grace Black says.

She'd heard that Eric spat on the shoes of the officers at the roadblock, she says. So, yes, the possibility that Eric was involved has crossed her mind. Actually, now that she's thinking about it, prosecutor Michael Satz might have mentioned something about the boy, just off the cuff. "He might have even just said, 'We're wondering about the boy in the car.'"

It's the missing pixels again.

"I would like to know the exact truth of what happened as well," Grace Black says. "If that is what you are trying to find out, you have my blessing."

The next day, my last full day in Florida, I'm back in Room 407 at the Broward County courthouse. Evidence.

"Here, can you hold this for a second?" Dave the evidence chief is asking me.

It's the jacket. His jacket. The one Jesse Tafero was wearing at the rest area that morning. The jacket both truck drivers saw him in. It is smaller than I would have thought, a mid-1970s tan, yellowish, not brownish, and belted, with a lapel collar and buttons. Among the photographs police found in the attaché case were a Polaroid of Jesse in this jacket, wearing a fedora, machine gun in one hand and pistol in the other. And a Polaroid of Jesse in this jacket with a ski mask covering his entire head. Faceless, eyeless, on his back on a bed, machine gun brandished at the ceiling, pistol toward the wall.

It's not a scheduled part of my visit, my hands on this garment. Dave just needs the jacket out of the way for a second while he puts a cloth down on the table. I hold the jacket with as little contact as I possibly can, just thumb and forefinger on each hand, all others extended far out of the way. And afterwards, I feel odd. I have now touched an object that Jesse Tafero touched. Something he wore. Not just any day, but that very day. Those very instants.

Next is the purse that Sunny had with her, the one holding her loaded .38 revolver. A designer monogram is on the purse's clasp: Oleg Cassini. When officers confiscated this purse at the roadblock, they found documents from the glove box of Trooper Black's cruiser inside. His FHP individual trooper inventory and a recall notice. The officer who drove Sunny and the children from the roadblock to the stationhouse told me that Sunny tried to insist on having the purse with her in the backseat of the car, but he'd refused. "If I'd given her the purse like she wanted, I wouldn't be sitting here right now talking to you," Lieutenant Gary Hill said.

Next: ammunition. Nine millimeters and thirty-eights and twenty-twos, rattling inside white paper boxes. Teflon-coated bullets too, the kind retrieved from the bodies of Irwin and Black. The Teflon coating is bright green. The box is marked "National Police Supply Company." These bullets were known as "cop-killers" because they could pierce armored vests.

But it's when I see the holster that I think, Oh, okay.

The case documents state that Jesse was arrested with the murder weapon strapped to his hip in a holster, and all along I've been picturing something basic off a gun shop shelf. But the item Dave puts in front of me is a fancy belt. It's tan leather, handmade it looks like, with an ornate image of a woman in a lotus position as its centerpiece, dyed with reds and greens and blues. A hand-tooled yoga-lady lotus hippie holster, if such a thing can be said. A leather pouch for two ammo clips is threaded onto the belt, plus a pancake holster, secured with just one snap. Easy access. That's interesting. But what really gets me is how personal it is. The handiwork on the leather, the details, the colors—this was *his* holster. That's perfectly clear. And when the Cadillac came to a rest at the roadblock, Jesse Tafero stepped out of the car wearing this holster, with the just-fired murder weapon and a clip full of armor-piercing bullets for the gun.

I pause for a moment as the crime scene flashes before me once more. Three months ago, when I stood outside Walter Rhodes's apartment building in the January sunshine of my first day here, I knew nothing about any of this. Piece by piece, the rest area has come to life. At its heart, detective work is a form of time travel. I have to be in two places at once. Now, in the present, with all my fears and flaws. And also *then*.

February 20, 1976. Just past seven o'clock in the morning. A beat-up green Camaro is parked in a rest area fifteen miles north of Fort Lauderdale on Interstate 95. Inside are an armed robber on parole; a fugitive convicted rapist and drug dealer; his girl-friend, a rich young woman with a history of drug dealing and a loaded gun in her purse; and her two children—a baby girl and a nine-year-old boy. In the car are five guns, a hatchet, a bayonet, and a Taser. Drugs: amphetamines, cocaine, Quaaludes, mari-juana, hashish, glutethimide. Thorazine. Pentazocine. Cigarettes. Beer. The sun has risen but the day is new and the rest area is shrouded in fog.

Trooper Phillip Black, on routine patrol, enters the rest area in his cruiser. With him today is his Canadian friend, riding along. Trooper Black pulls up next to the Camaro and parks. Then he and his friend Constable Donald Irwin step out into the mist.

The last items that Dave puts on the table are two paper parcels. Lunch-bag brown, stapled shut and labeled in black ink. Dave puts them out on the cloth gently, one by one. The parcels are worn and creased and crumpled. At first glance, nothing much. But inside are the bullets retrieved from the bodies of Phillip Black and Donald Irwin. Their last breaths.

I sit and look at those brown paper parcels for a long, long time.

Dad, you were taken from me at age seven, yet I remember everything you taught me about life, Christian Black wrote in memoriam to his father. *There will always be an empty place in my heart that can never be filled. I will love you always and make sure you are never forgotten.*

When I started this search, I knew I had to somehow find the nucleus of the case. The split seconds those shots rang out in the rest area. That is the instant I have needed to get back to. That.

Here it is.

Oh my God, I've been shot.

It only gets harder from now on.

PART TWO

But Which Truth?

17

Investigation 101

Along the coast road, Connemara is wild and in bloom. It is the last day of April, and I am standing in a seafront grave-yard in the afternoon. Already today Peter and I have searched along the strand beside the harbor and twisted through the streets of the quay, running up on abandoned houses and turning around on steep dirt roads that fall down toward the sea, clear like glass and cold blue below. We've stumbled onto this graveyard with its black headstones draped in bone-colored rosaries and ruins of a church, ivy-covered, sea-swept. Now a sharp wind is starting off the water as I make my way back through the long grass to the car. On the radio there is a report of a lashing storm, and we listen to the scratchy broadcast in the gravel lot at the cemetery beach, watching the Atlantic darken and the skies before us gather with rain.

Just a few weeks ago in Florida, finding Sunny Jacobs had seemed so simple. Peter found the registration information for Sunny's website, listing an address of "Muiceannach, Casla." No street name or house number, but on Google Maps the town of Casla looked tiny. On Facebook, Sunny's page had a photo of two horses in front of a green shed and a metal gate, with the caption "our morning visitors," another photo of the horses running across a rocky hillside with the caption "today in the garden," and a third photo, of a rainbow, taken through a window with a view out over a wooden deck to a body of water with houses on the far side. So, a house with a green shed, a metal gate, and a wooden deck, in a small Irish village near the sea. *Now it's time to live our fairy tale.* That's what the *New York Times* wedding story said about Sunny in Ireland, all those years ago. It had seemed like plenty to go on.

But now, after not even one full day in Ireland, we are at a loss. And lost. Casla is not tiny. There are so many houses on so many gossamer roads. Gray stone cottages with red doors, whitewashed cottages with blue eaves. There are gardens and cattle and rough stone walls. There are no wooden decks. No green sheds. And I don't know who I'm looking for. A martyr, sent to death row for a crime she had no part in? Or a murderer, hiding out in this wilderness of sea and stone?

Now I stare out at the Atlantic. I am not allowing myself to worry.

Peter is studying the map on his cellphone, and now he points to a lake, up away from the coast.

"What about this?" he says.

As soon as we turn north, the landscape changes. With the sea behind us, the world is a glacial emptiness glittering beneath a high wide sky. We pass the lake on the map and continue on, and a gap in the hedgerow appears. Peter spins the wheel hard, and now we are jolting along a paved thread, uphill. Brambles, trees, the black and blue of the sea.

"There's one," I say.

A shed with a green metal door. We rush toward it.

But it's too large, the color is wrong, there's no metal gate.

We round a corner, and a pony in a stone corral startles into a gallop. Behind her, another green shed.

We rush toward that one as well.

Now they are everywhere. We pass another graveyard and come back to the crossroads we started at, or the one we think we started at, and this time we turn left. This road runs out to the sea between two stone walls. A fierce wind buffets our little car. Out here, on the tidal flats, there are six houses, two to the left, two to the right, and—out at the end where the road stops and the water takes over—two more. One of the houses at the end has a white Mercedes in the driveway, and we rule that one out right away. Too fancy. But the one next to it is a tumble, with weather-worn white-washing and two silent chimneys. The houses on the far shore shine like sugar cubes in the storm light.

Peter drives slowly over the ruts as the gale blows in, the old stones by the road coming alive as moss meets rain. At the far end of the road, we ease down along a grass trail past the house. We can just glimpse into the front yard through the gate—a ram-shackle garden and rain-dark windows—and then, just past it on the left, a driveway leading to a green metal shed.

There is something in investigation that is close to a chemical reaction. It's a flush, a flash, a sting. It's rare, because most things are easy to find, and it's addictive, this jolt in the breastbone that comes only from finding something given up for lost.

"Oh God, we have to get out of here," I hear myself saying. Peter is already backing up and turning around. It wasn't my intention to talk to Sunny today.

"Wait wait wait wait wait," I tell him, fumbling for my iPhone and hurriedly snapping a picture through the rain-blurred passenger-side window.

On the way out, we pull over after the stone bridge to make sure. I have the photo I've just taken on my iPhone, and Peter has the Facebook images. They match.

"I can't believe it," I say, in a rush.

Now that we've found the house, it seems impossible that we stumbled on it at all. This falling-down cottage at the far ends of the earth. I look over at Peter, expecting to see the same look of relief on his face that I feel. But Peter looks concerned. He looks like it is going to pain him to say what comes next.

"What?" I say.

"There are no goats."

I stare at him, dumbfounded. Sunny and Pringle have goats, it's true—they write about them on Facebook. And it's true that the goats weren't to be seen. But ours was a very brief stopover. The goats were out back there somewhere, I feel sure of it. We just didn't walk around enough in the rain to find them is all.

"I think they've moved," Peter says, quietly, as if backing away from a lit fuse.

"No, they're just out," I predict, confidently. "We'll come back tomorrow and they'll be home."

But when tomorrow comes, I am too afraid to try.

Rain mists the windshield as we swing north from the coast road out into the flat expanse of the marsh. I try to steady myself, but it's a looming black dark fear, this fear. *How did I get myself into this I don't want to do it no.*

"Do you mind if we drive past?" I whisper.

"Are you okay?" Peter asks.

I nod, unable to speak. It's the house. It's kept me up all night. I know it makes no sense, but I had expected a tidier cottage. Someplace sweet and well kept, a pretty little haven out by the water. The fairy tale. Had I fallen for that somehow? This place is messy and untended, fending for itself in the rain and the wind. Everything, all of it, come to rust and ruin.

The road spins past a lake with wild swans, black water beneath a pale white sky.

"I don't know how I'm going to ask her," I say, when the house is well behind us.

The Taser the windshield post the bullet hole Steve Addis the car swap the Camaro Jesse's holster the murder weapon the green bullets the cocaine. All the facts from three months in Florida are crowding around in my head. This woman was caught on tape negotiating for a pound of cocaine. She's insisted over and over again that she and Jesse were innocent, but that is not what Robert McKenzie told me. The eyewitness who cannot forget what he saw. *The lady had to have shot them, because that's when they fall. I saw it, bam bam bam, it had to have come from the car.*

I look out the window. The stone walls across the green fields look like ossuaries to me right now.

"Say to her what you've said to everyone else, that you're here to find the truth about the case," Peter says. "Just say that."

"But I can't go in there with—" I stop, embarrassed.

"With what?"

"My soul," I say, in despair.

"You can," Peter tells me. "You have to. That's what this is."

The next day, and the day after, and the day after that, we are back at the house.

Sunday dawns gray with a light rain, and along the coast road heading out of Galway the sidewalks are busy with small children, tiny bright creatures waving their hands in the air. At Inverin we stop to buy flowers at the market, but the only thing on offer is a cactus inside a faded yellow plastic wrapper with the word *Happiness* written in faded script. We stop again in Casla town, first at a supermarket with a giant display of detective magazines—*I Have a Problem! I'm a Cannibal!*—and then at the gas station, which offers a choice: a giant bouquet of lilies and zinnias, or a lavender plant. We decide on lavender. We take the left turn at the hedgerow, and then we are out in the wilderness again, with the stone walls and the tidal flats and the rough Atlantic beyond. We arrive at the house and it is just the same as it was. Windswept, empty.

This time we venture up on foot to the front gate and peek through into the yard. There are rusted garden tools thrown about in the grass, tipped-over pots, plants that are in want of tending.

Through the windows, I can make out boxes on a living room chair, stripped beds, a yin-yang symbol on the kitchen windowsill. The house is cluttered, which makes me think they're still around somewhere, but there are no animals, which makes Peter think they've ditched it. I'm hoping I'm right, because if I'm not, I have no idea how we're going to figure out where they have gone.

On Monday, which is May 4, I wake up in our Galway apartment to a story in *Time* about Jesse Tafero. It's the anniversary of his execution today. My name is in the article—it quotes an article I wrote about the flames and smoke. I read it, feeling numb. *Time* concludes:

> After Tafero's harrowing death, the key witness against him admitted that he himself had pulled the trigger in the traffic-stop gunfight. Although prosecutors continued to insist that they'd gotten the right man, many concluded that Tafero was, in fact, innocent.

Out at the house again, we walk through the long grass right up to the sheds. We walk around the back deck and peer into the windows: empty milk cartons in the sink, cat food, a dirty fridge. Just before noon, I walk to the top of the road, near the house, and stand looking out toward the water, underneath the cat's-eye marble of the stormy sky. It has been twenty-five years now, exactly, since the door in the back of the death chamber burst open and the guards dragged Jesse Tafero in. I don't feel lost. I'm not giving up. I will see this through. But right now it seems like a long way to have come for an empty house and a landscape where pain and hardship have been set in stone.

"No. No! Do not tell them you're looking into a murder case. Listen to me. What you're going to do here is tell them you are Americans—okay, that's obvious—and that you're trying to track down information on your Irish heritage. Do you understand? Your heritage."

It's our new friend Liam on the phone. Peter has found him, an

Irish private investigator with four decades of experience and a web of sources and contacts across the island. I've called to ask him, PI to PI, for advice, and he's been charming, generous with his insights and with opinions too. All of it helpful, because, as I have been dismayed to learn, Ireland doesn't have the databases that we have at home. At home, if I need to find someone for a client, I can simply type the name into a giant computer network, press a button, and—well, it's not bingo, but it's close. But here all address information is tightly restricted by law. So there is—and Liam is now instructing me in no uncertain terms of this fact—no other option: It is time to go back to gumshoe basics. Time to get out of the car and start talking to people.

"Tell them you're doing heritage research and you've been directed to the Pringles," Liam says. Pringle is the surname of Sunny's husband. "You've heard there's a Pringle on the road. Do not under any circumstances mention the case or your project or the murders or his wife. That way, the neighbors will help you."

All the front gates of the houses along the tidal road are locked, or no one's home, or they say they don't know who I'm asking about. It's late afternoon by the time we find ourselves on the doorstep of handsome Aiden, a tall man with raven hair, broad shoulders, and a stately house just across the tidal flat. He listens intently as I recite Liam's intro, and then he immediately turns and points and says sure, the Pringles live right over there.

"Oh, but their red caravan is gone," he says, looking more closely. "So they must be away. Now, how are you connected to them?"

"It's a long story," I begin. I feel squeamish. I do in fact have Irish ancestry, but as far as I know I'm not related to any Pringles. I decide to start slow. "Somebody told us to ask after the Pringles—my great-grandmother was from Galway." True and true.

Aiden is looking at me with a polite but unmistakably quizzical expression.

"My great-grandmother's sister got married in Tuam to a Pringle, and I've heard the family then moved down here," I say, staring right into his clear blue eyes. "But after my great-grandmother moved to America she lost touch—it was hard, you know, she was a widow with eight children."

Handsome Aiden nods, and wishes us well with such kindness that I feel terrible.

But now we know we are looking for a red caravan.

One appears almost immediately. Outside the village pub in Casla town. A beat-up red mini-pickup truck, parked at an angle to the curb, as if the driver had exited at a dead run to the pub's front door. We pull up beside it, eyeing it.

"What is a caravan, anyway?" Peter asks.

On the roads coming toward us. On the roads behind us. Pickups, short-cabs, lorries. Carmine, crimson, vermilion, brick. As the light fades, we make our way back into Galway city, petals from the crab apples along the roadsides aloft in the gloaming.

It's the neighbor with the white Mercedes who finally tells us.

The next morning, Tuesday, we are down at the very end of the road again, at what has become clear—even to me—is their abandoned house. This time we've walked around the yard to the back deck and looked into the goat pens below, which are empty in the way that the house is, the leftovers of a life no longer lived here.

"Yes?" The neighbor opens his door with a distinctly unwelcoming expression. *Get the fuck out of my fucking yard* would be the direct translation from the Gaelic, I believe.

"So, I'm American," I begin, again. "I'm doing a bit of heritage research and I'm looking for the Pringles—are they still next door?"

"Ah, where are you from then?" He's softening. The start of a smile.

"California," I reply. Why? No idea. It just flies out of my mouth.

"Sunny is from California," the neighbor says, brightly.

"Who's Sunny?" I manage.

"That's his wife," the neighbor says.

"Small world!" Peter laughs, jumping in.

"It is indeed." The neighbor is smiling too. "Come in, come in."

And then here we are, sitting at his kitchen table as he bustles around fixing a pot of tea and putting out cake on pretty china plates. His kitchen has a spectacular view of Camus Bay, behind him. Some chat about my real-life great-grandmother Margaret Joyce, from County Galway—apparently the Gaelic-speaking Joyces, of which she was one, hail from a marshy patch in exactly this area—and then the neighbor has his cellphone out and he's reading an email from Sunny, saying that she and Pringle are in the United States and will be back May 5.

"But they've moved," he tells us.

"Oh?" I say.

"It's remote." He waves his hand in the direction they've gone, the next mountain over. We look out the window. Beyond the bay, the mountain is a gray granite monolith cast in shadows. Why did we want to see the Pringles again? he asks.

"It's for my father," I find myself saying. "He was the one who was corresponding with the Pringles, but he's fallen ill."

"Well, you could always say you found them, it won't hurt him, he won't know."

"Gosh, I could never do that," I say. Mainly because my dad died five years ago. But also because he was a meticulous attorney with a righteous respect for life's fine print.

So the neighbor drags his laptop out and gets Google Earth up and running and points out an infinitesimally tiny lane on the far mountaintop. I stare hard, memorizing, just as I used to do out in the Los Angeles desert, with my road map in my car.

"Do you think you'll still be here on May fifth, then?" the neighbor asks. "When they're back?"

"I hope so," I say, as Peter shrugs like, *Who knows?*

But we do know, even if this nice neighbor does not. Because May 5 is today.

And so we are on the road to Oughterard, a high barren stretch of moss and lakes, velvet and rock and sky. Below us, Connemara sweeps in grays and purples out to the coast. But in spite of my schemes and the neighbor's kindness, we can't find them. The mountain is too barren and the roads are too steep, and we are losing the light, the sun is sinking behind the far mountains, casting shadows across the emerald grass. I no longer have any idea what we are doing here, or what I am looking for. The only thing I know right now, after these days of searching, is that I have turned into a gray sky full of rain.

I made a mistake twenty-five years ago, when just before the execution I reported that story about Walter Rhodes, giving his— and the state's—version of events as the truth. I can see that now. For half my life, I realize, I have felt responsible for Jesse's execution because I wrote a story for the state's biggest and most powerful newspaper that completely failed to get to the bottom of things.

Even I can see how self-important that is. A journalist with the world on her shoulders? Really. But without understanding them, I have carried these feelings with me all these years. This private horror that maybe my own ego and incompetence helped fuel this fiasco. How is it possible that it has taken this, a search through the far western reaches of Ireland, across a tidal flat and a mountaintop, to figure this most basic thing out about my own heart?

That night, a pounding on the door wakes me. Echoing voices in the hallway, shouting. My heart starts beating so loudly I can hear it in my ears. They're just drunk, Peter says, sleepily, in the dark. But fear keeps me awake.

The next morning, out toward Oughterard again, we are picking our way along another threadbare road when a van is suddenly behind us, pushing us out of the way. It comes up so fast that I see it looming in the side-view mirror at the same time that Peter, who's driving, sees it too. The top of the van is a darker color, but below its windows, the van is red.

Peter pulls our car sharply to the shoulder. As the van barrels past, I catch a good hard look at the driver in my side-view mirror. A large man with silver hair and a silver beard.

I feel it again, the bright spike.

"That is Peter Pringle," I say.

The Irish Emigrant, May 1995
Freed After Fifteen Years

Peter Pringle, who was jailed in 1980 for the murder of a garda officer, has had his conviction quashed by the Court of Criminal Appeal. Following a bank raid at Ballaghaderreen in July 1980, Garda Henry Byrne and Garda John Morley were shot dead. Three men, including Pringle, were subsequently convicted of the murder of Garda Byrne and sentenced to death. This was later commuted to 40 years imprisonment without remission, in all three cases. For years Pringle maintained his innocence. In quashing the conviction the judges dismissed two of the three arguments put forward by Pringle's legal team. The one which was allowed concerned a tissue which Pringle used when he had a nose bleed in Galway garda station. In a 1993 statement, Det. Sgt. Thomas Connolly said that he handed the tissue to Det. Sgt. Pat Ennis. The latter denied that he had been given the tissue. At the original trial Det. Sgt. Connolly told the court that Pringle had said to him, "I know that you know that I was involved, but on the advice of my solicitor I am saying nothing." The Appeal Court now says that, had the disagreement about the tissue been known by defence counsel at the original trial, it would have been used to question Det. Sgt. Connolly's reliability as a witness.

A day after the court decision Pringle was released on bail of IR60k although this was objected to by Gardaí.

When I first read about Pringle and Sunny, I thought, Wow. Both wrongfully convicted of murdering police officers, both sentenced to death, both had their convictions overturned because their defense teams were not told of possibly exculpatory evidence. They must have a lot to talk about.

When I told a friend about them, he said, "Where did they meet? Match-dot-Con?"

As the red van shoves past us, for a long instant, we hang in between. Even the clouds above us seem to freeze in place. Only the van is still moving, up around the next curve in the road, about to disappear.

"There it goes—it's going," I say.

And with that, the world comes roaring back to life. Peter slams the car into gear and starts off after the van. It's a strand of macadam along a mountaintop, and we lurch and shudder past an abandoned house on our left and a large barn with a huge white bird in a cage on the right. Just ahead is the place where we turned back yesterday, an old farm courtyard with a stone barn and a cement mixer smack in the middle of the road. We'd figured that this was the end of things up here, that there was no going farther, but now we see that the road does continue, out along a long stretch to a promontory. Far ahead in the distance, we see the red van stopping in front of a house.

Peter finds a dip in the road, almost like a cradle, and pulls the car to a stop. As he does so, I feel a deep stab of panic along my breastbone into my stomach. It burns.

"Are you sure you're ready for this?" Peter says.

I stare at the road, willing myself to not be afraid. I nod. Yes.

"And you sure you don't want me to come?"

Of course I want him to come.

"I'll be fine," I say.

"I'll be right here," he says.

I lean over and kiss him and then, before I lose my nerve, I'm out of the car, walking.

It is indeed very remote, even in this very remote part of west Ireland; there's the spectacular view down the mountain toward the sea, there are the rocks on the hill in the high meadow to my right, there are the wildflowers growing in tangles along the old stone walls that line the road. That's it. No traffic, no people, no sound except the wind. As I walk, the Irish PI's warnings about Pringle ring in my ear. He said his sources were concerned that Pringle and Sunny are raising money—quite a bit of it. Publicly, the campaign is for the Sunny Center, a sanctuary for exonerated inmates they are planning to run here in western Galway, according to their website. They want $600,000. But Pringle was by his own account a member of the Irish Republican Army—well known for its "Once in, never out" creed—and then a leader of the Irish Republican Socialist Party, whose paramilitary wing has been banned as a terrorist group. That was why Liam, the Irish investigator, thought that maybe he should come along with me, armed and wearing a body cam. Then again, Pringle's son is a member of the Irish legislature, and Pringle himself has long since publicly stated that he is no longer a member of any group, terrorist or otherwise.

I shake it off.

The red caravan is parked in front of a tidy white cottage. As I approach, three dogs come hurling out from behind the house, and behind the dogs looms Pringle himself. Looking—well, I don't know him. But he does not look pleased.

"How are you?" I call out across the yard.

"I'm fine, and yourself?" A booming voice. He's a big strong tall man in his seventies, in blue jeans and a blue fisherman's cap. He has reached the gate, where I'm standing, and he's looking at me closely. He looks like he wants to know what the hell a windblown American with an armful of white roses is doing at his front gate.

"I'm fine. I'm sorry to intrude, but I'm hoping to speak with Sunny."

And with that, I burst into tears.

Pringle reaching through, unlocking the gate. "There, there." His voice softer now.

"Were you in that silver car, then? Did you follow me up here? Does your friend want to come in too?"

We're walking across the yard, around toward the back door of the house. His eyes are on me, intent and intense. It's not a dream-like quality, this walk across the front yard toward Sunny Jacobs's house, because dreams can sometimes feel real. It's a parallel track, running just alongside my real life but on entirely separate ground. Pringle takes me around back, ostensibly to show me the view but really, I think, to quiz me. What's my name? Where am I from? Who is the man I was with in the silver car? I get it. We are on the back half of the moon, and he—well, there's an element of distrust here that seems born of experience, whispered meetings in hidden rooms, night vision, no sudden moves. Or maybe it's just life out in the sticks.

Now I've passed the test, I guess, because we are heading toward the house.

"Ellen, what is your surname?" Pringle says suddenly, just as we reach the doorstep.

It will be a big problem tomorrow, me being me. Thank you, Internet. But for the moment, it's fine.

"Sunny, are you still on the phone?" Pringle calls out, as we step across the threshold of the kitchen doorway.

"No, I just finished." From the living room, Sunny Jacobs's voice comes floating back, high and squeaky and clear.

"This is Ellen from Michigan and she's come here to see you."

A small, plump, wrinkled, gray-haired woman in an oversized green sweater, sweatpants, and wire-rimmed glasses appears in the living room doorway, clutching a walker.

"All the way from Michigan?" Sunny Jacobs says.

I burst into tears again.

"Tell me, tell me," Sunny is saying. "Oh, baby, tell me."

We are sitting at her kitchen table and holding hands. It's a big wooden oval table in front of a picture window, with a view to the west out over the lakes and mountains beyond. The table is cluttered with mail and papers and teacups and coasters; a bookcase along the wall is crammed with more papers and boxes, semi-unpacked. Pringle is bustling around, eavesdropping and making tea, and Sunny is restacking things on the tabletop to clear room for the mugs. I'm still crying. Actually, I have taken my eyeglasses off and set them down on the table so I can weep.

"Did you know Jesse?" Sunny says.

"No, but I witnessed his execution," I whisper, and pretty much put my forehead right down on the tabletop.

It's hard to explain, but it's such a relief to sit here with my head on the table like this. Maybe because of all of the people I've ever talked to in my entire life about the execution, I feel that Sunny Jacobs is not going to judge my grief. I judge my grief.

"Oh, Ellen, I've talked about you," Sunny says. "I'm glad you found me. I've talked about you, not knowing it was you, so many times. I say, 'And the people who were there on behalf of the media said it was so horrible that ten years later they were still writing about it.'"

It's a line taken from *The Exonerated*, and I feel a twinge as she recites it. That line may refer to a piece I wrote about the electric chair for *Slate* in 1999, just before I testified in that last electric chair hearing. I've always felt uneasy that the line was in the play, because it's made me feel like I'm supposed to agree with what the play had to say about the case, when in fact my feelings are complicated. A small *uh-huh* takes shape now somewhere in my weepiness, but it gets elbowed out of the way by the tears.

"What an awful burden to carry," Sunny says, squeezing my hands. "Don't sit with it anymore. Let's share it. Because I've never gotten over it myself. You needed to come and I needed to do this with you. Really. It's huge."

I know I'm not here for her to comfort me. But right now it feels so good that I don't want to let it go.

"He looked very intense. He had a very, very memorable expression in his dark eyes," I'm telling her, about Jesse's last moments. She hasn't asked. "It was like he was very conscious of what was going to happen. He looked at each of us individually, like, *You're watching me, I'm going to watch you,* and that was very—it was individual, you know?"

"Oh, that was his intention," Sunny says. She's got herbal tea in her mug, I've got black tea in mine. Pringle is off somewhere. "You're not just watching something you can be detached from.

You are going to watch me die and you are going to feel it with me. He connected with your *soul*."

I don't want that to be true.

"I used to be afraid, actually, that Jesse would take me with him," she tells me, still holding my hands. "He was that powerful, and we were that connected. When they gave him the final death warrant, I got scared. I was afraid I'd be an empty shell left behind. There was a part of myself I had to reserve to myself, in order to survive, from then on."

When they were first sent to death row, Jesse painted her a circle on paper, and she stuck that painting on the wall of her cell and studied it every day. Because circles are perfect, and they contain the universe. Jesse was intense. He had an energy like nobody else's.

"He pushed you to come here. He made you come here! I have no doubt. I mean, how in the world would anybody find me here? Take a look around you! At the end of this road, you know? He had to have pushed you."

"I have kind of asked myself why," I say, reaching for a tissue from the box she's put on the table.

"I've given up trying to understand the whys," Sunny says. "I used to think, Why did this happen to me? Not out of self-pity, out of confusion. I just didn't understand. I was—and everybody else that knew me would say—the last person in the whole world that would ever be involved in any way with somebody getting killed. I was a hippie! And a vegetarian!"

Then she says, "Is that your husband?"

I look up to see Pringle outside the picture window, and yes, there is Peter right beside him. They are looking out over the garden, arms crossed over their chests, with Peter nodding and smiling, like, *Wow, nice goats!* Then they disappear from view and reappear in the kitchen, Pringle in the lead, striding across the room toward the door to the front parlor. As they come in, Peter shoots me a look that is such a perfect *Oh shit!* that I almost laugh.

Peter and I have no game plan. We have never exchanged so much as one syllable about him coming in. He has no idea what I've told Pringle and Sunny about why I'm here, and I have no idea what he'll say when Pringle starts grilling him. And now Pringle has shepherded Peter straight into the living room and is closing the door.

"Maybe you two can spend the night!" Sunny says.

"Oh, we'd love to, but I left my asthma medications back in Galway," I say.

That does happen to be true.

An hour or so later, and I am completely up a tree. Let's see: (1) I cried upon arrival, so that's not badass; (2) I've sat here at the kitchen table drinking tea and holding Sunny's hands, also not badass; (3) I have failed to ask one single question about the crime, and not only is that not badass, it's not even competent.

Right now, I can see that this is—well, *disaster* is a pretty strong word. But I have no clue as to how to get on track.

"So," I begin. Always propitious. I feel squeamish about it. Bait-and-switchy. The Weeping Detective. We are still at the kitchen table, and we've been chatting about nothing much for—Oh God. Two hours? Now that my grief episode is behind me, the tension I feel is a toxic ball of twine in my solar plexus. But I finally manage to say it. "My goal is to write the real true story of what happened."

"Good!" Sunny says.

Just then, Pringle, with Peter in tow, reappears and announces that they are off to buy dinner. Peter looks pale and strained, but he manages a quick smile. After they leave, Sunny gets out pretzel sticks. And as she eats them, she talks. Finally, I think. After so many years, it is time for the truth.

The feeling doesn't last long.

After about twenty seconds, it becomes clear that I am being given her standard speech. I've read pretty much an exact word-for-word version of this before. And I feel a little hurt. I can't quite believe she's going to try to blow me off. She spends a total of about three minutes describing the events leading up to that fateful morning—she and Jesse needed a ride, Walter was a friend of Jesse's, they stayed with Walter for a couple of days and she decided, *Wow, this dude is creepy*, and then her son Eric had a nightmare and she begged Jesse to get another friend to help, so he did, and Walter was giving them a ride to the other friend's house.

Then:

"It was February, so days were short, so the decision was made to pull over at the rest area and wait till daytime. The rest is pretty much history and I choose not to go through that again. You can read it in my book," she says. "Uh-oh, are those cows?"

Sunny is pointing out the window behind me.

I turn to look. "Yeah, those are cows," I say.

And that is that.

There's no going there, that's perfectly clear.

Pringle and Peter come back with pork chops and cook them up. We sit around the table, drink some more tea. Out the picture window, the mountains take on shadows like stone wings. We have dinner, we have dessert. They tell us about the time they took Kay Tafero, Jesse's mom, out to dinner in Los Angeles, to a restaurant that had a group sing-along between dinner and dessert. Pringle and Sunny both break out into "That's Amore"—*When the moon hits your eye like a big pizza pie*—and sway back and forth in their seats while they sing. We all laugh.

The entire time, I feel like there is a ticking bomb inside my chest, *ask her ask her ask her*. But I cannot. There's no point in trying, I can tell. All I'll get is another no, and I don't want one. I want to keep the door open. Plus, Pringle keeps looking at me like he's trying to see right through me.

After dinner I get up to help Sunny with the dishes. The dogs have been waiting for the leftovers and I put plates on the floor for them, as Sunny watches.

As the dogs are finishing up, there's a deep growl. It's Barney, the terrier, baring his teeth. Every tooth, top and bottom. He looks like he's smiling, but there's no mistaking that sound.

"That dog is going to bite someone," I say.

Sunny glances over.

"Oh, that's Peter's dog," she says.

She doesn't mean my husband. She means hers.

Near the end of our evening—we're back at the table again, watching the sun sink toward the mountains to the west—Pringle's voice suddenly commands the room. He's talking to me. "How did you know about Muiceannach?"

He's asking about our search for them at their former house, the one out at the end of that windswept spit by the water. Total silence falls while everyone turns to look at me. I can feel Peter's anxious gaze.

By doing a little bit of Internet research, I say.

"No. Because, you see, we *never* said where we lived online," Pringle says, very emphatically. He seems pissed off, like he's decided he's onto something. "So I'm very curious about how you found out we were in Muiceannach. Where online did you find it?"

"On the registration for your website," I tell him.

"Go on, bring it up, she'll show you," Sunny says, jumping in.

"I'll just put in Sunny and Peter and Connemara and let's see what happens," Pringle says, almost sarcastically. And he takes an iPad out and starts typing his own name into Google, saying it out loud as he types each letter.

The old address is not there. A low noise escapes Pringle, half groan, half growl.

"In America, the search comes up with different stuff." Sunny is explaining Ireland's privacy laws. "That's how she did it—in America." She's defending me. Or defusing Pringle—hard to tell. Pringle's not having it.

"Look, I'll bring the piece of paper with your old address on it tomorrow," I say, locking eyes with him across the table. They've offered to drive us around the countryside and we've said we'd be delighted. We've said we will be here in the morning, first thing.

Pringle relaxes, just a bit, and Peter and I use the moment to take our leave. Pringle walks us out. We can see him standing at the gate as we drive off.

All the way down the mountainside, I kick myself. Six hours! Six hours, and not one bit of information. I could fucking kill myself. Or cry.

"I would have been fired," I tell Peter, as he drives. "If I were still working for my old boss, he would have fired me."

The Irish hills glow with last light now around us.

"And I'm such a *liar*," I say. "Holding her hand like I'm some kind of penitent. Or pilgrim. I'm a liar and a thief."

Peter, for his part, looks pained. When we get back to Galway, he collapses on the couch, pale and tired. He is clutching his hands across his stomach, with his eyes on the ceiling.

"I don't think I can do that again," he says. "I had a little man inside my chest all day pummeling to get out and start asking questions."

"That's because you're honest."

"I just don't think I can sit there and pretend everything's fine."

"It's like that scene in *Roger Rabbit*," I say. "The one where Roger is hiding behind the wall and he hears 'Shave and a Haircut' and he just can't stop himself, the longer it goes on the more he starts trembling, and when the final *dun-dun-da-dun-dun* comes, he bursts out and screams, 'Two bits!' That's you."

Peter laughs, still looking pale.

"But you know," I add officiously, "really, you can't do that."

We rest for a moment, listening to the rain on the window-panes.

"Do you think Pringle thought we were double agents?" I say.

"Well, if we are MI6, we fucking suck at our jobs," Peter says. We both laugh.

But now I feel wretched too, and mad at myself. We've come all this way and we found her by going door-to-door in Gaeltacht Connemara and I sat with her at her kitchen table and held her hands? It makes me feel insane. And she's not going to talk. She'll never talk.

The thing is, the tears were real. That was the part that I did not plan out. Twenty-five years of anger and sorrow and fear came pouring out of me. And she held my hands as I wept. She, the person who might have caused all of this, for everyone.

That night I call Freya, my old friend and business partner. She suggests playing it cool with Sunny. Just go back there, don't ask any questions, keep it nice. Because there is a secondary strategy here. If Sunny won't talk to me about the murders, then maybe Eric will. The child who was in the backseat that morning. If Sunny really isn't interested in talking, don't give away your game, Freya says. Save it for Eric.

Peter agrees. I'm going to be nice, keep it quick, and get the hell out of Dodge.

That, in any case, is the plan.

18

But Which Truth?

We are late. Late, late, late. It's the next morning and we've stopped in the pretty little seaside town of Barna for pastries, and then dawdled north and west along the road to Oughterard, the wilderness around us changing color with each cloud overhead, the mountains in the distance a pale lavender line. I feel dread, pure and simple.

"We're just saying thank you and goodbye," I say.

"I don't feel well," Peter says.

"Exactly."

"No, I actually don't feel well."

"It won't take long," I promise. "Twenty minutes, tops."

Peter coughs roughly. Up ahead, the road unfurls, a black ribbon beneath the high wide sky.

At the house, we let ourselves in the front gate and come around the back. The dogs bark our arrival, but no one comes out to greet us, so we step inside, into the kitchen, calling out our hellos. Sunny is in the kitchen, looking out the back window with a blank expression, and Pringle is standing in front of her, on the phone. Neither of them makes much of a move toward us. We have upset them with our lateness.

Pringle is just hanging up the phone as I hand him the piece of paper I'd promised, the one showing the registration for the website. Pringle takes it and looks it over. I point out the town name to him, it's right there in black and white.

"My goodness, I didn't think that was possible," he says, reading it over. "Well done." He seems mollified, so maybe he's decided that Peter and I are not spies after all.

"She's an investigative reporter," Sunny says.

"I'm a private investigator, actually."

"And your husband? What does he do?" Pringle asks.

"He's my secret weapon."

Peter shoots me a *What did you just say?* look. Too late, I remember that he told Pringle yesterday that he worked in publishing.

"I also work in publishing," Peter adds, cheerfully, like it's a mistake anybody could make, what his or her husband does for a living. "Who wants pastries?"

Tea is brought out, plates are set, and soon we are back around the table where we sat for so many hours yesterday, chatting. The singer-songwriter and activist Steve Earle introduced them. The Shakespearean actor Mark Rylance is going to be at an event with them next week. The United States ambassador asked them to a luncheon, but Sunny decided not to go, it's impossible to do everything. Golden Globe–winning actress Piper Laurie helped Sunny write her memoir. Singer-songwriter Judy Collins was a Sunny in *The Exonerated*. Roger Waters, of the rock band Pink Floyd, just performed at a benefit in New York for the Sunny Center. At that benefit—a star-studded party—Sunny had mentioned just casually to a few people that she and Pringle could use a new computer. The next day, two brand-new Apple laptops appeared, plus an iPad, which now they're trying to learn.

Peter coughs and coughs.

Finally, after about an hour, it seems like it's time.

"Well, thank you so much," I say, pushing back my chair and getting ready to stand up. "We'll quit taking up so much of your afternoon—we'd love to stay but Peter's not feeling well, unfortunately."

Peter makes a big show of getting his Kleenex out and blows his nose.

But Sunny's not budging. She keeps her seat and she motions for me to do the same. Her eyes are interesting—they're green and hazel and brown, and they can seem sparkly, but they also go flat and blank, like those metal gates in front of store windows in New York City that roll down at the end of the day. Completely metallic. They're metallic now.

She wants to hear the thing about Jesse again, what I said yesterday about him looking at everyone while he was being strapped into the electric chair, and then she wants to know what I thought of her book and the play *The Exonerated*.

My plan is still to keep it nice and get out of here. It's clear I'm not getting anywhere with Sunny, and I don't want to say anything now that will tip her off that I hope to talk to Eric. In investigation, surprise is a basic element. Like hydrogen.

"He just looked at everybody," I say, about Jesse. "And I saw him looking at us, and I knew he was doing it, that he was going to look at everyone. It was very clearly like, 'I see you, and I see you watching me.'"

"Nothing was said?" Sunny asks.

"At the end they gave him the microphone. And that's when he said his last words. I don't remember what all of them were, but I remember that he said, 'The laws that go against me today can go against you tomorrow.'"

"He said the laws that went against me can go against you tomorrow," Pringle repeats. "Well, that's so true."

"We've said that so often," Sunny says.

"So often we've said that," Pringle says.

Right. *Can we go?*

Now Sunny wants to know what I thought of her book and of the play.

"I think the book is really from your heart, it's really very much your story," I say, carefully. Actually, I think the book has a strange, maybe forty-five-degree tilt to the facts of the case, but I don't tell her that.

Sunny nods.

"And I thought *The Exonerated* was a very, very effective, moving, emotional work of theater."

She nods again.

"But very honestly, I think the play doesn't tell the entire whole story of the case."

"Absolutely. It can't, though. They had to condense it." Sunny seems relieved, actually, that this is what I have to say about it.

And I'm relieved too, because in 2003 I wrote a piece for the *San Francisco Chronicle* excoriating *The Exonerated* and calling Sunny Jacobs an unexonerated gun-owning convicted murderer, and a liar. Awkward! But she doesn't seem to have read it, or if she has read it, she's certainly taking it in stride.

"I know that technically they don't allow people to say they're exonerated, you know, unless it was like DNA and they're released," Sunny says, as if she can read my mind. That was exactly the point I made in my *Chronicle* piece—the plea deal that got her out was a special kind of guilty plea called an Alford plea, not an exoneration. "But if you win your habeas corpus, you're an innocent person from there on, right?" Sunny continues. "And so, at that point, you're exonerated."

She then launches into a long description of her plea, which ends with Pringle grabbing that new free iPad of theirs and reading the Wikipedia entry about Alford pleas.

It's a really, really long Wikipedia, at once confusingly vague and teeth-grindingly repetitive. As Pringle makes his way through it word by word by word, I can feel myself start to shake, just like Roger Rabbit in that scene I was so know-it-all about with Peter last night.

I've read Sunny's Alford plea, obviously. I brought a copy of it with me to Ireland, in fact. Her Alford plea, while allowing her to maintain her claim of innocence, required her to agree under oath that the state could prove certain evidence against her in court, and one of those pieces of evidence was that she had "admitted that she fired a shot from the Camaro." As Pringle drones on and on with the Wikipedia entry, the *ask her ask her ask her* from yesterday returns. It's now or never, I can feel it. Now or never to ask Sunny about the Taser dart found in the weather stripping of Phillip Black's cruiser.

It's a crucial piece of evidence. The Taser is what likely set the whole deadly rampage off, according to the prosecution. The state's theory was that Sunny fired the Taser and the gun at Trooper Black while he was attempting to subdue Jesse, and that in the ensuing confusion, Jesse freed himself, grabbed the gun from Sunny, and continued firing at both Trooper Black and Constable Irwin. The fact that a Taser dart was found in the weather stripping of Black's cruiser substantiates the theory, the prosecutors argue. But they have no evidence regarding who fired the Taser, or when. None of Walter's confessions reference the Taser, and while it was featured prominently in news reports about the case circa 1976, it's never mentioned these days. The Taser is mentioned ten times in Sunny's Alford plea, however. That's why I want to know what Sunny has to say about it now.

Pringle is still in his Wikipedia monologue. In Henry Alford's case, he's explaining, the prosecution had strong evidence for conviction, so the United States Supreme Court "held that his guilty plea was allowable" while Alford himself swore he was innocent.

"But isn't that like extracting a false confession?" Sunny asks.

"Yes," Pringle says.

"Well," I say. "The evidence in your plea that they made a big deal out of was, first of all, a Taser."

I put the question directly to Sunny, looking right at her. I want to see what her reaction to the word "Taser" is. And she does have one. It's small, but when I say "Taser," her upper hairline flinches back a tiny, tiny bit, and her eyes go absolutely flat.

"Oh, yes," Sunny says.

"But the point is, Sunny, if I may interject here," Pringle says. "At the time when you were coerced into accepting this Alford plea, there was no evidence upon which the state could have proven you guilty. So therefore, your Alford plea is false."

"But they do make quite a big deal about the Taser," I say.

"Because they didn't have anything," Sunny says.

"Well, what do you remember about it?" I ask.

"What is she asking about?" Pringle says, about me.

"A Taser, there was a Taser," Sunny says to him, pronouncing the word as if she personally had never heard of such a device before—*What is this thing they call a Taser?* Which is odd, given that she herself purchased the Taser, four months before the murders. She went to a weapons store in Tampa and told the owner she was a divorced nurse living with two small children out in the sugarcane fields and needed some protection for her home. Rita Pendel, that was the name she gave. The gun shop owner testified to it at trial.

"All I know is, I was in the backseat of the car with the kids, and after the word came back that Rhodes was on parole, there was gunfire," Sunny says, matter-of-factly. "The policeman drew his gun, he said, 'Nobody move.' I have no idea who started the gunfire. He was the only one I saw with a gun, was the policeman. But when I looked up, Rhodes had a gun, and was ordering Jesse to get us out of the car. So, I have no clue."

"When you looked up, what were Rhodes and Jesse doing?"

"I don't want to get too much into it," Sunny says. "But anyway—and I don't think it has relevance to whether or not Jesse should have been executed—when they ordered Rhodes out of the car and they took the gun from between his feet, they took his ID and then they had him stand sort of to the front of the cars."

"And you were—?"

"I was still in the backseat with the kids."

"So you were in the backseat and you were watching this happen?"

"Yeah. Then the cop came around to get Jesse's ID. And Jesse didn't want to give him his ID. And they argued about it. And then finally he got Jesse out of the car, and they were kind of dancing around together. And then, um, the word came back on the radio that Rhodes was on parole. And at that point, the cop pushed Jesse, took his gun out, and said, 'Okay, nobody move. The next one to move is dead.' And then there was gunfire."

"Were you looking out when it started? Were you already down?"

"No. I was watching what was happening. And then as soon as the gunfire started, I covered the children. And there was firing, and I heard all the sounds."

"So there was a Taser fired at some point in that. Do you know where or when that happened?"

"I have no idea."

"So when you say 'dancing,' were they—"

I'm trying to zero in on the instants before the shots rang out. Trooper Black pushing Jesse away, reaching down, drawing his gun out of his holster.

"I'm not doing that. I'm not doing that!" Sunny says, with sudden vehemence. She waves both of her hands in the air, as if she wants to block me out.

"I want to know—"

"*I am not doing that.*"

Peter and I are on the road toward Oughterard again. The road is taking us into a dark forest, so thick and dense that it is like a shadow on the hills. Around us, meadows tumble away from the road, sheep scattered across them like dice. It is now three o'clock in the afternoon. Sunny had a doctor's appointment, and so Pringle has given us a set of keys to their house and told us to come back in two hours with a roast chicken.

"Why are we going back there?" Peter says.

"Because we said we would."

It's the only reason. After Sunny shut me down about the Taser and about Jesse grappling with Trooper Black, we chatted quite a while longer, but mainly about Pringle's theory that the warrant to transfer Sunny back to jail after the Eleventh Circuit overturned her conviction was improperly issued and therefore the entire legal basis for her Alford plea was void. It was a long bout of the kind of detail-mongering rabbit-holing that clogs up discussions in criminal cases, the logic that "if my conviction was illegal then I can't possibly have committed the crime," but Pringle was in his element, boasting about his jailhouse lawyer skills, which he says won thirteen people—"they weren't all innocent"—freedom from the Irish prison system.

When I agreed to return for dinner, my secret plan had been to buzz over to Galway, grab my copy of Sunny's Alford plea, race back out here, and go over it with her line by line by line. Peter, though, disagrees.

"You've already asked her what happened, she's already said she doesn't know," Peter says. "She's not going to go over that again. Come on, why don't we just call them and say thanks but we have to be back in the city?"

"We can't."

Who am I, Miss Manners? Although I have a bad feeling about this too.

"You should tell them about the *Chronicle* piece," Peter says.

"You don't think they already know?"

"Oh, no way," Peter says. "If they knew, they'd have thrown you out of there. You need to be the one who brings it to them. That's your best chance now."

"Well, they didn't know their website registration was public. So maybe they aren't too great at the whole Internet thing." I say it to the trees outside the window. I can't look at Peter, because I know he's right. The thing is, I don't want to tell them because I don't want them to read it. Specifically, I don't want them to read it in front of me.

On the newsstand in the small roadside store we stop in, there is a headline in *The Irish Times* about the murder the previous day of a former IRA commander in Belfast. Nine o'clock in the morning, on a sidewalk, on his way to work, five shots: one to the back of the head, four to the face. He'd allegedly been involved in the murder of another man in a bar ten years earlier, and the IRA had wiped down the place afterwards so there'd be no forensic evidence. Seventy people in the bar when the murder occurred, and wouldn't you know, nobody saw a thing.

We can't find a roast chicken, which seems like a fool's errand out here anyway, so we get lamb chops and an apple tart and race back again. There's construction on the road. We are late.

At the house, Sunny is in the kitchen, bent over the desk along the far window, reading something on her iPhone. Pringle is nowhere to be seen.

"Hi, Sunny," I say, putting the groceries on the countertop next to the sink.

Sunny does not look up or give any other indication that she's heard me.

"So sorry we're late—that took much longer than we thought. But it's beautiful!" I say.

No response. It's like we're not here. Finally she puts the phone down and comes across the kitchen, toward the sink. She still has not acknowledged our presence in any way.

"Everything okay?" I say as she passes me. She looks pale, and drawn, and grim.

"I'm just tired," she says.

At dinner, Pringle breaks up a strained silence with a long story about the time all the prisoners on his wing threw their piss pots at the guards and shit dripped down the wire mesh along the stone walkways. And the time that the little Napoleonic guard made everyone watch the television channel that he wanted, not the channel the prisoners wanted, and later that same weekend the guard was leaving a boxing match and someone pulled up alongside him in a car and blew the back of his head off with a gun.

"They didn't kill him, though," Pringle says, looking from me to Peter with a highly instructive expression. "They turned him into a vegetable for nearly a year. When the news came down, the whole prison erupted in cheers."

Afterwards, the warden was walking the new chief guard along the rows, and a voice from Belfast rang out. "Hey, John"—the new chief's name was John—"you're next!"

Pringle kicks back in his chair and laughs.

As soon as dessert is finished, Peter and I are more than ready to take our leave.

"Well, thank you so much," I begin, for the second time today. Our car is locked inside the yard, behind the big metal fence around their house. We actually need their permission to go.

"Oh, no," Sunny says. "Not until you've answered a question."

Peter gives my trembling knee a steadying pat underneath the table.

"Because while you were late, I told a friend in Florida about this great lady who stopped by, and she sent me this piece you wrote," Sunny says. "And I thought, *Oh good*, because you can read it aloud, I love when people read what they've written aloud. But then I read it."

That thing that I feared, them reading the 2003 *Chronicle* piece right in front of me? It's happening now.

Exonerated Blurs the Facts about Death Penalty Case

In *The Exonerated*, Tafero's story is told by an actress playing Sunny Jacobs, Tafero's lover and his co-defendant in the crime he died for. In the play, their tale is simple: Jacobs and Tafero, young and in love, catch a ride from ex-convict Walter Rhodes. In cold blood, Rhodes shoots two police officers, frames Tafero and Jacobs and sends them both to death row to save his own skin. Jacobs is exonerated after Rhodes finally confesses, but it's too late for Tafero, who dies in the electric chair.

In creating *The Exonerated*, according to the program, playwrights Jessica Blank and Erik Jensen "spent countless hours in dusty courthouse records rooms, pawing through thousands of microfiche files and cardboard boxes full of affidavits, depositions, police interrogations, and courtroom testimony. . . . With a few exceptions, each word spoken in this play comes from the public record legal documents, court transcripts, letters or from an interview with an exonerated person."

But in researching the Tafero case, Blank and Jensen seem to have missed evidence that did not fit their story. For one thing, Sunny Jacobs, who owned the gun used in the murders, was not exonerated. According to court records, she entered a plea of guilty to second-degree murder and was released with time served after an appeals court found that prosecutors had withheld potentially exculpatory evidence from her defense. And Tafero's own lawyers argued in court that only Jacobs could have started the shooting, if eyewitnesses were to be believed. "The entire incident might never have occurred if she had not fired the first shots," the lawyers wrote, in a brief I found at the Florida State Archives.

That's just mean, Sunny says, when Pringle has finished reading it. "As an investigator, you can't go in with an agenda. Otherwise they're not going to talk to you."

"Oh, but I do have an agenda here," I say. "What I really want to do is find and print the entire whole truth. It is the thing that I've realized is the thing I have to do. And that's—"

Sunny cuts me off. "But which truth?"

"I really need to know what happened."

"Whose truth do you accept?"

"I like to believe that there is an objective absolute *something* that happened."

"I don't think you can know that. I don't think that's knowable," Sunny says.

"Okay, there are all those facts," Pringle says, stepping in. "And then there are the interpretations of facts. And there's truth. But you know, my truth may not be your truth."

"It depends on your purpose, too," Sunny says. "If you do a scientific experiment, it's well known that the experimenter's viewpoint affects the result of the experiment. You know this, right?"

"You mean, an observed particle behaves differently?" I ask.

"Yes. And that's what's going to happen to your truth. Whatever you want it to be, you will affect it," Sunny says. "It's the nature of the universe. There's really no way, in my opinion, to ascertain The Truth. Because it will change according to people who are examining it."

"I've been an investigator for nineteen years," I say slowly. This whole discussion has, frankly, caught me by surprise. I had expected Sunny to say, if she said anything, something along the lines of *You want to know what really happened? What really happened is Walter* fucking *Rhodes killed those officers.* Not "I don't think that's knowable" hitched to a debate about the nature of truth and the universe.

"What I do is go out and find the facts," I say. "The lawyers fit them to their case. The lawyers will take a fact and turn it into an argument, but a fact is a fact. You know, the car was red or the car was green. One or the other."

"But that's a different kind of fact," Sunny says. "When it comes to, like, who killed Cock Robin. Who did what. Like in our case. We might as well take it. How would one ever know? I was there! I don't know. And that's the truth. I don't know. When I looked up, Jesse was standing in the middle of the cars, he looked like I felt, you know, and Rhodes was running around the car with a gun in his hand, ordering Jesse to put me in the backseat. Now, some people would say that's not a fact. But I'm saying, that's a fact. That's what happened. So they might not accept my facts, so what's a fact? It's not a case of red or green or light or dark. It's a question of things that happened that—I don't know."

The thing is, when Sunny was interviewed by the police that morning, right after the Cadillac crashed into the gravel truck and everything came to a halt, she never mentioned Walter having a gun in his hand. As far as I can tell from the case documents, anyway. That's a fact, if now we're talking about facts.

But it's not the fact I'm interested in right now. What I want to know now from Sunny is about another piece of physical evidence, one of the most important pieces of physical evidence in the entire tragedy: that piece of metal I saw in Room 407. The bullet hole in the windshield post of Black's police cruiser.

The police put a rod in that bullet hole and drew a straight line to the backseat of the Camaro, where Sunny—by her own account—had been sitting. Voilà, the prosecutors said. But the defense lawyers disputed that, saying there was no way to tell how the cars had been parked, since after the murders they'd stolen the cruiser and driven it away. In terms of exact angles, it was a good argument. But the one thing that remained unchallenged—and unchallengeable—is the basic trajectory. Back toward front, low to high. Four decades haven't eroded that piece of evidence at all. It's metal. It's unmistakable. I saw it myself.

"But here's the, here's the— Okay," I say. "At your trial, Jesse testified that he saw Rhodes shoot from a position at the front of the car. Right?"

"Right," Sunny agrees.

"So what I don't understand is how, if he's at the front of the car, how do you get that bullet through the windshield post?"

Sunny knows exactly what I'm talking about. Bullets don't reverse themselves in midair. She leans forward.

"Rhodes moved. He *moved.*"

"But that's not what Jesse testified to. Jesse testified that Rhodes shot from this position from the front of the car. So that's under oath at trial, right? So I figure that he's telling what he saw."

"But I told them, I did see him move."

Saw him when? Sunny's whole story is based on her claim that she didn't see anything after the gunfire started. I must look skeptical, because Sunny adds, "I wasn't wearing my glasses, so I can't swear to anything."

And anyway, that bullet hole in the cruiser? "It couldn't have possibly come from me. You couldn't anyway. You could not, in the back of a two-door car, be able to do anything effective. Even if you had a gun or whatever."

"But Jesse was standing between the cars," I say. "And so it could have come from him. And Jesse testified that it came from

Rhodes. So that's what I'm trying to figure out. That is actually the question I am trying to answer."

"Like, which one?" Sunny says.

"Right. Exactly," I say.

"I mean, in that case it could have been both. They could have worked together. They could have," she says. "Right?"

I pause for a moment, steadying myself.

So it is possible that Jesse Tafero was guilty.

According to Sunny Jacobs, no less.

You know everything and you don't know anything, and you have to decide when to flip the switch. I decide that the time has come to flip the switch. To test her with a few facts from the case file and pay attention to what she says. I'm listening for honesty. For evasion. For truth versus lies.

My first question: the missing bullet casings. Six gunshots killed Trooper Black and Constable Irwin, but crime scene investigators only found the casings for three bullets. "That is one of the mysteries to me. I just don't understand it," I tell Sunny. Walter has said Jesse picked up the casings from the ground outside the Camaro where Black and Irwin lay dying, and police later found fourteen casings in little Eric's pockets, but I don't mention that. I want to hear what Sunny volunteers.

"Were the guns automatics?" Pringle wants to know.

"Yeah, they weren't six-shooters," Sunny says.

"An automatic. So there would be casings," Pringle says knowledgeably.

"Right, and there weren't any," I say.

"That's strange. There were no casings?" Pringle says.

"See, that's the point, though," Sunny says. "I don't think it's going to be possible to really ascertain what happened."

My next question: the truck driver eyewitnesses, who swore they saw Rhodes standing with his hands in the air when the gunshots went off. What about them?

"It was very, very foggy," Sunny says. "From the distance those trucks were from the cars, under those weather conditions, they couldn't have seen."

"And if they had seen, they couldn't have identified the person," Pringle offers.

"They wouldn't have known which man it was," Sunny says. "They're both tall, slim, dark-haired men. So that—"

"He could have seen Jesse standing there," Pringle says.

"And you know eyewitness testimony is not reliable," Sunny says.

Well, why was Jesse arrested with the murder weapon?

"He explained that himself," Sunny says. "He said that when he got in the car, Rhodes handed him the gun and picked up the new gun that had been placed in the police car, that had been taken away from his feet."

"Did you see that happen?" I ask.

"I was in the back," Sunny says.

"So then, no?"

"At this point in time, to be honest, it would be hard to say if I really saw or if I just remember it from being said."

That is such a sudden burst of apparent honesty that I feel grateful.

"Thank you for that," I tell her.

"Yes, and that's why I say again I don't think you're going to be able to achieve either of those goals. Either the yes or the no," Sunny says.

"I'm emotionally prepared for that. I am." I have no idea what I'll feel, actually.

"So then what happens?"

"I don't know."

"So then that's the answer," Sunny says. "That to me is the whole point of this exercise. The system was misused and as a result countless people were victimized. And someone *may* have been put to death who was innocent, or at least was entitled to a new trial. And that is a fact, he was entitled to a new trial. That is a fact. So on what we can say are *facts*, that's the only conclusion we can come to, and that's actually helped me enormously."

"What has?"

"That the only real *fact*"—she leans hard on the word—"is that the system was abused."

She continues, bitterly. "Guilty people get help when they get out. Innocent people get nothing, and then they're supposed to start their life again. And there's always going to be people who think, *Oh yeah, a technicality* and *Maybe they just had a good lawyer*. There's always going to be that and there's always the stigma. . . . It's horrible. There's no help, there's no apology, there's no big thing in the papers saying 'We made a mistake, this woman was absolutely innocent, we apologize to her, we want her community to know that she was an innocent woman wronged by the system.' That doesn't happen. It's horrible, and it just goes on and on and on."

She pauses.

"Even you did it, you know?" Sunny Jacobs tells me. "And that's, like, horrible. Horrible. That someone would doubt what we went through? Jesus Christ."

It's past ten o'clock now and the light is fading. We are finally taking our leave.

"Before you go, I want to tell you something," Pringle says.

He motions to me to come closer to him.

"This is something I learned about myself in prison," he says. "I learned that I cannot stop breathing voluntarily. You know, I could kill myself, but I can't physically stop breathing except for a few minutes. I have to breathe. I can't intellectually stop breathing. So what is the meaning of breath? Where is my breath coming from?"

He inhales and exhales. Inhales. Exhales.

"My breath is my spirit," he says. "Your breath is your spirit."

"I've been afraid of my breath." I don't intend to say this.

"Of course you have," Peter Pringle tells me.

19

If Anybody Moves, They're Dead

We drive down through the green fields. Our hotel in County Clare is an old manor house, and if I stand on the front lawn and look hard enough I can make out the blue wink of Galway Bay, where we just were, off in the distance.

Upstairs, Peter unpacks and then goes to get a drink in the bar while I run a bath. It is afternoon and the spring light is clear and cool, like water. This bathroom is white marble, with celadon walls above the stone wainscoting and a tall old window looking out over the garden. I sit on the edge of the tub in my hotel bathrobe for a long while, watching steam curl in white wisps against the porcelain and the stone. When the tub is full, I pour in a cup of bath salts and the water turns—I can't, in the moment, quite decide. It is either the color of wine and roses, or of blood.

If I close my eyes now, I can see it, all of it, start to finish. The van, the white gate, the way I held on to her hands that first morning as I wept, Pringle's hard blue stare, the near-dogfight in the kitchen, her grim, flat blankness when we came back from the coast. The words, too, jostle and echo. But it all feels at such a distance. I feel lighter than I ever remember, expansive, as if I've swallowed clouds. It's not until I've slipped underneath the pale red water that I realize what it is that I've lost, in meeting her. In talking with her. The anvil of anger—and guilt and fear—that I've carried for so many years: it's gone.

Which means the ghost must be too.

In the morning, I begin writing a letter. The words surprise me:

> Dear Sunny, I just want to thank you so much for talking with me. I really feel that meeting you and talking with you has opened up my heart and started me on the road away from anger and sorrow toward peace and gratitude. Thank you. I'll be honest, I think you know more than you are going to tell me, but that's okay with me. I can handle it now.

Downstairs, a peat fire glows in a stone fireplace, and antique puzzles in ruby velvet boxes stand stacked on polished walnut tables. After I draft out my letter, I sit for a long time looking out onto the front gardens and the emerald lawn.

What does it matter? she'd asked me, over and over. *What does it matter to you if Jesse was innocent or not?* Now I find myself asking the same question, marveling at it, like a new taste on the tongue. What does it matter? The place within me where the anger lived feels like a suddenly empty room. I feel like I could open every door in my soul and find nothing but gorgeous parlors with parquet floors and high ceilings, gilded light falling across the walls. For years and years, before I met Peter, I dreamed almost every night of walking through the same imaginary city, across broad staircases that led out to the sea. In those dreams, whenever I was inside, the apartments were in disarray, with sheets thrown over the furniture, trash scattered on the floors. Now those rooms have been cleared out. I had no idea how much worry and fear I had crammed away and carried with me over the years, but now that it's gone, it feels amazing.

I try another draft.

Dear Sunny, I think the trauma has been very complex, and I guess I was caught in it, and now I can see that you were as well. I don't know where this journey will take me, but talking with you has brought me such peace.

My phone is on the table in front of me, and I reach over and pick it up. What if I just called her? To say hello? To chat, see how she's doing, what she's thinking about, what she thought of me.

Can I really just let it go? I don't believe this is me writing this, but yes, I think I can. That is amazing to me. Can I let it go without finding out what actually happened? Yes. That's an extraordinary place to have found myself at. A crossroads, and a path forward. Something I'd never dared see.

Maybe it is as Sunny said yesterday, at her kitchen table. Maybe everything does depend on how you look at it. I've always firmly believed in an objective reality, but maybe my insistence on that has stood in the way of my coming to terms with what I witnessed. Maybe that is what I need to resolve.

That afternoon, I find a spot on a corduroy couch opposite the fireplace. Around me the room is candlelit and shadow-cast, with rain against the windows outside. Peter is out for a drive, down to the cliffs and the sea, and I have the place to myself—the lunch visitors have gone, dinner is still a few hours off. I order a pot of tea and as I wait, I decide to get out my notebook and go over the notes I took while talking to Sunny in her kitchen.

As I read, a line catches my eye. It is something I completely missed the first one hundred million times around.

We're talking about the minutes leading up to 7:32 A.M., when Trooper Phillip Black shouted the code 10-24 into the radio and then the radio went dead.

Here's what Sunny says:

They finally got Jesse out of the car, and they were kind of dancing around together, and then the word came back on the radio that Rhodes was on parole, and at that point the cop pushed Jesse, took his gun out, and said, "Okay, nobody move. The next one to move is dead." And then there was gunfire.

I can hear her voice in my head. We were at the kitchen table. I had just popped the question about the Taser. Her eyes had just gone that flat hazel, locked into mine, and I was about to get her *I have no clue* response for the second time. I'd been so focused on her response about the Taser that this got lost.

I flip back quickly through my notes, and see that she repeated this exact same statement, almost word for word, at least three times. Just before the shots that ended his life, Sunny told me, Trooper Black drew his weapon and said, *Nobody move.*

The policeman drew his gun. He said, "Okay, nobody move." . . .
And then there was gunfire.

The pot of tea has appeared in front of me, but I pay it no mind. My head is spinning. A uniformed policeman with a drawn weapon. How did I not see the significance of that before? This is by no means the first time I've heard this particular fact. Walter Rhodes told me this in 1990, and testified to it at trial. Both truck drivers swore they saw it as well. But even so, I wasn't ever sure that it actually happened like that. That Black actually had drawn his gun and told everyone to freeze. According to Walter, Black said: *If anybody moves, they're dead.*

It just seemed too dramatic to have actually happened. I'd written it off as a bit of collective embellishment. Too many people who'd watched too many Westerns. But hearing Sunny say she too saw Trooper Black draw his gun just before the gunfire started—it makes me think, So it did go down like that. Black did draw his gun. Which means that whoever fired the shots that morning somehow got the better of an experienced uniformed police officer with a fully loaded and drawn weapon. How could that possibly have happened?

I flip back through my notes again, with Trooper Black and his weapon in mind. Sunny told me that Jesse was "dancing" with Black, and that Black pushed Jesse and then Black drew his gun. The two truck drivers saw Jesse in the grip of Irwin, bent over the FHP cruiser. So how does Jesse break free of Irwin's grip, get hold of a gun, and shoot Black, before Black—standing right there, with a drawn weapon—shoots him first?

Sunny also told me that Walter had been ordered to the front of the car, and that Walter might have had a gun hidden in the waistband of his pants. The two truck drivers testified that they saw Walter standing with his hands in the air while the shots rang out. So if Walter did have a gun hidden somewhere on his person, how does Walter drop his hands, get the weapon out from its hiding place, and fire at Black before Black—again, standing right there with a drawn weapon—shoots him first?

Black was a veteran police officer and a former U.S. Marine who had trained with the elite corps and who, as his widow said, liked to draw himself up to his full height and joke that he was "lean and mean." How could Jesse, restrained by Irwin, or Walter, standing with his hands in the air, get the drop on Black? Exactly how Quick Draw McGraw could they be? Now that Sunny's told me that Black had his gun drawn, the only thing that seems possible is that the first shot had to have caught Black by surprise. It had to have come from someone that Black was not pointing his weapon at. Someone that Black didn't see, or didn't see as a threat.

In my mind's eye, the last moments of Black's life float into focus. The white winter fog, Black reaching into his holster, drawing his weapon, taking a step back and holding the gun out in front of him. Jesse struggling with Irwin just across from the open door of the Camaro. Walter, farther away, putting his hands in the air. Sunny and Eric and the baby inside the open door of the Camaro, in the backseat. Watching.

Nobody move.

If anybody moves, they're dead.

"It couldn't have possibly come from me," Sunny told me yesterday, about the shot that ripped through the windshield post of Black's cruiser. "You couldn't anyway. You could not, in the back of a two-door car, be able to do anything effective. Even if you had a gun or whatever."

Effective. Such a strange choice of a word.

The Florida Highway Patrol Investigation Report for that morning, written by Corporal C. J. Wippel, ends with the following statement, capitals per the original:

> During the investigation, it was revealed that certain errors were made. These errors are in NO WAY POINTED OUT IN A DEROGATORY MANNER, but as an aid to the possibility of preventing another situation happening in the future. . . . The greatest error made by Trooper Black was that he FAILED TO RECOGNIZE THE DANGER POSED BY THE WHITE FEMALE.

I close my notebook, push it across the table away from me, and turn to look out the window at the rain.

No wonder she wanted me to agree that the truth is subjective. To accept that there is no way ever to know what actually happened. That first shot must have come from the back of the Camaro, is how it looks to me now. I can't see any other plausible explanation. Not if Trooper Black had his weapon drawn, which of course he did. It's in the case record. Walter Rhodes saw it. The truck drivers saw it. And Sunny Jacobs herself just admitted it to me.

So now I know what comes next. Since Sunny cannot or will not tell me, I am going to have to go find her son.

In Australia.

20

The Playground

Dawn, the Indian Ocean.

The jet shakes as it descends and in the thin morning light the trees on the streets of Adelaide below are dull brown. It's fall here. That seems impossible. Yesterday we were in Singapore, looking out the window of our high-rise hotel at two tall buildings that stood between us and the harbor. One, blue glass, shone with the reflected light of the rooftop pools scattered like sapphires far below; the other, its twin, was an abandoned shell, construction dust blowing off its balconies and trees growing up through the top floors. Two versions of the same stories. Before that, London, Dublin, the ephemeral green of County Clare.

We land hard and taxi to the terminal. Drug dogs in the jetway, leashed, panting; soldiers with guns at the luggage carousel. The airport lobby is tiny, a chrome-shiny postage stamp with a coffee shop. Peter and I walk across an empty plaza to the rental car kiosk, leaves skittering ahead of us, pushed by a brittle wind. I fumble in my pockets for my gloves and then remember that I ditched them days ago as we were leaving Ireland. The regret I feel about this is enormous, as if the very fabric of my life has been torn.

I have a photograph of Eric that police took after the murders. Eric is nine years old, wearing a white T-shirt that is too large for him. It hangs off his thin collarbones. He has dark eyes, long eyelashes, dark hair, and his expression—he's looking right into the camera—is hard to read. Stunned. Suspicious. Or as if he has just seen something terrible. Which is why I am here. Eric was sitting next to his mother in the back of the Camaro at the rest area. I want to know what Eric saw.

At the airport exit, we turn south, toward a place on the map called Encounter Bay. We've decided to try the addresses we've found online for Eric right away, so we know what we're in for. Eric moved Down Under after falling in love with an Australian woman, the Internet tells me. But there will be no knocking on the doors of isolated farmhouses here, that is immediately clear. No genealogical yarns. The outskirts of Adelaide are a mishmash of strip malls, office buildings, apartment complexes, and eucalyptus trees. The road is wide and well marked; the hills up ahead are low, covered in pale gold grass and evergreen shrubs. Except for the roundabouts and the fact that we're driving on the left, it looks like—

"San Mateo," I say, leaning forward, gesturing. "That's what this is. The stretch south of the airport, west of the 101." Twenty miles from where I used to live in San Francisco.

"Or Hayward," Peter agrees. Twenty miles from his old house in Oakland.

Hayward is a fine place. It's just weird, to have come all this way to find a world so exactly the same, only upside down.

On the morning of the murders, the police made note of Eric's cool demeanor, particularly in view of the blood on his shirt and the photographs they found in Jesse's briefcase, the snapshots of Eric brandishing a pistol and cradling a machine gun. Gunshot residue tests on Eric's hands came back positive for having handled a recently discharged weapon—same as Sunny's test results—and there was talk about charging him with first-degree murder. But that did not happen. Instead, the county kept Eric in juvenile detention for two months and then sent him to live with his grandparents. During the entire time he was in custody, Eric does not appear to have told anyone anything at all. Some of the police took a very dim view of that behavior: "The boy had the attitude of a hardened criminal," Captain Valjean Haley said. But other people who came in contact with Eric were more sympathetic. Eric's social worker described him as innocent, lovable, and "brainwashed" in her report. "I get the impression that Eric honestly wants to be a child and yet he can't," the worker wrote. A teacher called him "extremely intelligent and sensitive," an imaginative daydreamer who knew "a great deal more about adult life than most children his age." Police detective Fred Mascaro, who was in charge of Eric during the time Eric was in state custody, told me he thought Eric was scared of his mother.

You don't have to talk to these people, Sunny told Eric at the police station that morning. *Tell them you want a lawyer.* Several officers and the social worker heard Sunny say that to Eric, and Sunny wrote it in her book. Sunny's family did hire a lawyer for Eric, and he handed out the lawyer's business card when anyone asked him a question. But I hope Eric will talk to me now. He is my last chance to fill in the missing pixels. I've spoken to every other person who might have seen what happened at the rest area on February 20, 1976, and is still alive, and to friends of Jesse Tafero too, and they've all had something different to say.

Time passes. Memories fail. I don't expect any one person to remember everything. I tell witnesses so right up front. But I do want the truth. I once did a case in which a patient was suing her psychiatrist for implanting false memories. My assignment was to go to talk to the patient's ex-husband and ask if he had assaulted her, as the patient now believed. I can't remember, the husband said. If that was a lie, it was a savvy one. I had no way to know.

Over the years, the thing I've figured out is to talk to everyone about everything. That's the only way to navigate the fallibility of memory. Because if we cannot or will not face the truth about ourselves, sometimes other people can—and do. The trick is to gather those stories together and see how they fit. Our lives live on in the stories other people share with us, in what they remember, in what they know.

The address we have for Eric turns out to be a ranch house in a quiet suburb just south of the city line. Peter parks our rental car down the block. I walk up the steep short lawn to the house and knock. Nobody's home.

Then Peter and I sit in the car, looking out the windshield. What is today? Tuesday? Friday? It's noon in any case, the sun sharp like a laser beam, but cold. The pine trees in the park across the way cast shade like pools of water on the dying grass. The blue shadows of the oncoming winter.

The next morning, I set out alone.

It's Saturday and the roads are empty, the kind of gray-day fall weekend where everybody stays home and does laundry. Saturdays like this used to make me so lonely, this sense of everyone else being cozy at home, and this landscape is not helping: It's the same low hills and open sky as the highways I spent way too much time on when I was first working as a detective. Back when I was starting to understand that we keep secrets not only from each other, but from ourselves.

I was nine, as well. The same age as Eric was that morning. I never think about it, or talk about it. Even Peter didn't know until I told him this winter, after I found the social worker's report about Eric in the files of the Broward County State Attorney's Office. I thought I'd put it all well behind me. But when I was nine years old, I was assaulted by a gang of boys in a Central Park playground. They backed me up against a wall and came at me. It hurt. I was afraid. It's not one of those memories you hear about that someone has completely repressed. I remember it. But I never—I don't know. Never thought it was that big a deal.

Until now. Now, every time I think about Eric being nine years old that morning, when I think about what a nine-year-old might know, about what a nine-year-old might remember, might have felt—this old memory of mine, it comes to life. I'm right there again, and there's nothing I can do but the same thing I did while it was happening. Which was to turn, pull myself up over the par-apet on the high concrete bridge where they'd trapped me, and throw myself over the edge.

Their hands, pulling, grabbing. The ground, so far below. I told myself: *Go*.

Investigation is not about empathy. That's a mistake people make. It's about control.

Eric doesn't live at the ranch house address anymore, a young woman with blue hair and a tattooed throat tells me, when I find her at home. She looks like she's going to burst out laughing. "Sorry! Wish I could help you!" she says, with an enormous smile.

At the next address, down a hillside, another young woman smiles widely when I ask for Eric. "He used to live here," she tells me, radiantly.

Wow, people are nice here, I think, as I get back in the car again. Must be an Australian thing. Kindness to strangers.

"Well, now, that's an accent," the woman who answers the door at my third and last address says. She's never heard of Eric. "Where are you from, Canada?"

As the light fades, I wind my way back through a whirl of wrong-side-of-the-road roundabouts and then down along a long stretch beside the sea, which is turning to silver as the sun sinks low. Maybe this thing about being nine—I'm just realizing—is why I feel hopeful about talking to Eric. That day in the park is some-thing I remember so clearly, unerringly the same memory every single time—not in photo-perfect detail, but always the same—and maybe, I'm thinking, maybe it's the same for him. Something gets cemented, and try as you might, there is no escaping it, even if you really want to. So maybe Eric really will have the answers that I've sought for so long, and from so far away.

And I am pretty sure I know where Eric will be tomorrow. He'll be visiting the sixteenth century, and my plan is to find him there.

21

The Kingdom of Lochac

In Adelaide, the sixteenth century can be found most Sundays in a park off Brand Street, just around the corner from the motorsports shop and the McDonald's. Here, on a rectangle of grass bordered by stone cottages and shaded by gum trees, the gentle people of the Barony of Innilgard, Kingdom of Lochac, practice their arts: rapier fencing, arts and sewing, heavy combat. It's a Renaissance Faire for serious history buffs. Among the participants, I hope, will be Eric. Or, as he is known here, Lord Marc de Montfault.

It's just past noon when Peter and I slip our rental car into a parking space opposite the jousting grounds. Already there are knights on the field. I can tell they are knights because they're lurching around in long felt tunics, trying to whack each other with wooden swords. It is perhaps ironic that our information about Eric's interest in the past comes from the most modern of media, but thanks to Facebook, we know that Eric and his partner and daughter are all members of the Society for Creative Anachronism, a worldwide celebration of all things medieval that was founded in Berkeley, California, in 1966. Here in the Kingdom,

Lord Marc de Montfault is a Frenchman living outside Paris in the sixteenth century, and his partner is the lovely Bella Lucia da Verona, an expert seamstress who also runs a Yahoo chat group for those who, like herself, are medieval Venetian courtesans.

I had resisted the idea of engaging Eric here in the Kingdom. Interviews conducted outdoors in crowded places—particularly, I'm guessing, those full of fellows fetched up in felt—are not usually conducive to intimate conversation. But Peter has insisted, saying that this is our best chance at finding Eric in Adelaide. We have only one photo to go on, from Facebook. A pirate in his late forties who looks something like Sunny.

"Uh-oh," Peter says, as he turns the car off.

The swordsmen are wearing beekeeper-ish mesh masks that completely cover their faces, and shiny full-metal helmets. If it's a pirate under there, I have no way to tell. We decide to walk around the park to think.

The stone cottages of old Adelaide are beautiful. They're like San Francisco Victorians shrunk down to one story, made of golden sand, and overdecorated with gingerbread. They remind me a little of New Orleans as well, with their ornate porches and wrought ironwork, but really I've never seen anything like them, this perfect marriage of frill and solidity on these silent sun-stilled streets. Which makes it all the more jolting when we finally come back around the corner to where we started and—

"Right there, by the tree, in the baseball cap," I say. My missing puzzle piece.

It's his cheekbones. Even from this distance. High curved cheekbones that look like Sunny's. I'm surprised by the ponytail and by his solidity. I thought he'd be skinny, somehow. And he is wearing a Tampa Bay Rays baseball cap and green camo pants, which seems about as un-Renaissance as a person can be.

In a quick conference, we decide that Peter will walk up close under the guise of being a "bloke" in search of the "toilet" at the park building. I retreat to the car to watch out the front windshield, my heart pounding.

Peter is coming back now, giving a discreet thumbs-up.

"It's him," Peter says, as he gets in the car. "American accent, zombie T-shirt."

Ah yes, zombies. Zombies are another Eric interest, thank you again, Facebook.

Peter has gotten back in the driver's seat now.

Don't tremble, I tell myself. No point in trembling.

"What?" I say.

When Peter was a kid, he had a collie. The collie, Cameron, had long legs. Sometimes Cameron slept on Peter's bed at night, and during the night Cameron would lie with his feet against the wall and his back to Peter, and slowly stretch his legs out until he pushed Peter right out of bed onto the floor.

"You're doing it, aren't you," I say, looking at him.

Peter reaches over and pulls the door latch on my side open.

"I'll be waiting right here," he says.

He pushes the door open a little wider.

I zip my coat tight, climb out of the car, and head toward the clod of knights on the lawn.

Eric is by a tree, deep in conversation with a young man wearing a brown felt tunic and a leather neck guard. Both of them are holding swords. They are so intent on their conversation that they don't look up as I approach.

"Eric," I say, totally interrupting. I don't say it as a question.

Eric turns toward me. I recognize his brown eyes from his long-ago mugshot, but his expression is so different now that he looks like a new person. The man standing in front of me is so robust that he is almost rectangular; he is hale and hearty and exuberant, his eyes radiant and friendly.

"Hello!" As if there couldn't possibly be a nicer surprise than me, barging in like this.

"Can I talk to you for a second?"

"Sure!" He's still smiling.

"I'm writing a book about Jesse."

"You're kidding!"

"No," I say. "So I really need to talk to you."

"That's excellent," Eric says. "Somebody really needs to. Because so many people, they look at his criminal record and they judge him. He was nothing like the man that a lot of people judge him to be. He didn't have the easiest upbringing, he had a hard life, he didn't exactly have the best influences chumming around with him, but he was a good person. He did some really dumb things, but in our youth we've all done something we look back on and say, are you kidding me? He was a really good guy, he was a good person, he loved my mom and my sister and I. And the way he was treated, nothing, it's beyond criminal. I mean, they treated him like an animal. Less than an animal. They don't usually shoot a gazelle, drag it down on the ground, and kick it unconscious."

He says it all in one burst.

We stand there for a moment. A gazelle?

"I witnessed his execution," I say. Tentatively.

"Oh, you're the lady my mom told me about!"

But before I can quiz him about what, exactly, his mom told him about me, Eric continues. "It's good you're doing this, because somebody's got to tell people."

That happens to be what I think as well. But what? Tell them what?

"He really took time to be a dad to me," Eric is saying. "He actually got me a pair of World War I model kits, Eddie Rickenbacker's plane and the Red Baron. And he painted on a sheet of parchment paper an aerial view of an airfield." Eric pauses for a moment. "He was a good guy. He really cared. He had a good heart. He really wanted to be something modern society doesn't recognize anymore. He wanted to be an honorable person. I mean, it was a dream of his. He wanted to be a samurai."

"With swords?"

"Not the swords so much."

"A knight?"

"Exactly," Eric says. Nodding. "And that became one of my things as well."

It's always such a crapshoot, an interview. Eric was almost seven when his mom and Jesse got together in mid-1973, and the murders happened when Eric was nine and a half. That's only about thirty months total, much of which Sunny and Jesse seem to have spent on the run, living a life of drugs and guns. Eric is now forty-eight years old, he's been married and divorced, he has a new partner and grown daughter, and he is living in Australia, as far away as a person can get from Florida without pitching a tent on the South Pole. I'd thought that perhaps Eric might have gained a bit of distance from the whole terrible situation, maybe have a slightly analytical perspective on it, but immediately I can see that, no. You can take it with you, apparently. Across the world, even. Although I'm one to speak.

"Were you able to visit Jesse in prison?"

"Starke Prison? Oh my God. That place, it looks like a Civil War–era prison. It's horrible, it's filthy, it's built to intimidate—it's stone and steel and bars and barred doors—it really does, it looks like a place you store munitions, not humans. It was freezing in there. Every time we'd go to visit, it was freezing. Even in the summer, it was cold."

"And you were a child."

"I was. I was. I mean, honestly, I've been working for so many years to get over the fact that, you know, you see a police officer or a police car or any sign of them and—you know?"

I'm really just letting him talk now, trying to get over my own nervousness. I can see Peter watching me and Eric from our rental car, parked across the street from the Kingdom. This all feels like it's happening very fast—coming here, finding Eric, standing here talking to Eric, listening to Eric talk about the police, with felty fellows all around us, slicing, swaying.

"In America, honestly, it used to drive me crazy, I'd be driving down and I'd see a police car in traffic and I'd be like, 'I'm not doing anything wrong, I'm an honest citizen, I'm obeying the law!' But still I'd feel like I've got to watch out for them. Because I mean, honestly, when they took us prisoner over at the roadblock site, it was ridiculous."

There's something in what Eric has just said about the police that has given me a *pay attention* vibe. But try as I might, I can't grasp it, and now we've moved on.

"It's already come out in declassified documents under the Freedom of Information Act that the CIA brought in the majority of drugs in the sixties," Eric continues.

"Is that crazy?" I say. It's an actual question.

"And since then, both the bombing of the World Trade Center and the planes hitting the World Trade Center, I mean the only reason that the United States government hasn't been made to answer for those is because the CIA's answer to everything is *you saw nothing*. They're like Jedi."

I wait.

"The fact is, I'm not a demolition expert, but I've seen enough building demolitions because it's always cool when you live in a city and you've got nothing better to do in an afternoon and they're going to implode a building—"

"Eric," I say. To get his attention. "There's been a lot of talk about Jesse's innocence."

Eric looks directly at me, intense.

"He was!" Eric says. "He was standing— Okay, come on."

And with that, Eric spins around and starts off, with his sword, away from the knights, toward the street. I race to catch up.

We reach a blue station wagon parked along a curb at the edge of the park. Eric strides up to the car and takes a spread-'em stance up against the driver's-side window, one hand on the car roof, the other behind his back, as if someone is trying to cuff him.

Jesse was like this, at the car, Eric says, looking over his shoulder at me.

"Over the patrol car?"

"No, over our car."

That's odd, I think. The two truckers and Walter both remember Jesse pressed up against the patrol car. Jesse himself testified that he was being held at the cruiser. But I'm interested to hear Eric unimpeded, uncorrected, so I don't stop him.

"Where were you?"

"I was in the backseat, with my mom and my sister," he says, pointing. We both look at the interior of the car as if they're all there still.

"Okay, so then what happened?"

The officer threw Jesse over the car and was holding him down, Eric says.

"Was that the Canadian officer who did that?" I ask.

"No, the uniformed officer. The Canadian was out about over there." Eric points to a spot behind me.

That's odd too. The two truckers and Walter and Jesse all testified that Jesse was being held by the guy in the white T-shirt. But no matter. Let's hear it.

"Where was Rhodes?"

"Rhodes, while the altercation was going on, he walked around like this."

With that, Eric walks along the side of the car to the front, and then across the front to about the location of the headlight on the right. If this car were the Camaro, the position that Eric is standing in now would be about one foot in front of the headlight on the car's passenger side. I am standing by the door on the driver's side, so I'm standing where Jesse was when the shooting stopped. Eric, as Walter, is diagonally across the car hood from me, about ten feet away.

"The officer yelled at Rhodes, 'Get back over here!' And that's when everything let loose and the whole, you know? I didn't see him actually shoot. But Rhodes was the only one with a gun."

It's that one detail. The part where Eric says, "The officer yelled at Rhodes, 'Get back over here!' "

I think I remember seeing that in the court documents somewhere. I'm not one hundred percent certain, but in this moment, it seems to me that yes, I think Trooper Black did motion at Walter with his gun and tell Walter to move. So how does Eric know that? He's wrong about Jesse being held over the driver's-side door of the Camaro. He's wrong about where the Canadian officer was standing. So obviously he hasn't bothered to pretty up his story—he's telling me what he remembers. What he himself heard. Right? He heard Trooper Black tell Walter Rhodes to move. The location that Eric remembers Walter standing is exactly where crime scene investigators found a bullet casing that morning. One of only three found at the scene. The only one found outside the car. And Eric saw Walter holding a gun.

Jesus God.

It's like a thunderclap has gone off in my head.

I watch Eric at the front of the car. He has his hand in the air, like he's got a gun in it.

I can see it so exactly, right now.

Walter Rhodes got out of the car with a gun hidden on his person, walked around to the front of the car, and when the officer admonished him, Walter "pulled it out and started shooting over the top of the car," just like Eric is saying.

The day feels like it's gone black-and-white. Eric is so intense. Definite, descriptive, confident, committed. There at the front of the car, with his hand in the air, it's like he's reliving it, playing it out from a part of himself where it's been hidden all these years. And now it's alive, this memory, in full motion. I can feel it. It's alive for me as well.

"He shot them, you know. He shot them dead and left them in huge pools of blood." Eric's voice bounces and echoes around me. *Walter Rhodes*. Just like Eric says.

I ask Eric to draw what he remembers for me, to be sure.

We sit side by side on a fence rail along the edge of the park. Eric has my notebook and is sketching, head bent. I'm watching him and every so often taking notes, writing upside down on the same page that he's drawing on.

"And the patrol car was like this," Eric is saying, pointing.

"The cruiser was parked *behind* the Camaro?"

"Right."

But it wasn't, actually. Every other witness—Walter, the truck drivers, Jesse—said that the two cars were parked parallel.

I take the notebook and squint closely at what Eric has drawn. In addition to the two cars, Eric has marked where everyone was standing—Jesse, Walter, Black, Irwin. He's got them all labeled, with arrows pointing where everyone was and where they were moving to.

Every single thing in the drawing is wrong.

The knights are in heavy combat now, beside us, staggering slightly on the uneven grass, tilting to and fro. Eric is watching me as I try to think of what to say. *Do you realize that what you've drawn here conflicts with all the police reports and with what every other person who was there that morning has said?* I decide there is nothing for it but diving into the facts, one by one, and seeing how he responds. He still seems friendly, but there's a wariness growing, I can tell. He's got his sword across his knees and now he's tapping it, lightly, as if to make sure it's still there.

I feel a bit thrown as well, especially after what happened just now at the car. That lightning bolt I'd felt of complete trust and belief. Of revelation. Before coming here today, I'd wondered if Eric was going to be defensive. To evade, to bluster. *But which truth?* And then he'd turned out to be so open, and so convincing. But now I wonder if Eric actually knows the basic facts of the case at all.

I start with the Taser dart, the tiny barbed fishhook stuck in the police car window.

"Do you remember a Taser being fired?"

Eric looks blank. Pleasant, but blank.

"There was a Taser dart in the trooper car," I prompt him.

"That's weird," Eric says now, musingly. "I've never heard about that, I don't think. That's very strange. I don't remember the presence of any Tasers and I'd seen Tasers because, you know, I'd seen the police use them."

"Well, and your mom had one."

"She did?"

"Yeah, she bought one."

"I didn't realize that. The only time I'd ever seen a Taser was when they allowed the public in when the police were testing them."

I try to imagine a police-sponsored Taser test that allowed children in the audience. Aside from the scene in *The Hangover*, that is.

"It was kind of weird, I thought it was very neat, it was like a *Star Trek* phaser set on stun," Eric is saying. "It was a wonderful thing, because, I mean, they had this large officer, a federal marshal or something, and they had him go charging at a female officer who was about your height and build and she just said 'Stop!' and he didn't and so she let him have it and so he fell on the ground."

"Just like that," I say.

"It's amazing, the innovations," Eric says, with a touch of dreaminess.

It seems possible that he's got no idea about the Taser, sure. Or maybe I've hit a wall.

I think for a moment.

"Did you see the officer draw his gun that day?" I ask.

Yes, Eric says. The uniformed officer had his gun out when he first opened the door to the Camaro, right at the beginning of everything. But then the officer "holstered."

"Holstered?" I ask. "He put the gun back?"

Eric nods.

"The officer was showing off," Eric says. "It doesn't take a professional psychiatrist or any expert to see that. He wanted to show off for his buddy from Canada by rousting a carload of people. They might have some dope, they might argue with him, he might have to ticket them and haul them off, and look like the big man. Like John Wayne."

I watch Eric for a minute.

"So one of the things they made a big deal of was there was a shot through the window trim of the cruiser," I try next. There were photographs, I say, illustrating the angle of the shot: from the back of the car toward the front. "That doesn't match at all with what you just said," about Walter firing from the front.

"The thing is, because the police concealed so many things and fabricated so many things, it would take nothing to move things a little bit before they take the pictures," Eric says.

What about the casings that were found in the car?

"There were no casings in the car."

The gunshot residue tests that determined you'd handled a recently discharged weapon?

"That's horseshit."

The guns?

"Both of those nine-millimeter pistols were owned and possessed by Rhodes," Eric says, forcefully.

But I saw the sales receipt myself, in Room 407. A faded white rectangle with Sunny's name written on it in blue ink, just above the serial numbers of the guns.

"One of the other things they made a big deal about was Jesse being arrested with the murder weapon. Do you remember how that happened?"

"Yes." Eric takes a deep breath. He looks down at his hands, and then right at me. "After Rhodes made us get in the police car and we got to the parking lot, he closed the slide on the weapon—on the pistol that had been used—and handed it to Jess and made Jess take it while pointing his other gun, the loaded gun, at him."

"This was in the parking lot?"

"Yes. Rhodes forced Jess to take the empty weapon and help him. Otherwise Rhodes was going to shoot him, he was going to shoot Jess, and shoot us."

He pauses and takes another deep breath.

"That must have been terrifying," I say, because Eric seems so upset.

"Yes."

"Did you see that happen?"

"No, I didn't."

We look at each other, neither of us moving.

"But I'll tell you what I did see. The entire time we were riding in the police car and the entire time we were riding in the old man's car, Rhodes had me in the front seat with him and he had the gun pointed at my head. Literally like this."

Eric pulls his left hand back, cocks his thumb and index finger into a pistol, and holds it point-blank against the side of his head.

His own imaginary head.

Everything Eric has told me so far, every single thing—who owned the guns, whether there were casings in the car, the gunshot residue tests—all of it is factually inaccurate. According to the case record, which means according to the police reports and everyone who testified under oath. And on the day of the murders, Eric never mentioned Walter having a gun, let alone that Walter had pointed that gun at his head. Not to the social worker who was following his every move and writing up everything he said, and not to the police officer who interviewed him on tape at the police station right after the arrests at the roadblock. I know this because I read the notes and transcript this winter at the Fort Lauderdale courthouse, and then I talked to the police officer myself.

Now Eric and I are sitting in silence.

Around us, the afternoon is getting colder. We're in the shade of a big gum tree, in a blue shadow that feels stronger than the fall sunlight, dark-edged, deep. The shadow might be the reason I am shivering. Eric has edged away along the fence and he's not looking at me.

"They held me without charging me," he says suddenly, to the ground in front of him. He's talking about the months after the murders when he was held in juvenile detention. "They threatened my mum and Jess that if one of them didn't confess they were going to make a case against me at nine years old." Late one night, police grabbed him, cranked his arms up hard behind his back, marched him in front of a judge, and interrogated him, Eric says. "They were trying to make me say what they wanted."

"What did they want you to say?"

"They wanted me to say that my mum and Jess did it. And it was ridiculous. It was absolutely ridiculous."

"Eric," I say. "What do you remember about when the gunfire started?"

"My mum was holding my sister, and she put her arm around me and pulled me down like this and laid over us. And Jess was incapacitated like this."

"You don't remember anything about a Taser?"

"No. I have no memory of my mum ever buying or owning a Taser."

"But do you remember hearing one or hearing about one from that morning?"

"No. When you mentioned it, it was the first mention I've ever heard about a Taser."

"It's the mystery piece of evidence. That's what I don't understand," I tell him. "There's a photograph of a Taser dart in the side of the patrol car and there were fired cartridges and they made a big deal out of it in the trial, they fired one in the courtroom—"

"I've never heard about that. I mean, honestly, they tried to say so many things. They tried to say so many things that are patently untrue. It's just garbage."

"You think the Taser was made up?"

"I think it was made up. I think they probably fired off one of their own Tasers and put it out there and put it in as evidence."

So that's where he's at, I think.

"You know, I looked through a bunch of papers in the case," I say. I am starting carefully, not entirely sure how to say this, even though I know that I have to ask. "And, Eric, there's a report in those files that says you told your social worker at one point, quote, 'My mother made me do it.'"

The sentence hangs in the air.

"That is such—that is such a load of *fantasy horsecrap.* Oh my God, which psychologist supposedly wrote that one?"

"It's a report by your social worker."

"I don't even remember ever seeing a social worker at all. I would never have said that. That is an absolute lie."

"So what do you think they were getting at, then?"

"They were trying to piece together any possible shred of a case to try them on. The fact was, they had no case."

I suppose that if you take away the bullet hole through the windshield post, the ownership of the guns, the fact that Jesse Tafero was arrested with the murder weapon, the eyewitnesses who saw the shots coming from the car, the Taser dart in the police car, and all the drugs and weapons in the Camaro, then that might be true. I could sit here and punch through every single wrong fact that he's told me, one by one. But I don't. Because now he seems very upset.

"It's been a real struggle not to be consumed by anger because of what Rhodes and Satz and the rest of them did," Eric is saying. He knows the events of that morning affected him, he says. He's pretty sure he has post-traumatic stress. He feels like maybe he will never be right again. As he talks, he's looking at me with a steady, flat gaze. It's the look his mother gave me in Ireland.

"It took me years, quite literally it took me until about—when I moved to Australia, I finally was able to stop walking around armed. When I lived in America, I had to at least have two knives on me all the time. I had to be able to protect myself. Because no one else would. I mean, what do you do when your early years, when nine years, nine of the first years of your life, you're taught that police are there to protect and serve you, that you can trust them, when anything happens run to a police officer, they won't hurt you, they're there to protect you, and then you have over-whelming proof positive that you can't? That that's not the case, that they're there to take advantage of you, hurt you, try to kill you, take the people you love away from you, to hurt and kill them, to lie, to cheat?"

We sit there for a while after that, underneath the gum trees. Beside us, on the lawn, the knights in heavy combat cross swords, but their cries are muffled underneath their masks, and all that I hear is a dog barking in the distance and a radio from one of the limestone cottages, tinny and faint, as if from long ago.

22

Investigator Strait

In the kitchen, Peter turns on the kettle. It's gray this morning—gray sea, gray sky. This echoing apartment is on the edge of the ocean, and a brittle wind rattles through. I'm raking over my notes. And kicking myself, because I am sure I fucked up.

It was intense with Eric yesterday. I should have pressed him more. I should have backed off earlier. Did he really not know about the Taser? Or that the Camaro was full of drugs? He is so sure now that Walter had a gun—*Rhodes was the only person with a gun*—but that is not what he said on the morning of the murders. Fresh out of the Camaro and the Cadillac, he told police he did not see anyone with a gun. "I wasn't looking," he told a detective at the police station. Did Eric tell the truth now, or then? And my unbearable trembling while he was talking. Racking, painful, and freezing cold. Why?

At the end of our interview, I asked Eric for his phone number in case I had follow-up questions. Now I punch the numbers in carefully. Standard procedure would be to drop by his house, but I feel like it's okay to give him some advance notice, given that we talked for two hours and wound up shaking hands.

"Who is this?"

"It's Ellen, I talked with you yesterday. How are you?"

Eric is silent. That is never, and I mean never, a good sign.

"Eric?"

"Yeah, yesterday was really upsetting for me."

"Oh God, I'm so sorry."

Silence.

"Eric, I am so sorry, but this is important. There are some photos I'd like to show you and—"

"No," Eric says. And hangs up.

In the living room, I find Peter sitting at a little table that's been built into one wall, like a two-top diner booth. I slide in opposite him.

"It's not like the detective's oath is 'First, do no harm,'" I tell Peter.

"But if he's told you no, isn't that harassment?" Peter says.

"No. It's persistence."

"Anyway, what does it get you? He doesn't remember."

"But what if I can get him to remember?"

"How? By breaking him apart?"

I spend the afternoon in an empty bathtub on the phone. The apartment is so cold that I have two sweaters on, but from the tub I can at least look out the window at the seafront and its Norfolk Island pines, tall cylindrical evergreens whose rigid fringes mock the breeze.

"It's his life, and maybe this is how he's chosen to deal with this," Freya is telling me from the other side of the world.

"By not knowing anything?"

"That could be the choice he's made."

I want to let it go. I want to let it go. I want to let it go.

But at four o'clock, with the light fading, I decide I must try. Peter has come up with a new address for Eric—found it on a website registration—and so I collect my case documents and photographs and we take off. I feel dread. All the way across the city, I'm hoping the address is going to be a bust like the others, but then we pass a sign announcing the town line of his suburb and there it is, his house number, shiny in brass on a tall fence with a closed gate. I ask Peter to drive past the house, and he does, pulling in down the road a bit.

I try to imagine walking over there.

The conversation yesterday was so tumultuous—the gun Eric remembers being pointed at his head by Walter, the Taser he is sure was planted by police. As we sat together in his Renaissance kingdom, he'd also told me that as the carjacked Cadillac barreled down on the roadblock that morning, it did so in a blaze of gunfire from two hundred police officers armed with automatic weapons and as helicopters "stitched the top of the car" with gunshots from above. "They wanted a riddled car with six dead bodies in it so there would be no one who could say what happened," Eric told me. "So they could say whatever they wanted."

Back in Florida, I'd talked to Corporal Jack Harden, is the thing. Harden was the Florida Highway Patrol officer who commanded the roadblock that morning. It was Harden who fired the double-aught buckshot through the Cadillac door into Walter Rhodes's left leg, crashing the Cadillac and resulting in the arrests. There were no helicopter gunships that morning, just three police sharpshooters on the ground and a fixed-wing airplane keeping an eye from above, Harden told me. The pilot, Trooper D. G. McDermid, had been assigned to do routine traffic patrols that day and had been at the airport when the call came in that Black and Irwin were down. He'd shadowed that getaway Cadillac from a thousand feet up, coordinating all the officers who were trailing the car. McDermid was the reason that nobody in the Cadillac knew they were being followed. They were trapped at the roadblock by a decorated Vietnam War veteran pilot and the element of surprise. Not by strafing automatic overhead gunfire.

And Eric's extraordinary admission, after his long recollection of Walter pointing a loaded gun at Jesse to make Jesse take the murder weapon. "Did you see that?" I'd asked Eric. "No, I did not," Eric had responded. Yet the memory was so detailed, so specific. That's what you're supposed to look for in telling fact from fiction. Depth. Detail. Emotion. Complexity. Eric sounded as if he had lived it, but he'd dreamed that one up.

I watch the road around us for a while. The weeds on the median strip, the Monday rush-hour traffic, the traffic lights up ahead, changing, changing again. And it occurs to me, sitting here, all the way at the other end of the earth from my home, watching this intersection that could be anywhere, with its dinged-up streetlamps and battleship sky, that the man who was the boy in the backseat of that Camaro is not and never will be, in fact, my missing puzzle piece. My pixel. My grail.

And so this is it. This workhorse thoroughfare running down to a place on the map called Investigator Strait, a southernmost shore of a southernmost continent, out toward the ice, toward Antarctica, out across the water to where it's always winter and sometimes never gets light. This, right here.

This is the end of the road.

PART THREE

Gone Ghost

The Boxes

At home, I walk from room to room, opening windows. The house is dusty and it feels cold. Outside, a beautiful Michigan summer day is under way, blue skies and birdsong and a freshwater breeze. When we left here for Florida in January, snowdrifts covered the fences, and when we left for Ireland six weeks ago, the trees had just the lightest lace of green. Now it's June and the woods behind our house whisper with leaves.

It's been two years since we traded the big city for this clapboard house amid the orchards of the Michigan lakeshore. Peaches, corn, garden tomatoes, blueberries, black raspberries, fresh cherry pies. Narrow roads stung into silence by the heat; afternoon thunderstorms and the way everything shines afterwards, sun-struck, rose and gold. It's been a refuge for me. Now I'm back from the other side of the world and I don't recognize a thing. This could be someone else's house. Look, a couch. That's a nice place for it, there by the fireplace. Sweet. Harmonious. No bullets or bloodstains. This must be someone else's life.

This morning we were having breakfast on the porch and I

started crying and I could not stop. It felt as if the bones along my back were going to break. Are you okay? Peter asked.

I guess so. I'm not sure. I don't think so. No.

I'd been so certain I could find out.

Upstairs, on my office desk, the phone rings. Work comes in: a Fortune 500 company needing to know if employees are selling stolen goods on eBay; a multinational corporation worried about possible mob-related fraud in a major real estate deal. I'm glad to have the cases and I like my clients—I've worked for some of them for two decades, through bad times and good. But right now I feel like every ounce of whatever it is that makes me a private detective got lost somewhere along my travels overseas.

After that day outside Eric's house in Australia, we did not come straight back home. We could not. In planning the trip, we'd had to allow plenty of time to find Eric, just in case, so our flight back to the United States wouldn't be leaving for two more weeks. We were marooned at the far end of the earth. We fled north, to the Great Barrier Reef.

There, a sandy path led out the back door to the sea. At the beach the water was silty, rolling in one long wave toward the shore. Mountains rose in the distance, pitchforked up against the high wide sky, and underfoot, translucent crabs spun sand into lace, an intricate pattern of perfect spheres. At night, orange-footed jungle fowl in the rainforest around us screamed in the dark, a series of piercing shrieks that ended in mad laughter, again and again. Every night, I lay awake in the pitch-black, obsessing. *How could he really not know? How do I get him to remember?* That's the way police coerce confessions, I reminded myself. *Tell me the things that I tell you are true.* I did not know I had that in me. I did not want to. And from there it spiraled out and down, to every mistake I'd ever made and every bad relationship I'd ever been in to every pet I'd had and loved and lost. An assassin stalking me inside my own head. *The Polaroid of him and Jesse and the machine gun, I should have—*

At dinner on our last night there, at a restaurant on a deserted road out near the beach, I thought I saw birds in the sky as night fell, but then I realized they were bats. Under the streetlamps, their wings were translucent, veins through flesh, stretched tight from bone to bone.

Later, we walked out to the beach to look at the stars. The heavens glittered in the black velvet above us. I wanted to see the Southern Cross. I'd always wanted to see it. I waded into the sea and stared up at the sky. But all I could see was the spangle out over the open ocean, and the moon, a bright path across the dark water, out into the deep, leading away from the shore.

Today in Michigan, crows are calling in the woods surrounding our house. I can hear them in my office upstairs, where I am going over my notes.

What you are doing is pointless and hurtful. That is what Irish told me, at the very beginning. *Quixotic* is how investigator Walt LaGraves put it. *Impossible,* Sunny Jacobs said.

"I wish I'd never started this," I told Peter this morning, on the porch. Before this year began, Jesse Tafero had been a ghost whose presence was just a vague feeling of foreboding. Now I've met his friends and his lover and a man who'd been the boy who idolized him. I know about his dreams and his drugs and his brutal assaults. I know everything, it seems, except what actually happened at the rest area. Which was the only thing I'd wanted to find out.

All that time in the rainforest, I told myself to give it up. *Okay, maybe I won't ever know. I guess I am going to have to figure out how to live with that.* But as soon as I got back home, I realized: no. If I stop now, things will never get better. All I will have done is free up the ghost. Even now it is so much stronger. Swaggering, in full living color. Viscerally painful. Bringing with it my own terrible memories too—that's something I never expected, starting out. And me, without my defenses. I guess that was always a risk. The downside of trying. I just didn't realize it until right now.

I have never once lost a case I've worked on. Never. I have always, before this, been able to put my feelings in a box and get things done. I once sat for hours with a man who had been shot four times in the head and left for dead *by my client*. I got that man to talk to me. But now, in the one case that really truly matters in my life, I've come up empty. Weak. I'd had that moment of lightness in Ireland, when I thought I could leave it all behind me, but then the facts of the case caught up with me again. I feel deeply depressed.

Sunny and Eric both say they didn't see the shooting. They both say Walter made Jesse take the murder weapon, but they didn't see that happen either. Eric says Walter shot the officers from the front of the Camaro. Sunny says Walter shot from behind the Camaro. When they looked up after the shots stopped, both of them, they saw Jesse standing right there at the open Camaro door, and Walter with a gun, telling them to get in the police car.

Sunny said she didn't recognize the name Ricky Cravero. Did not recognize the name Marianne Cook. She did know Jack Murphy, but when I asked why a guy like Murphy—a celebrity both in and out of prison—had taken an interest in Jesse's case, I got that flat stare again. "Jesse was special," was all she said.

And the Taser. Sunny and Eric knew nothing at all about a Taser. They were, both of them, very definite about that.

The Taser dart in the police car is a critical piece of the tragedy. The catalyst—for the murders and everything after. Either Sunny or Eric not knowing about the Taser? Could be. A quick detonation in the backseat, obliterated by the chaos that followed. But could you really fire a Taser and not remember? Seems unlikely. So possibly Sunny or Eric lied to me. I get that. But to make sure I understand all the angles, I am going to take it as truth that both Sunny and Eric did indeed have "no clue," as Sunny put it, about the Taser. In that case, who did?

Walter Rhodes. He was standing at either the front or the back of the Camaro. He had his hands in the air, dropped them, fished the Taser out of its hiding place, fired the dart into the patrol car, dropped the Taser, then found and fired the gun.

Jesse Tafero, pinned up against the cruiser. Jesse broke free, got hold of the Taser, fired it, dropped it, then got hold of the gun and shot some more.

But what were Phillip Black and Donald Irwin doing while this was going on? Watching?

After the murders, officers found the Taser and its expended cartridge in the stolen Cadillac. But the Taser's holster—its black plastic carrying case—was still in the Camaro, in a denim handbag behind the driver's seat. Where Sunny had been sitting. Or maybe Eric. Because when we talked down there in Australia, Eric told me he'd been sitting right inside that open door himself.

Into all this come ten boxes of files from Walter Rhodes.

One day about a week after we get home from Australia, I come back from the farmers market and find the boxes in the garage, stacked there by the delivery guy.

This past spring, Walter mentioned these files to me in a letter. During my travels, I'd been in contact with Walter's friends about them. But there was never a point I was certain I was going to get them. Or that I wanted them. I didn't want to appear to be on Walter's side, and I didn't want to be indebted to him. Also, I did not want the files in my house for the simple reason that the trip I took to see Walter in 2003 still freaked me out.

But I needed them. The Broward County Circuit Court files were a mess; I'd looked through everything that the Broward State Attorney's Office had given me but I knew it wasn't every single piece of paper they had; Jesse's trial attorneys no longer had their files; and I am still—after half a year now—tracking down the rest of the court exhibits in the case. And I have not been able to get prosecutor Michael Satz to agree to an interview with me.

I stand for a moment looking at the boxes. Then I get down on my hands and knees and start cutting the tape. It takes me fewer than five minutes to find what I'd been hoping might be in here somewhere: the attorney-client files of Ralph Ray, the lawyer who represented Walter Rhodes in 1976.

Attorney-client files are confidential. It's not a negotiable concept. The client may waive confidentiality and allow the disclosure of information he provided to his attorney, but the attorney may not, period. We work with attorney-client materials all the time in our investigation practice, always when the client has given us permission to do so. Walter has waived confidentiality in giving me these files, so it's fine for me to read them. And I am very interested in what Ray's files might have to say. It would be information that Walter told to his attorney in confidence. It might be the closest version to the truth of anything that I've found thus far.

The Ray files are a thick stack of manila folders with xeroxed papers tucked inside—billing records, handwritten time slips, handwritten case notes. Some of the handwritten case notes appear to have been taken by Ray during his attorney-client conferences with Walter Rhodes in the days immediately after the murders. Those are what really get my attention.

I take the Ray files into the kitchen and start reading, standing up. I take the first few pages pretty casually, just a few more of the tens of thousands of pages I've read so far on this case. But then suddenly I'm in a frenzy, flipping forward, flipping back, turning the files clockwise and counterclockwise to get at all the little scraps that are stapled in there, leaning close. Because I feel all of a sudden—again—like the world is upside down.

Walter Rhodes testified, under oath, at two trials—at Jesse's trial and at Sunny's—that he was standing with his hands in the air at the front of the cars when he heard gunshots, turned around, and saw Sunny in the backseat holding a gun in her hands. Then, he said, he saw Jesse rush over, grab the gun out of Sunny's hands, and continue firing at the police officers. This testimony was the crux of the state's case.

But here, right here on my kitchen counter, I am reading a handwritten note from Ralph Ray's files that says:

Conf w/Rhodes
he doesn't think Sonia shot—thinks
maybe Jesse fired all shots—

The note is not dated, and it's not initialed or signed, so there's no way to know for sure when it was written, or by whom. But the note references a doctor who, according to Walter's medical records, treated him at Jackson Memorial Hospital on February 25, 1976, five days after the murders. That's the day that Ralph Ray was appointed to represent Walter, according to Ray's billing petition in the case. The billing petition states specifically that Ray and Walter conferred on that date, and the handwriting on the note about the "Conf w/Rhodes" looks the same as the handwriting on the telephone and time slips in these files for Ray. At the time he took Walter's case, Ray was close to forty and had been in private practice in Fort Lauderdale for about four years; prior to that, he had spent most of his career working as a lawyer for Broward County, including as an assistant state attorney in the prosecutor's office. After Jesse's and Sunny's trials, Ray rejoined the State Attorney's Office and worked as Michael Satz's chief assistant for the next three decades, a move that both Sunny and Walter later challenged in court as a conflict of interest.

Another note in the file, in different handwriting, accompanies a drawing of the crime scene.

After 1st tussel cop called
1st shot he thinks was troopers.
thinks Jessee fired all shots.

So, Walter Rhodes told at least two people in his attorney's office that he thought Jesse Tafero fired all the shots.

This was not the only scenario for the murders included in Ray's files. One day later, on February 26, 1976, Ray had a telephone call with prosecutor Michael Satz. According to Ray's case file notes, Ray learned in the call that the "girl said she fired 1 shot—threw gun out and Trafero [sic] grabbed it and fired." That is exactly what detective Angelo Farinato claimed Sunny had confessed to in his handwritten "Statement from Sonia in Vehicle Feb 20 1976." That same day, Ray spoke again with Walter, and this time Walter told him Sunny fired one shot and then "Jess" shot five times. Then, on February 27, 1976, Ray spent two hours at Satz's office and learned that Walter had told police Sunny fired "at least two times."

But according to these notes, the first thing Walter told his lawyers was that he did not think Sunny fired at all.

How then did Walter end up testifying to two juries under oath that he heard gunshots, turned around, and saw Sunny with a gun in her hand? Was it because that is in fact what Walter saw? Or was his memory "refreshed," as the saying goes, to fit the police or prosecution theory of the crime?

Walter's testimony was a key part of the prosecution's case, and helped send Jesse and Sunny to death row. But now I see that when Walter first spoke with his attorney under the protection of privilege, he had something completely different to say.

24

Shattered Glass/Shiny Gun

"Now, obviously, she fired this first shot at the trooper."

On the old cassette tape, Walter's voice is deep, and raspy. Gravel mixed with honey. After reading Ray's notes, I rifled through my files to find the tapes of my interview with Walter in 1990. I'm listening to it now in my basement, surrounded by the boxes Walter sent. I want to know what he told me—what I once completely believed.

"Her bullet, from her gun, went through him, right here, through his body," Walter is saying, on the tape. "It slammed into this car that I'm leaning against like this. I heard it hit." He sounds so confident that, even in this moment, I halfway believe him again.

I called attorney Ralph Ray to ask him about Walter, and about the notes from his case files that contradicted what Walter testified to at trial. Ray flatly refused to talk about any of it. "It is what it is," Ray told me. No, he wasn't interested in talking about Walter. No, he did not want to look at his notes. No, I could not change his mind about that. "I'm not real comfortable agreeing or disagreeing with anything Walter Rhodes had to say, or with anything he may or may not have said," Ray told me.

In my basement, Walter is still talking. "Tafero breaks away, and he jumps over there to where the woman's got the gun like this, and I see him clearly grab this gun by the barrel. And he says something like 'You stupid goddamn bitch,' or something like that. I don't recall exactly what it was, but he was cursing at her. And I don't know whether he was cursing at her because of her shooting, or cursing at her because she stopped."

I reach over and shut the tape player off.

This winter, before I left Florida, I met with the man who in 1976 hooked Walter Rhodes up to a lie-detecting machine.

Carl Lord. Police polygrapher. Built like a drinking straw, and friendly. Amused. He had a wet bar in his Space Coast living room, and we sat there on barstools side by side with his polygraph report in front of us on the granite countertop. In 1976, at the prosecution's request, Lord strapped Walter to the polygraph apparatus and asked him four questions about the murders of Phillip Black and Donald Irwin. Then Lord wrote up the test results in a memorandum that the federal court later ruled the prosecutor should have turned over to Sunny's defense attorneys. It was one of the main reasons the court threw out Sunny's murder conviction. Why? Because Carl Lord reported that Walter Rhodes "could not be certain whether or not Sonia had fired at all."

In news stories about Sunny and Jesse, this polygraph has a special status. Sunny's lawyers learned about the polygraph report shortly after her trial in 1976, and they used it as a main argument in her appeals from that point forward. But in the popular mythology of the case, the polygraph is depicted as a long-hidden piece of evidence that, once discovered, set Sunny free. When *The Exonerated* was presented at the Edinburgh Festival Fringe in 2005, for example, the festival's newspaper reported:

Despite these efforts, though, Tafero was executed. Then, two years later, Jacobs was freed, in large part based on the theory that Rhodes was actually the lone killer. It emerged that evidence in the couple's favour had been held back, including a polygraph test taken by Rhodes, which had been falsified.

Actually, Sunny's attorneys did not argue that Walter's polygraph test had been falsified. Exactly the opposite. Carl Lord's polygraph report stated Walter "could not be certain whether or not Sonia had fired at all," and her attorneys told the court that Walter must have been truthful on the test—because it meant the difference between life and death to him. Passing the polygraph was a condition of Walter getting a plea deal, and if he flunked, he too faced the electric chair. That's what Sunny's attorneys wrote: "His life literally depended on the results of the tests. It is hard to imagine a stronger motivation to recount the events in a manner consistent with what he considered the truth."

With the polygraph report on the counter in front of us, I asked Carl Lord about it.

"Why did you guys polygraph Walter Rhodes?"

"Because he was the one who squealed," Lord said. "Do you know how a polygraph works?" It's an interrogation, Lord explained. The machinery records the subject's body friction when you ask questions. It's not about surprising someone. You take it very slow. You make them feel comfortable. You tell them how the instrument works, and you go over the test beforehand and make sure they understand exactly what the questions will be. There are control questions and test questions. You instruct them to tell the truth on the control questions, and on the test questions too. Then you compare the way the answers look on the chart.

Control questions, from Lord's notes: Were you born in Alabama? Do you live in Florida now? Did you ever go to school? Are you wearing a blue shirt? Is your first name Walter? Have you in the last two years committed an undetected crime?

That last one, it's a control question, but it's a trick too. Its purpose is to find out what someone looks like on the graph when they lie, Lord said. Because everyone lies on that question. Everyone strapped to a machine for a law enforcement polygraph, anyway.

Test questions: Did you see, for sure, Jesse shoot both police officers on February 20, as you told me? Did you, yourself, fire at either officer on February 20? Did you help anyone in the shooting of the two officers on February 20? Did you tell the truth on the statement that you gave to Captain Valjean, to the best of your knowledge and memory?

"What did you find?" I asked Lord.

"There was no question. He was not the shooter."

I looked at the list of test questions again.

"Hold on," I said. "I'm not seeing a question about Sunny on this list. Did you test Walter about Sunny?"

No, Lord said. But before hooking Walter up to the polygraph machine, Lord interrogated him—that's standard procedure. And in that pre-test interview, as Lord called it in his report, Walter said "he saw Tafero struggling with Trooper Black, heard a loud report, and then saw Tafero go to the backseat of the Camaro, take out a gun, and fire four times at Black and two times at Irwin. He could not be sure whether or not Sonia had fired at all."

I asked Lord to explain.

"I said to him, 'Did you *see* Sonia fire?' He said, 'I don't know if she did one of the shootings.'"

"So Walter couldn't be sure," I clarified.

"That's what he said," Lord told me. "He wasn't sure. I tried to tell that to the nitwit who was going to try the case. Michael J. Satz.

"He's an asshole," Lord added, about Satz.

"Should Satz have turned your report over to the defense?" I asked Lord.

"He definitely should have," Lord replied.

According to Ralph Ray's files and the appeal brief filed by Sunny's lawyers too, the plea deal that Walter made was predicated on Walter passing the polygraph. And about two weeks after Carl Lord wrote a report saying there had been "no deception" on the test, the Florida Department of Criminal Law Enforcement issued a new finding in regards to the gunshot residue tests. Its previous finding had been that tests on Walter's hands were consistent with him "having discharged a weapon." Upon reconsideration, the crime laboratory found that the elevated levels of antimony and lead found on the back of "Mr. Rhoades'" left hand were not from firing a gun but from having been wounded there by a lead projectile during the gunfire at the roadblock.

The department now was of the official scientific opinion that the gunshot residue results for Walter Rhodes "are consistent with his having handled an unclean or recently discharged weapon." And Walter Rhodes now had a deal. In return for testifying against Jesse and Sunny, Walter would not face the electric chair.

In Carl Lord's Space Coast living room this winter, he and I examined the polygraph charts together. The machine had printed out Walter's physical reactions to the questions onto a sheet of graph paper, and that paper—I found a copy in the State Attorney's Office's files—when laid out on Lord's black granite bar countertop, looked like the readout from a hospital heart monitor, peaks and valleys across the page.

"This guy answered the questions truthfully," Lord said, at first.

But then he stopped, looked at an answer, looked back at the question, looked at the answer again.

"There was something he told Captain Valjean that wasn't truthful," Lord said.

On the morning after the murders, Walter gave a statement to Captain Valjean Haley of the Palm Beach County Sheriff's Office. That statement was the basis for polygraph test question number four: *Did you tell the truth on the statement that you gave to Captain Valjean, to the best of your knowledge and memory?* Walter talked to Haley from his hospital bed, coming off a night of morphine and intense pain.

HALEY: Let me interrupt at this time. When the shot went off, did you actually witness the shots?
RHODES: I actually witnessed the shots.

HALEY: Who had the gun in their hands or whose hands was the gun in when the first shot was fired?

RHODES: When the gun first went off, Sonia was the one holding the gun. . . . I am not clear, it was after she shot him, I think this is to the best of my knowledge, I am not a hundred percent sure. To the best of my knowledge, she fired two shots, there was three shots fired off at the officer, I know, I believe then Jesse pulled the gun from her and shot him one more time and then he shot the other cop twice.

To the best of my knowledge, she fired two shots— Since Walter told his attorney under the protection of privilege that he did not think Sunny fired any shots at all, yes, it certainly seems that Walter may have lied to Captain Haley from that hospital bed.

But Walter also told Haley that "I didn't kill them, I didn't pull the trigger and I am innocent of that charge." So that could be the lie that Lord detected, too.

Sitting here now in my basement in Michigan, with Walter's voice coming out of the tape player beside me—*And then when she fired, it dawned on her at that second the seriousness of what's happened, and she froze*—I tally it up. Walter told his attorney one thing, testified twice to another, recanted that testimony on numerous occasions, recanted the recantations, and may have lied during a lie detector test. This is the State of Florida's star witness, in trials that sent two people to death row. And I still need to go talk to him. Again.

As I'm leafing through the files from Walter's attorney, getting ready to put them away, a sentence fragment catches my eye. It looks like Ray's handwriting, just two lines at the bottom of one page, in the same folder as a long list of notes about photographs police took at the rest area crime scene.

"Holy shit," I say out loud.

I saw crime scene photos this past winter at the State Attorney's Office. But only the ones I was allowed to see—due to privacy laws, I was not allowed to see any that showed the deceased officers, lawyers at the office told me. At the time, I had not thought that restriction was a big deal. Now I do.

I rip through all of Walter's boxes. Yes, there are crime scene photos, a more complete collection than I was allowed access to in Fort Lauderdale. I find the photographs Ray's sentence fragment seems to have been referencing. I stare. I bolt upstairs to find Peter.

"You have to look at these." I hand him a stack of close-ups of the Camaro at the rest area, taken right after the murders. Constable Irwin, covered in a bright yellow tarp. He's in a pool of blood, with his feet at the rear wheel of the Camaro. There's a pair of handcuffs on the ground near him, and some stray bullets. And all around him is shattered glass.

"See?" I say to Peter. I'm pointing to the glass. "That's glass from the driver's-side door on the Camaro."

"Okay," Peter says.

"The glass is to the rear of the door. At the back of the car. All of it."

We examine the photo more closely.

"None of the glass is in front of the open door. None. Glass breaks in the direction it was hit. And look."

I hand Peter the piece of paper from Ralph Ray's files.

Window to Camero [sic] *drivers' side was smashed (someone firing from front of the car)?* the note says.

"From the *front* of the car," I say.

Peter nods. He squints at the Camaro's front tire. "What about that, right there?"

He's pointing to the photograph. I have to lean in even closer to get a good look. But once I do, there's no mistaking it. That, right there, next to the front tire of the Camaro, just over from where Walter Rhodes was standing, on the ground next to Phil Black's cream Stetson hat, is a little pistol. It's not either of the 9mm semi-automatics taken from Walter and Jesse at the roadblock, or the .38 Special from Sunny's purse. It's another gun, one virtually unremarked on in the voluminous records of the case: a .22 mini-revolver.

A tiny, shiny gun.

25

What Kind of Strange Fate

"What if I have been just centrally wrong about this whole thing?" I ask Peter.

It's evening on our screened porch. In the woods around us, a soft chorus lit by fireflies. I've gotten word that I've been cleared for a prison visit at Jackson Correctional Institution. The day after tomorrow, I will be leaving for Florida to go talk to Walter Rhodes.

I've spent the last week in the basement, trying to figure out about the shattered glass, that little gun, and Walter Rhodes. *Someone firing from front of the car?* That is exactly what Jesse Tafero testified.

Ballistics: A North American Arms .22 short is the world's smallest and lightest five-shot mini-revolver, according to the manufacturer's website. Not much bigger than a credit card, barrel included. At the rest area, that tiny gun was found fully loaded there on the ground. So maybe Walter fired it and reloaded it and then cast it aside. Can a bullet fired from a .22 short shatter a car window? It's a gun with a small, light short-range bullet, good for putting tiny holes in empty Coke cans—but lethal too, according to the Internet. Maybe the bullet hit the car window at exactly the right angle to explode it. The fact is, I do not know if I've stumbled onto a red-hot clue or a red herring. But I do know that I cannot give Walter Rhodes the benefit of the doubt. Not again.

After Walter was paroled in 1994, he got his hands on a twelve-gauge shotgun, a knife, ammunition, handcuffs, Mace, and two swords. He cleaned out his bank account, rented a car, and took off to hunt two people: the doctor who amputated his leg and Michael Satz, the prosecutor. That's what Walter wrote in his memoir. "I'm now a wanted fugitive—a convicted double cop killer who has absconded from parole with a car full of various weapons, with the intention of shooting someone." Walter's wife called the parole board to warn them. An old memorandum from the Florida Parole Commission in the boxes Walter sent me has that down in black and white: "Mrs. Rhodes is concerned subject may attempt to pursue these people in Florida."

And in 2003, when police in Washington State arrested Walter, they searched his trailer—the one I spent the night in—and found a .22 caliber rifle sawed off into an illegal handgun, live ammunition, a pair of handcuffs, and a Florida Highway Patrol badge. Walter Rhodes bought the badge from a flea market as a memento, according to the arrest report. "He only had short contact with the Trooper but there was a connection, there was something in the Trooper's eyes he connected with," the report said. A *keepsake*, I thought. It's what the commander of the police roadblock told me, when I interviewed him this winter: "All police shootings, they always take something," Corporal Jack Harden said. Up there in the Washington woods, Walter had the .22 and the FHP badge hidden in a black bag in his bedroom. In his *bed*.

I have not been wrong about my fear. I see that now.

That night, Peter and I get into a terrible argument. I don't want him to come to Florida, and I am wasting no time telling him so, even though I don't understand why.

"There's not going to be anything for you to do," I say.

"I don't need anything to do. I'll wait."

"But I don't know how long it's going to take at the prison. You're going to be stuck in a crappy hotel."

"I'll come with you and wait in the parking lot."

I explode. "Have you even *been* to a fucking prison?"

I cannot deal. I do not want to go. This trip is doom incarnate and it's a stupid fucking mess and I never want to fucking think about any of this ever again. It has wrecked my life. And even so, I can't stop. I have come much too far to stop now. I need to see this through.

"It's not a fucking *vacation*," I tell him.

A long silence follows.

"Wow, that hurts," Peter says eventually. "You know, Ellen, I'm not some random guy with one dream and one dream only, which is to go to Florida in the last week of July and now by God I have my chance. I want to go because I care about you. About *you*."

And? That's what I want to say. *Well, you can take that caring feeling and—*

The day in 1990 when I went for the first time to talk with Walter Rhodes, the route I took from the highway to the prison was a two-lane blacktop that ran for miles through a grove of orange trees. In my rearview mirror, I could see the white stripes on the pavement behind me vanishing as I went around each bend. I was twenty-six, confident, ambitious. Naïve. I did not know it, but that was the last day of the life I would have had. An abyss was about to open up in front of me, and not only would I have no way to get across it, I had no way back. I would be stranded, uncertain, and totally alone. I feel it all again, right now.

"I love you," Peter says. "Let me help."

We exit the terminal into the rental car lot and stand for a moment in the bright light and the heat. Alabama in the last days of July. Walter is in prison over the Florida state line, serving out the remainder of the three life sentences he was given in 1976 for his role in the murders of Black and Irwin. He has been back in prison since he was arrested as a fugitive in 2003. Walter has said this reincarceration is my fault.

On the way into town from the airport, Peter and I pass faded brick buildings with boarded-up windows, railroad tracks, a shotgun shack sliding off its foundation deep underneath a stand of shade trees, a yellow velvet couch on its front porch. The rains come all of a sudden, big heavy drops falling hard.

That night, I reread all of Walter's statements. Accusations, confessions, recantations. *I actually witnessed the shots. When the gun first went off Sonia was the one holding the gun. I cannot be sure that Sonia fired a pistol first—she was definitely the first to shoot but it may have been the Taser she fired. She may have had the Taser in one hand—pistol in the other.* "He doesn't think Sonia shot—thinks maybe Jesse fired all the shots." *I heard two, for sure two shots. . . . She had the gun in her hand, like this. She had both hands on it.*

Now a thought hits me with the smack of a baseball going over the far fence.

Walter Rhodes is either lying about all of this to cover up his own role in the murders—or he doesn't know. This star eyewitness may have sworn to something he did not actually see.

But would he admit that to me?

As I'm reading through the documents from Walter's boxes, I open a file that I haven't opened before and— Oh God. It is a photograph of Jesse Tafero after his execution. Naked on the autopsy table. Dead. I sit frozen in front of my computer screen, staring. How could Walter possibly have this? I've seen this photo before, but not for twenty-five years. It was part of a report that the State of Florida did in 1990, after Jesse's execution. The photograph shows Jesse's dead body from the viewpoint of the top of his head: his scorched scalp, the bridge of his nose, his bare shoulders, bare chest, bare feet. The burn mark on his scalp from the flames covers most of the top and left side of his head. The burn is charcoal black around the edges and raw red in the middle. The burn, plus his nakedness, the naked body on the slab, the charred corpse: for me, here right now, in this hotel room, in the dark, waiting until it gets light enough to drive to a prison and talk to the man who put Jesse Tafero in the electric chair—I don't know. All of this has been a lot, but this—*this*—is too much.

After that, I don't sleep much. In the morning, I'm ready early. Peter, sleepy in striped pajamas, gives me a hug as I head out the door.

Once I cross the Florida state line, the prison appears suddenly on the right: guard towers behind barbed-wire fences, coils shining in the sun.

In the lot, I park next to a battered white van. The driver turns to look at me and smiles, prison visitor to prison visitor. Blue tattoos cover the white skin of her face. I smile back. I walk across the lot to the administration building. A guard appears out of a door marked ARTILLERY and points me down the hallway to the warden's office. She greets me from behind her desk, which overlooks the prison gates.

"Is it okay with you if we lock you in the room alone with the inmate?" she asks.

Her question sets off a mini-movie in my head: the visiting room with Walter in April 1990, right before Jesse's execution. Walter sitting at the table in his blue uniform as I smoked my cigarettes and tapped my ashes on the floor. Walter telling me, that day: *I guarantee you, there's some people that can lie so good that you could not bust them.*

I tell the warden it won't be a problem.

I go through a metal detector, and a prison guard hands me an alarm to press if I need immediate help. I follow her outside to a pathway between a row of barracks. Up ahead of us, the main building of the prison looms. There are inmates everywhere, in blue jumpsuits. Working, not talking. The guard hands me off to a prison officer in a pink polo shirt. We walk a few steps toward the main building, and the officer says, "There he is."

He is almost sixty-five now. He's pale, with white hair, stooped in his prison uniform, wearing a thermal undershirt despite the heat and leaning heavily on a cane. Frail, thin. He sees me and smiles quickly and then turns his head away.

"They only told me five minutes ago it was you," Walter Rhodes says.

In silence, Walter and I walk behind the prison officer over to one of the barracks buildings, into an entry hall packed with men—crammed together, sweating—then quickly down a corridor to a small windowless room. Inside the room are four long tables and a lot of chairs.

"You have one hour," the officer says. I hear his footsteps receding down the hallway. I am alone in a prison visiting room with Walter Rhodes. Again.

"Long time no see," Walter Rhodes says, in his raspy voice. He draws it out, each word an island. An accusation, perhaps. *Long. Time. No. See.*

"Yeah, I know," I say. Even to me, my voice sounds cold.

I take a seat, setting out my pen and paper and documents, trying to gather my thoughts. In this moment, I have known Walter Rhodes longer than I've known a lot of the people in my day-to-day life, and I've carried his story—the part of the story that we share—with me all these years. For such a long time, I was convinced that he'd been sentenced too harshly for the crime of standing with his hands in the air while two police officers were gunned down. But then Walter falsely accused me, and to me he became a liar, pure and simple. And with that, at the moment in 2003 when I turned my back on this case, I shut a door against him and against all of it, the world and its abundant sorrows.

When I first came to Fort Lauderdale this past winter, it was the most extraordinary sensation. It was the relief of finally admitting that I needed to know, after half a lifetime of pretending this mystery did not matter much to me. It was the genuine liberation of deciding to care. It's late July now; I've been on the road talking to people since January. That's seven months—it's a long time, too long—plus the previous twenty-five years as well, all of it an entanglement that I did not anticipate and certainly have not dealt with well. Now I'm back where it all started: in a Florida prison, facing the witness who testified against Jesse Tafero, trying to figure out the truth.

This time, though, I'm not a young reporter whose knowledge of the case has come from old newspaper clips. And I'm not a newly minted private detective with the script of a hit play ringing in my ears. Today I am not at the mercy of my impressions. Dousing, divining. I have read the entire case file. I know it cold. I have something much better to work with: evidence.

Walter's white hair is shorn to a shadow on his scalp, and his eyes are coal black, so dark I can't tell iris from pupil. Sitting across the table from me, he has his arms crossed over his chest and he's squinting, like he's trying to figure me out too. For an instant, I'm back at the rowboat again, on the shore of that mountain lake, in the far northern wilderness, with the wind in the trees behind me and the night coming on. I pause for a moment to run a quick internal check. No. I am not afraid. Not here. Not now. I decide to skip the pleasantries.

"So we only have an hour and I want to get to the facts," I say.

Just like that, we are back at the rest area. It is almost seven-thirty on the morning of February 20, 1976. Walter is standing up at the front fender of the FHP cruiser. Constable Irwin has Jesse up against the cruiser, trying to get handcuffs on him. Trooper Black is stepping back and drawing his gun. Walter looks at Black, looks at the drawn gun, puts his hands up and turns around. Facing away. Sunny is sitting in the backseat of the Camaro, with her nine-year-old son and the baby.

What happens next?

Over these last months, the more I've thought about it, the more it's started to seem to me that it was Jesse Tafero who fired the shots that murdered Black and Irwin.

I'm at least eighty percent sure of this right now. Both Sunny and Eric told me that when they looked up after the gunfire stopped, Jesse was standing at the open door of the Camaro. In that position, Jesse would have had one dying police officer on each side of him, based on the bloodstains on the pavement and the narratives in the police reports. So if it was not Jesse who fired those shots, it was someone with extraordinary marksmanship, shooting Trooper Black and Constable Irwin with pinpoint accuracy while leaving Jesse Tafero, standing directly between them, completely untouched. Like an action-movie superhero, immune to bullets. It's possible, I guess. In a million-to-one world.

But even though I'm feeling increasingly certain about Jesse's role in the murders, I still do not know how the shooting began. Jesse didn't start it. He couldn't have—he was up against the police cruiser, restrained by the doomed Donald Irwin. So was it Sunny, in the backseat of the Camaro? Her frightened little son? Walter, from the front, with the tiny, shiny gun?

"I think there's still a question of how it got started," I tell Walter now.

In 1976, Walter Rhodes told two juries that as he was standing with his hands in the air facing away from the Camaro, he heard gunshots, turned around, and saw Sunny in the backseat of the Camaro with a gun in her hands.

"She looked scared. She had the gun in her hand, like this," he told the jury at Jesse's trial. Then Jesse ran over, grabbed the gun out of Sunny's hands, and continued firing, "boom, boom, boom, at both officers," Walter testified.

At Jesse's trial, prosecutor Michael Satz used his opening statement to tell the jury the same thing: "Trooper Black drew his gun. There was more scuffling, and what happened was that there were some shots from inside the car. Rhodes turns around. He sees the gun in Sonia Linder's hand. He sees Tafero scuffling, and getting away, and running over and firing the rest of the shots."

The gun in Sunny's hand is a crucial piece of Walter's testimony. Without it, the testimony of the truck drivers—that the shots came from the backseat of the car—conflicts with Walter's testimony that Jesse shot the officers from outside the car, and the state's case falls apart. "That's what really got the conviction, was Rhodes," the officer who commanded the roadblock that morning told me. He's the one who shot Rhodes in the knee. "If I'd have killed him, maybe they would have walked." But after studying the case file and finding the notes that Walter's lawyer took, I think there might be a problem. I think Walter Rhodes did not see what he testified to at all.

"Because when you really look at it," I tell Walter now, "if you think about the time between when Trooper Black pulled his gun and said, 'If anybody moves, they're dead' and the time the first shot came out, you had your back turned and your arms in the air."

"Well, when he pointed the gun at me, I put my hands up—I'm facing him. Then I turned my back," Walter corrects me.

"Then you turned, okay," I say. "My question is, I want to know exactly how it got started. And I've read a lot of what you've said about it. You've said a lot of different things over the years. So I don't know if you actually saw what happened at the very beginning of it."

"Now, here's the thing. The trooper is between me and her," Walter says.

At the rest area, the white mist is starting to break as the sun rises higher over the horizon. Walter is standing at the front of the two cars. Jesse, in his tan jacket, is being held at the police cruiser by Constable Irwin. Sunny is in the backseat of the Camaro with little Eric and the baby. The driver's-side door of the Camaro is wide open, and Trooper Black is standing between the Camaro and the cruiser, inside that open door. From where Walter is standing at the front of the cars, Walter cannot see Sunny in the backseat, because Black is directly in Walter's line of sight. Black draws his weapon, and Walter turns around and faces away.

"So when the trooper turned and went like that"—Walter mimes holding a gun out in front of him—"apparently she must have had a gun or something, because the gun fired."

"See, this is the thing, though—"

"Her gun fired."

"It's the *apparently* part," I tell him.

"I didn't see that, though, because of him."

"Exactly," I say.

A pause.

Walter is watching me.

"So here is my question," I say. "You can't see her—"

"I can't see through him—to what she got in her hand, or anything," Walter agrees.

"Right. So can you say that you know what happened?"

"I can't say—except for one thing I can say. Somebody fired a shot."

Somebody.

On the table next to me, I've got a manila folder with the notes from attorney Ralph Ray. I've brought the notes for this moment.

"So you at some point, you initially"—I'm stumbling a bit here because I don't want to mess this question up—"you told Ralph Ray that you didn't think Sonia fired any shots."

"No, I did not tell him that." Instantly. Vehemently. "I damn sure didn't tell him that."

I take the copy from Ray's file and push it across the table to him. He leans close, reading it. *Conf w/Rhodes—he doesn't think Sonia shot—thinks maybe Jesse fired all shots.*

"I would never have made this statement," Walter says, pushing the paper back toward me.

"You did at some point, and I'm just curious."

"If I did, it was because I was probably delirious on morphine and I wasn't in my right mind."

"So this is not something you currently agree with."

"No," Walter says. "I definitely don't agree with—it's possible I said that, but I don't believe I would have said that, because of the fact that I know that somebody fired something from that backseat."

"So you don't think it's that they tried to corral you," I say.

"No. They never tried to manipulate me into—"

"Into saying that Sunny was involved?"

"No. No, they didn't do that. No. I think they were sincerely trying to find out what the answers were."

But Walter's statements significantly changed over time in ways that matched the developing physical and eyewitness evidence. In the statement he gave to Captain Valjean Haley on tape and under oath the day after the murders, Walter said he "actually witnessed the shots" and that Sunny "may have fired" all the shots that killed Black from the backseat, a statement that closely matched truck driver Pierce Hyman's statement that the shots came out of the Camaro. Three days later, Haley visited Walter again in the hospital, told him the results of the gunshot residue tests, and took another statement. This time, Walter said: "I cannot be sure that Sonia fired a pistol first—she was definitely the first to shoot but it may have been the Taser she fired." This was a better match for the test results, which did not show that Sunny had definitely fired a gun, but it directly contradicted what Walter had told Haley under oath and on tape just days earlier, when Walter said that to his knowledge, he had not seen a Taser used. Then, on the witness stand at Sunny's trial, Walter told the jury that he was turned with his back to the Camaro, heard two or three gunshots, "jumped and immediately looked" toward the Camaro, saw Sunny holding a gun "in two hands," and saw Jesse snatch it out of her hands, lean against the driver's seat, and fire four or five shots at Black and two at Irwin. This version was an exact match for the state's theory of the crime.

Walter liked and trusted Captain Haley, he is telling me now. "I always had a good impression of him. I think he was a straightforward man. I really believe he was an honest man. He was almost like a father-type figure, or maybe that was the role he was playing to get me to talk." Haley visited Walter in the hospital, he brought Walter cigarettes, he gave Walter paper to write and rewrite his statements. At the hospital, Haley informed Walter that a Taser dart had been found on Trooper Black, Walter says. Actually the dart was found on the trooper's patrol car, but this news from Haley was what gave Walter the idea that a Taser had been involved in the murders, Walter is saying. Before Haley mentioned the Taser, Walter thought the only weapons used were guns. And Haley told Walter that Sunny and Jesse were blaming him for the murders, according to Walter's memoir and Ray's notes. That was a lie. Jesse was stonewalling the cops, and when Haley himself had interrogated Sunny, she claimed not only that she did not know what had happened at the rest area, but that she had no idea who Jesse or Walter were.

I reach over now and show Walter another note from Ray's files. Someone in Ray's office—likely Ray himself, based on the handwriting—jotted down notes from a conversation with Walter, probably on the day Ray was appointed to the case. The note says that Walter thinks his first handwritten statement "is the more correct version."

The case file has two handwritten statements from Walter Rhodes. One of the statements is dated February 24, with Captain Haley's name written in at the top. This statement is the one that mentions the Taser, contradicting what Walter had told Haley just three days earlier. It also states that one of the officers was Canadian—something Walter surely learned from the police after the murders. And it states that Walter "heard shots" and then saw "Jesse struggling to get the gun from Sonia or from between the seats." The other handwritten statement is undated and it does not mention a Taser or that one of the officers was Canadian, which makes me think that this statement is an earlier, more spontaneous, less carefully crafted one. And, importantly, this statement has the gunshots starting *after* Jesse got the gun, not before:

> Then Jesse started to scuffle again and he just pulled away from the officer and that's when the shots started—Jesse reached in and got a gun either from Sonia or near her and turned around and fired at both officers.

"Yeah, there was a little confusion in my mind at first," Walter says, looking over the documents. "But I believe I saw her with her hands on the gun like she was trying to hand it to him."

But you also told Captain Haley that you didn't see Jesse get the gun from Sunny, I say. "You said, 'I couldn't see, his back was to me.' " I read that statement to Walter. "You even told Haley that Jesse might have gotten a gun from just 'the area where Sonia was at.' " Not from out of her hands.

"Looking at this objectively, maybe that is what I saw," Walter admits. "I didn't see, and then the rest of my mind put the rest of this together afterwards. It's not impossible." Now he's thinking over his statements in which he said he saw Sunny holding the gun. Those, "my mind may have created after several days of re-hashing this and getting feedback from Haley. You actually—you can actually—start believing things that you really didn't see."

Exactly, I think. Rehashing. Without a lawyer, in a hospital bed where your leg has just been cut off, and with the help of hints, lies, and other feedback from a friendly police captain. You can actually start believing things you really didn't see. And then maybe you swear to those things under oath in open court at trial and send two people to death row.

On March 1, 1976, ten days after the murders, Walter's attorney Ralph Ray had a telephone call with Haley, discussing the case. Ray's notes of the conversation were in the boxes that Walter sent me, and I have them with me now. Haley has passed away, so I can't ask him about it, and in any case he quit the sheriff's office just a year after the murders, amid an investigation into his al-leged misconduct off-duty at a hard-drinking Delray Beach bar. And Ralph Ray refused to talk to me, so I can't ask him either. It's up to what Walter remembers.

The note says:

Dr. Gold—WP Beach = hypnotist Valjean has used.
- Defendant wanted to prove to Vjean that he'd been telling the truth to him.

I slide the note across the table to Walter, and watch him read it. "Were you hypnotized?"

"I wanted them to use the truth serum or hypnotize me or do something. They said they couldn't do it."

"So you never saw a guy named Dr. Gold."

"No, I never saw a doctor at all, except for medical," Walter says. I make a note. *Not hypnotized.*

But later Walter will write me to ask, "Was I hypnotized by this Dr. Gold? I really want to know."

I will make another note. *He does not know.*

In 1985, the use of hypnotism was banned by the Florida Supreme Court in a lawsuit brought by Ted Bundy, who alleged that testimony given at his trial by witnesses whose memories had been "hypnotically refreshed" was per se tainted and unreliable. The Florida Supreme Court agreed. The court ruled that hypnotized witnesses would not be permitted to give testimony in criminal cases going forward in Florida, and ruled that all cases currently on appeal in which witnesses had been hypnotized were subject to mandatory review.

Why ban hypnotism from the courtroom? In its ruling, the Florida Supreme Court cited California, which had spelled its concerns out clearly: A hypnotized witness "will lose his critical judgment and begin to credit 'memories' that were formerly viewed as unreliable, will confuse actual recall with confabulation and will be unable to distinguish between the two, and will exhibit an unwarranted confidence in the validity of his ensuing recollection."

Here in the prison visiting room, Walter Rhodes is still on the subject of Sunny and the gun and Jesse and the Camaro. "But the thing I do know and what we all know is that Tafero did get that gun and he did shoot it, and so therefore he had to get that gun from somewhere—and it wasn't in a vacuum, it didn't come from another dimension, you see. Maybe I made the leap in my mind, but I know this: He got that gun from the direction of where she was. And the crux of the matter is that she cannot be innocent. She fired first."

I pause for a moment, thinking.

I can't say—except for one thing I can say. Somebody fired a shot.

"What about Eric?" I ask Walter now.

Eric was in the backseat too, and some of the police officers who investigated the murders thought maybe Eric was involved, I say. So maybe it was a child with a Taser who sparked the tragedy. Not Bonnie. Not Clyde.

"Well, it just doesn't make sense to me that Eric would take the initiative. I can't possibly even fathom he did it. It never entered my mind once."

"But what about 'My mother made me do it'?" I ask Walter. I show him the statement from the social worker.

"I don't think Sonia told him, 'Look, when this guy turns around with this weapon in his hand, I want you to fire the Taser at him.' She didn't know what was going to happen. She couldn't have known what was going to happen. The only thing she knew was going to happen was we were probably going to be arrested."

A flash. I'm in Adelaide, sitting with Eric on the fence. Eric has just been telling me about watching the officers and Jesse from the backseat of the Camaro.

"My mum was holding Tina and she grabbed me and pulled me down like this and laid over both of us," Eric is saying. "Apparently she saw something I didn't."

"Oh, so she pulled you down before it started?"

"Before the shooting actually started."

So now I'm wondering. Was it the Taser Sunny saw? Jesse, lunging toward her to grab a 9mm semiautomatic? Or was it Walter, standing at the front of the car with that tiny, shiny gun?

I take the crime scene photos out now and slide them across the table to Walter. Pictures of the Camaro at the rest area. The blood, Constable Irwin, the shattered glass at the rear of the car, the shiny gun at the front.

"Do you know how the window got blown out?" I ask Walter now, pointing.

Walter seems taken aback. He hasn't seen a photograph of the Camaro in—forever. He had these files when he was on the outside, but he never looked at them, he says. He cannot believe the condition of the car. That it is such a shit heap.

It was from the trooper's gun, Walter says, taking a photo and looking at it up close. But he always thought it was the windshield that got hit, he tells me.

I make a note. Black's .357 Magnum service revolver was recovered in Jesse's attaché case at the roadblock, and when forensics examined the gun they found one bullet missing. Black's hands tested negative for gunshot residue, so the state's theory was that the gun accidentally fired at the rest area, probably when Black dropped it after having been shot himself.

"Was the trooper in front of the car window?" I ask Walter. "Because the glass got blown backwards." I point out the shards to him, glistening on the pavement in the blood.

"Well, obviously he must be in front of—but I didn't know what the bullet hit, I think I was thinking that the windshield got hit because I didn't look."

"And how did that get there?" I ask, pointing to the tiny gun by the Camaro's front tire.

"What is it?"

"That's the twenty-two. The derringer."

"Okay, well, I don't know how that got right there," Walter says. I watch him.

"It doesn't make sense that it would be right there," Walter says, staring hard at the photograph. "I'm pretty sure you'll find it wasn't fired, right?"

Yes, the criminalist did find that it had not been recently fired, I tell him.

"Did anyone try to get fingerprints off that?" Walter asks, still looking at the photo.

"They really didn't do anything with that piece of evidence."

"That's crazy," he says. "That doesn't make sense."

I'm not kidding myself this time. Despite reading his ten boxes of documents and his five hundred handwritten pages of memoir, I don't know Walter Rhodes. Everything I've learned has actually made Walter more of a stranger to me. *I have been so wrong for so long,* I wrote in one of my many notes to myself while reading his files. And I've made enough mistakes where Walter Rhodes has been concerned. I don't need to make any more. But even so, his question just now about the fingerprints on that derringer—it's got my attention.

When I was with Sunny in her kitchen, I asked her about the Taser. We were at her table, we'd been talking about her Alford plea, I said that the plea had made kind of a big deal about a Taser, and I asked her what she remembered about it. And Sunny replied, "I have no clue."

That is what's striking to me right now. *Did anyone try to get fingerprints off that?* That is what Walter asked. During two days of conversation in Ireland, I'm just realizing right now, Sunny did not ask me a single question about the Taser. Not one. Not: *A Taser? Really? How do they know? When was it fired? Did it hit anyone? Did anyone get fingerprints off that?* A mystery weapon in a murder case she was sent to death row for, that she has spent more than twenty years talking about onstage and onscreen, and she had zero curiosity about it? Less than zero. She did not want me to talk about it either.

I think back to that afternoon in Ireland, nearly three months ago now. We were at her kitchen table, and Sunny was telling me that Trooper Black pushed Jesse and then took his gun out and said, *Okay, nobody move. The next one to move is dead.* "So there was a Taser fired at some point in that," I had told Sunny. "Do you know where or when that happened?"

"I have no idea."

"So when you say 'dancing,' were they—"

But that's when Sunny began waving her hands at me, and raising her voice.

"I am not doing that!"

Now in this windowless prison conference room, Walter Rhodes is watching me.

"They took pictures of Black," he begins. On the slab, after his murder. Naked, propped up against the wall with his legs straight out in front of him, with metal rods running through his body, showing his wounds. The path of the bullets, entry to exit.

Those photos prove the first shot came from the back of the car, Walter says.

I've heard about these photos before. From Michele McCain, widow of Jesse's defense attorney. But she told me the photos prove that it was Walter Rhodes who murdered the officers. *It had to have been someone tall.*

Those photos are not in the files you sent, I tell Walter now.

Investigator LaGraves showed them to him, Walter says. "I could have sworn I had them," he tells me.

No, I say. And I asked for them from the Broward County State Attorney's Office, but they said no too. Privacy reasons.

Well, there were clay dummies made from the photos, and used at trial, he says.

As soon as he says this, I realize that I know it already. I saw a mention of the dummies last winter when I read the transcript of Jesse's trial, and months ago I asked the State Attorney's Office to see them. But that never happened, and with everything that has gone on between now and then, the dummies have slipped my mind.

I've been staring at my notebook, but I look right at Walter now. There's a question I've needed to ask him for a long time.

"You talk a lot about all this," I tell him. "To the police, the prosecutors. To me."

I say it sharply, in a knowing tone, thinking of *The Exonerated*. In the play, Sunny says that immediately after the murders, while she and Jesse were being questioned, "Rhodes, from his hospital bed, was negotiating a deal. He'd been in prison before, he knew how the system worked."

I bring that up to him now. "Even on the morning of the murders," I tell Walter Rhodes, "you were talking right away."

"Because I felt like what happened was wrong," Walter says. Forcefully. "The truth is, Tafero could have just thrown down with the gun and handcuffs." Brandished the weapon, instead of pulling the trigger. "It wasn't necessary to kill them."

A knock on the door—it's the guard. Time's up.

"I didn't turn you in," I say to Walter as I gather my papers to go.

Walter nods now, and says he believes me. He says he knows who did. He was taking photographs of UFOs, he says. That was what tipped the government off. He was sending the UFO pictures to a guy who he's positive was in the CIA. "He had a secret project set up around Earth to capture secret UFO photos—I think he turned in a report about the photos I was taking, and then somebody would have checked me out. I knew that was a risk, and anyway, that really has no bearing on all this."

"Well, I just wanted to tell you that," I add, after a moment.

I look up now, right at him. He is looking at me.

"Do you know how long it's been?" Walter says.

"Yeah, it's been about thirteen years," I say, rounding up. "I see you and talk to you every thirteen years."

"What kind of strange fate is that?"

The road south from the prison to the Gulf of Mexico is a shimmering strip through a pine forest. It's just us here, me and Peter and the pavement and the trees up ahead, closing into a triangle where road meets trees meets sky. We drive for hours. We pass a prison road gang wearing the same blue jumpsuits as at Jackson this morning. The car temperature gauge says it is one hundred degrees outside, and we roll the windows down to see what that feels like. Just as we do, the rains come again, pouring down from above with such force that the road disappears. We are on the big bridge over Apalachicola Bay, flying out toward the Gulf of Mexico, when the lightning begins.

"Is it safe?" I ask Peter, looking down at the roiling black water.

"Oh, it's the safest place we could be."

Three months from now, scientists will announce another step in the verification of quantum entanglement, the theory that Einstein derided as "spooky." In a lab in the Netherlands, researchers will prove that "objects separated by great distance can instantaneously affect each other's behavior." A newspaper will characterize this step as a peek into "an odd world formed by a fabric of subatomic particles, where matter does not take form until it is observed, and time runs backward as well as forward."

I will read that story and think it an accurate description of what my life has been. This year in particular.

That summer after the execution, I used to come out to this bridge all the time. I'd drive down from Tallahassee and hit it mid-morning, the concrete roadway cracked beneath my tires, sunlight like silver coins along the tops of the waves. I didn't have air-conditioning, so I drove with the windows down. Sometimes when I reached the top of the span—up and out for that brief moment when the world seemed to drop away—I'd think about crashing through the guardrail down into the water below. After Starke, the line between life and death seemed so thin. How easy to slip over into the abyss. Did I have any idea, though? That I might find out life—this life—wasn't just for other people, but for me?

Peter is driving, watching the rain. Without taking his eyes off the road, he reaches his hand over and puts it on my knee. We ride like that for a while, up and over the bridge. Here on the other side, coming down toward the sea.

26

Metal Rods, Running Through

In the morning, on the way to the airport, I call the State Attorney's Office.

"I've talked to Sunny Jacobs and Eric and Walter Rhodes," I tell an assistant state attorney. "I really think Mr. Satz should talk to me too."

"How is Walter?" she asks me.

"He's gotten old," I tell her. Look, I continue, Walter told me yesterday that he was shown photographs of Trooper Black taken after the murders. I know those photos are protected under privacy laws. But what about the clay dummies?

"We're still having trouble finding them," the assistant says.

Pause.

"I also talked with Carl Lord and Robert McKenzie," I tell her. The polygrapher and the one surviving truck driver eyewitness.

"You do your homework," the assistant says.

"I need to speak with Mr. Satz," I say. "And I need to see the dummies."

A week later, I get a call. They've located the dummies.

The week after that, I am in Deerfield Beach, Florida, at the north branch of the Broward County courthouse. It's just down from the retirement village where Jesse and Walter and Sunny carjacked the Cadillac that morning. I meet Dave the evidence chief in the courthouse lobby and follow him down a corridor through a door that he badges his way through and then through another door that needs an actual metal key to open. We step into an enormous warehouse, big as an airplane hangar, lined floor to ceiling with shelves of neatly labeled brown paper parcels, all tied up with manila tags. Trial evidence. Life and Death. Facts.

Dave disappears down into the shelves. He comes back carting two big wooden crates.

For the eight months that I've been working on this, I've not yet been able to understand the trajectories of the bullets that took the lives of Trooper Black and Constable Irwin. I read the medical examiner's autopsy reports and the trial transcripts but those have been opaque, and in interviews I've been told, *Well, you know it all depends on the position of the shooter versus the falling object of the body*, as if death were a physics equation, which I suppose in some way it is. The one specific thing I've heard was what Michele McCain told me, which was that the photographs of the slain troopers proved that the shots that took their lives were fired at a sharply downward angle. The dummies in these crates were made from those photographs, which is why I want to see them.

When I'd imagined the dummies, I'd seen them as department store mannequins, life-size and smooth. These are much smaller and made of pale white clay, roughly formed. They are lying on their backs in the crates. They have surprisingly lifelike faces, with eyes and noses but no mouths. I can see the metal rods, running through.

Back at home again, we act the dummies out.

I am in our garage in Michigan. Peter is here too, and our friend John, who introduced us and married us. He's visiting from

California. Right now John is at the front of our blue Mazda station wagon, which is standing in for the Camaro. John is between the car's headlights, about two feet in front of the hood. Peter stands next to the driver's-side door of the Mazda. The door is open. Peter is facing the rear of the car. I am behind him, toward the rear of the Mazda, a little to his right.

At this moment, I am Donald Irwin. I am crouching down in a deep squat with my hands extended, reaching forward. In that position, I am looking straight up. That is the state's theory—that Irwin was shot after Trooper Black, as he was reaching for Black's gun on the ground.

Peter is standing directly above me, at the open car door, the position where Sunny and Eric—and Walter too—say Jesse was standing when the shooting stopped.

John, up at the front of the car, is standing in the position where Jesse testified Walter was standing when Walter shot the officers.

"Okay," I say to John.

The dummy for Donald Irwin had two metal rods piercing it. The first metal rod went straight down into his eye. Go on, try it. Tilt your head all the way back and stare at the ceiling. Now take a pen and hold it directly perpendicular to your right eye. That is what the rod looked like. Irwin was wearing gold-framed aviator eyeglasses. The bullet went straight down through the right lens of his spectacles, shattering the glass without damaging the frames, down into his eye socket, fracturing the bones of his face, through his eyeball, and traveled downward and backwards out the back of his head into the base of his neck, where it lodged near his spine. The second bullet went straight down into the top of his left shoulder and exited his back.

"Hold the gun below your waist," I tell John. At trial, Jesse said Walter had the gun there, "down by his private parts." At his crotch. "Now," I continue, "can you shoot me through the eye, straight down?"

"No," John says.

Peter walks to John's position at the front of the car and gives it a try. Peter is taller.

"I can shoot you through the eye, but it goes out through the back of your head. Not down into your neck," Peter says.

It feels odd but also helpful, to be so cold about this.

"What about now?"

Peter is back at the open door of the Camaro, where Jesse was standing. He is standing directly above me. I am crouching, craning my neck back to keep an eye on him, still reaching on the ground for my friend Trooper Black's gun.

Yes. Straight down. My eye socket, my eye, my skull, my neck, my back.

Straight down into my shoulder too.

Phillip Black was shot four times. The coroner could not determine the sequence of the wounds, but all the bullets entered Black on the left side of his body.

He was shot in the head. That bullet sliced sharply downward, entering the back of his skull, traveling forward through his brain and exiting from his right ear. That wound caused Black's death.

He was shot in the neck. That bullet sliced sharply downward, entering on the back left side of Black's neck, exiting through his right armpit. That wound also caused Black's death.

He was shot in his right shoulder, possibly while he was falling to or on the ground. The metal rod for that shot ran straight down into his body from above, like a marionette string. Like the shot into Irwin's shoulder.

And he was shot in the front of his left arm, the bullet traveling to the right and lodging behind his spine in his neck. That shot went in an upward trajectory. As had the bullet hole through the cruiser's windshield post.

We're standing up now, Peter and John and I, closing the car door, turning back toward the house. I feel dizzy.

There is no way that anyone standing in front of or behind the Camaro could possibly have shot Donald Irwin straight down through his eyeglasses or shot Phillip Black downward into his head and neck. Not possible from the backseat of the Camaro, either. No way. That is perfectly clear. It had to have been someone standing above them at the open door of the car, firing down toward the ground.

The person who was standing at the open door of the car the instant the shooting stopped was Jesse Tafero. That is what both Sunny and Eric told me, when I asked them for the truth.

Jesse Tafero. In that moment, standing there at the door of the Camaro, Jesse was a fugitive on the run from the law. He was a convicted home-invasion robber who had brutally beaten and sexually assaulted two young women. He was a karate athlete who'd studied with the most feared sensei in the Florida prison system. He was a drug dealer associated with a notoriously violent gang of cocaine traffickers. He'd been startled awake by police in a car full of guns and ammunition and drugs—amphetamines, cocaine, Quaaludes, marijuana, hashish, glutethimide, and Thorazine. He had more than forty pieces of fake identification with him, including stolen passports and driver's licenses. He refused to tell the officers his real name or address. He was a psychosexual sociopath, the Florida Department of Corrections would later determine, and so paranoid and so strung out on drugs in this moment that he could not think, reason, assess, or recognize reality, according to his own lawyers. He was shortly to be arrested with the murder weapon strapped into a hand-tooled holster around his waist. His own lawyer would be terrified of him and believe for the next four decades that indeed he was guilty. And when the shooting stopped that morning, Jesse was standing alone, directly between two mortally wounded police officers, both of whom had just been shot straight down into their heads.

There is no doubt in my mind now. None. Jesse Tafero fired the shots that took the lives of Trooper Phillip Black and Constable Donald Irwin. He was not innocent.

I'd watched a murderer die.

27

On the Road

"Hello, Ellen," the email from Michael Satz's office begins.

It blinks into my inbox on a bright September morning, not long after my afternoon in the garage. Outside my window, it's still summer, but the trees are a fading green that means fall cannot be far behind.

A few nights ago, a prison friend of Walter Rhodes left a message on my home telephone. A convicted murderer, just *checking to see if you need anything,* as the message said. I do not know him. I don't want to know him. I'd not given him my name, or my number. Or, God forbid, my address.

A few hours later, the Ringwraiths came for me. Burning-eyed, bolting through the dark forest, branches catching at their billowing cloaks. I screamed so loud I woke myself up. I woke Peter up too.

Our friend John has gone back to California and last week his house burned down in a wildfire. Everything he owned is now cinders and dust. It does not matter, he tells us. His husband died last year, and after that, the house—it's not important, he says.

I feel helpless. I am helpless. I keep seeing Trooper Black on the pavement, fallen, bleeding. Constable Irwin, his eye socket shattered, the metal frames of his eyeglasses perfectly intact. I see Jesse Tafero too. It's odd, but I can see him more clearly than ever now. I have clarity, but not peace. It is seven o'clock on a May morning, and in the back of the death chamber, the door bursts open. Three men—two guards and a prisoner, bald, shackled. The prisoner is struggling but the guards are strong and they are ready for this. They have him by the armpits and they march him into the chamber and they slam the door shut behind them. Then they turn him around and make him look at the chair. Jesse Tafero, murderer, looks at the electric chair. And startles backwards.

That is how it ended.

I still do not know exactly how it began.

In Phillip Black's autopsy, the medical examiner noted a small rip in Black's uniform shirt, one inch long, near his heart. Grace Black pointed to that spot on her own body, when we were talking about the Taser. Pressing down on her own bones, her eyes searching mine.

Oh my God, I've been shot.

Mr. Satz is available to meet with you, the email says, and names two possible dates. I pick the later one, and pack my bags. On the way from my house in Michigan to the State Attorney's Office in Fort Lauderdale, there are a few last people I need to talk to.

Two days later, I am in a West Virginia trailer park. The person I'm looking for here was married to Eric many years ago, when they were both just out of their teens. I'm hoping she can help me now.

Do you remember a Taser being fired? That is what I asked Eric, down in Adelaide.

That's weird. I've never heard about that, I don't think, Eric replied.

I'm not trying to pin blame on Eric. He was nine years old that morning. A child. It feels odd to me, uneasy, to insist on knowing what that child may have done when the man today denies it, or does not know. Still, this matters. *My mother made me do it.* That is what Eric told his social worker, according to her report. *Somebody.*

That is who fired the first shot from the backseat of the Camaro, according to what Walter Rhodes now says, which is not what he testified to in court. The State of Florida based its case on Walter's testimony, but he did not see. "No, I did not," he told me, when I asked him directly. So I still need to find out the rest of the story. Exactly what happened. This has never been a guessing game for me.

In Australia, when Eric told me he knew nothing about a Taser, I simply could not tell if he was stonewalling or telling the truth. And then he started talking about how he'd always carried weapons and how the police were out to get him and the whole thing, from the Taser to the casings to the social worker's report, was just one big conspiracy against him and his mom. I'd gone to the Kingdom of Lochac expecting to meet a forty-eight-year-old man, but it suddenly felt like I was talking to a terrified nine-year-old child. That's the thing I did not understand as it was happening. His fear, resonating. Radiating. It sparked something in me. I can see that now. For I too was once a terrified nine-year-old child, hunted and cornered and attacked. That day at the playground, fighting back, scrambling, clawing, catapulting myself into thin air. *I had to be able to protect myself. Because no one else would.* That's what Eric said to me, and as he said it I could feel it, as painful as a scar catching fire. The whole thing threw me so hard I backed off.

I have been so angry with myself since then. For being soft. Letting him off the hook. Not confronting him with case photographs and documents. I've been proud of myself too. In that moment on the fence rail with Eric, caught between being a private detective and being a human being, I chose to have a heart.

Now it's time to find out if I made the right call.

"Yes?"

A woman about my age in pajamas, blinking into the sunlight from the doorway of her home. Short dark hair, warm brown eyes. If she is surprised to see a stranger on her doorstep asking about her long-ago ex-husband and a capital murder case, she sure doesn't show it. Debbie has not had any contact with Eric since 1999, she tells me. No ill will, but the way it ended wasn't the friendliest. Sure, she'll talk to me.

"I'm all about being honest," Debbie says, stepping out onto the rickety porch. "I'm not somebody who puts things out of my mind. I'm a person who continues to process them."

"I am too," I tell her. Because somewhere along the way here, I've stopped burying my feelings about all of this. About everything. It feels unreal to admit that out loud.

Eric talked about the murders very openly, Debbie says as we sit down. It was one of the first conversations they ever had, and the case was always part of their lives. Even when money was super tight, they kept a working telephone so that Sunny could call from prison, and Eric went down to Florida a couple times a year to visit her. When Debbie and Eric's daughter was born, Jesse sent them baby booties knitted by one of his condemned-men friends on death row. But growing up without his mother was very hard on Eric, Debbie says, and he felt "a certain amount of anger that all of this happened in the first place. He wished she had taken up with someone who was more stable, not somebody who was a parole violator. He felt that robbed him of a normal childhood."

Yes, of course it did, I think. But I don't say that.

"What did Eric remember?" I ask, instead.

"He remembered a lot. He remembered them getting awakened in the rest stop—the cops, the Canadian and the Florida cop, very abruptly getting both Rhodes and Jesse out of the front of the car. He remembered one of them very roughly manhandling Jesse at the front of the car."

"Which car?"

"The Camaro."

See, that is what Eric told me. That's why this is important.

"Eric was watching what was going on with Jesse," Debbie is saying. "He didn't see where Rhodes had gone. Then all of a sudden gunshots started, and Sonia covered him up."

It's so interesting, this recall that everyone has about this case. It's like we've all lived it, every one of us, for all these years. It's shared, collective. Have you ever heard water running underneath a city street? This case is like that, I think. Lift up the drain grate, step into the flow.

"Did Eric ever talk about a Taser being at the scene?" I ask Debbie.

Debbie looks mystified.

"No, I haven't heard anything about that."

I take the picture of the Taser dart in the police car out of my bag and show it to her.

"I've *never* heard about that at all."

"It looked like a flashlight. Did Eric mention a flashlight?"

"No." Debbie is still looking at the photograph.

"The theory is that the Taser was fired from the back of the car and then Jesse burst over and grabbed the gun, but nobody knows."

"Again, when you mentioned the Taser, it was the first I'd ever heard about it."

"It really wasn't something he ever—?"

"No!" she says. Emphatically, not impatiently. She is almost laughing at my obsessiveness now. *No!*

I take the small roads, heading south. As I approach the Virginia state line, I fly through a tunnel, a long deep darkness that ends in a slingshot out along a mountain ridge. The first leaves of the changing season flutter across the roadway, like exhaled breath.

Eric never mentioned a Taser to his wife. I believe her. For all of the dozen years they were together, not one word about the stun gun or the dart. So when I asked Eric this spring about the Taser and he said he'd never heard of it, he was telling me his truth.

All my soul-searching and second-guessing, the insanity and turmoil of those weeks on the reef, with the night-screaming birds and the silty sea—all of that, for *nothing.* But oddly everything feels a little easier now, with this new tiny bit of certainty. *That was his truth.* Maybe instead of obsessing, the thing to do is to accept that truth, just as it is, I tell myself. Take the no and move on. Move beyond.

How did it start, then? I ask myself as I drive.

There's the derringer. The tiny, shiny gun. In truck driver Robert McKenzie's statement to police, he remembered seeing Jesse trying to keep Trooper Black from frisking his front pocket. *The officer reached for him, reached for his pocket, and he jumped back. . . . The guy, his hand, went down at his left pocket, trying to keep the officer from searching him.* That tiny pistol was found on the ground very close to where Trooper Black and Jesse had struggled. "Dancing," as Sunny called it. The derringer was found fully loaded and the police laboratory said it had not been fired. I know I've made mistakes before, but that gun just does not seem like a prime suspect to me. For sure, though, *somebody* fired the Taser. The dart in the police car speaks to that.

As the miles flash past, my mind starts to spin.

In Sunny's book, she writes about watching Jesse arguing with Trooper Black at the open door to the Camaro. Sunny is sitting in the backseat with the children. She is scared. "I knew we were in for trouble now. Jesse had already violated his parole. He would almost surely go back to prison."

The TV movie *In the Blink of an Eye* has that moment too, I'm just realizing. Sunny watching anxiously from the backseat as Jesse fights Trooper Black. And in the movie, as Jesse struggles with the officers, Sunny turns suddenly to Eric and asks her little boy to find something for her.

"It's okay, honey," Sunny says to Eric in *Blink*. "Try to find Tina's bear."

Eric ducks down, searching. Then:

"Found it. Here," Eric says, handing it to her.

And the gunshots begin.

Right. I know I'm obsessing now. I promised myself I would not do this. Maybe it's the road, this long drive, the sun sinking lower in the sky. But: There was no bear in that Camaro. No toys at all, according to the crime-scene property inventories that are part of the case record. And I know *Blink* is not a documentary. It's a made-for-TV movie. Still, a disclaimer states right up front that the movie is told "from the perspective" of Sunny Jacobs. *Blink* is her account of the murders. *Stolen Time* is too. They are what she says happened.

So I have to wonder: *Found it. Here.* Is that an admission? Something handed by Eric to Sunny just before the gunshots started. *He would almost surely go back to prison.* A disturbance, a disruption, to free her lover. The Taser looked like a flashlight. It was a device so new that it had not been classified in Florida as a firearm yet. "Unlike a gun, firing the Taser is not likely to be final," its glossy pamphlet purred. "Its sole purpose is to protect you and your family from harm." Although not if it's followed by six blasts from a 9mm semiautomatic handgun, I think bitterly. If Trooper Black noticed the Taser in the backseat of the Camaro, would he have known the danger he was in? One of the darts lodged itself in the window frame of the police car, but the other dart did not. *Oh my God, I've been shot.*

But that is conjecture. Eric does not remember. Sunny has "no clue." I do not know.

Ten hours later, I am talking to another ex-wife. At least I think she's an ex-wife.

"Who?" she says, when I tell her I'm hoping to talk to her about Walter Rhodes.

"Never heard of him," she says, when I ask again.

Walter Norman Rhodes, I say. Walter. Rhodes. I am about to give up when I remember Walter's old nickname.

"Oh, *Rusty*," she says. "I used to be married to the bum."

She's chain-smoking and in a wheelchair, the former Mrs. Rhodes, sitting in front of a computer screen in her living room in a small Southern town, a black velvet headband on her shiny silver hair. I've stopped by well past dark, but she doesn't seem to mind. She does not want me to use her real name, though, so I'll call her Kate.

It's been a long day, but I'm here because I need to make sense of Walter's magnum opus. All the UFO sightings. The scheming spiders and screaming flies. In his memoir, Walter wrote that when he was first arrested in Miami in the late 1960s, he saw Jimmy Hoffa in the police car next to him. Jimmy Hoffa! So I need to know if these visions are the product of a mind that's been incarcerated for forty years—or if Walter saw those things back when he was the star witness in two capital murder trials.

Kate and Walter met in karate class in 1974, she is telling me. "I broke his hand." They lived in Maryland for a while and then moved down to Florida, to that little apartment in Fort Lauderdale. No, she was not in the CIA, despite what Walter claimed in his memoir. One day in early February 1976, she came home and found Walter in bed with another woman. "You told me you didn't care what I did," Walter protested. Kate threw a lamp at him, got the next bus out, and she never saw him again—because right after that, Walter met up with Jesse in Miami for that drink, which soon led to the Camaro and the rest stop.

Jesse Tafero, she says musingly. "He was kinda eerie."

She and Walter used to go out to a house in the Everglades to party, she says. A friend of Walter's had a big house—she names the same person that Walter does in his memoir—that was so isolated they could do whatever they wanted. Sometimes Jesse was there, "always looking for an angle. Looking for a scam. Always talking about winning a game. And he was always looking at you like he was undressing you. He had a very short fuse, and a dead cold stare. It gave you a chill. Jesse Tafero, that is one man this world is better off without. He was a predator in every sense of the word." That whole group, she says, was "heavy into trafficking narcotics."

Walter included, she says. She doesn't know the details of exactly how it worked, but Walter used to go out to the Everglades and help with the drug boats. Two or three times a month, sometimes overnight.

So much for Walter's claim in his court filings that he was only driving Jesse and Sunny around, I think. In his M.O., Walter wrote extensively about the drug runs and Everglades partying that Kate is talking about now, but when I read those pages, I assumed he was making that shit up. Speedboats, trips to Bimini, going out on nights when there were twelve-foot swells because the Coast Guard wouldn't brave it, grocery bags full of cash. Orgies in the sauna at the party house, so many drugs laid out on the coffee table that it's a miracle everyone didn't OD. Bragging, boasting—but apparently it wasn't fiction, or at least not entirely. No wonder Carl Lord, the police polygrapher, told me Walter hit the ceiling on that trick test question about "undetected crimes." Which was how Lord knew the polygraph was working.

"Cocaine," Kate adds, when I ask her what kind of drugs.

"Did he talk about UFOs?" I ask Kate.

"Constantly," she says. "We'd be out riding in the car and he'd look up in the sky and see something blinking way, way up there, and he'd say, 'I wonder if that's a UFO. I wonder if there's life beyond.' He was spacey. He had a vivid imagination."

So I know Jesse and Walter met in prison, I say now. But how did they end up in the same group of people out there in the Everglades?

"Have you heard of Murph the Surf?" she asks.

Jack Murphy, I write in my notebook. "I've heard of him."

"It was an association that was built when they were in the cell-block together." Before the murders, obviously. "Jesse Tafero was friends with Murph the Surf. Jesse introduced Rusty to Murph the Surf, and they all became compadres in jail. It was pretty much through Murph the Surf's okay that Tafero befriended Rusty and looked out for him." Kate pauses. "It was a hierarchy," she says, about that prison friendship. "The only self-esteem Jesse had was he was given authority by Murph the Surf. He was given authority in and out of jail—but how they did it, that kind of stuff, I don't know."

"What did Walter tell you about the murders?" The case file has billing slips for phone calls between Walter and his wife in the days after his arrest. In his M.O., Walter writes that one call was so devastating that they both wept.

"As far as I'm aware, Jesse was the one that did it," Kate says. "That's what Rusty told me when it first happened."

"Did he say Sunny was involved?"

"No, she was in the backseat with the children."

"Did Walter ever confess to you?"

"No."

"Do you think he would have, if he'd murdered the officers?"

She nods, slowly, and takes a long drag. "I said, 'Tell me what happened.' And I told him, 'What do you need, I'll do anything.' He had no reason to lie to me. He knew I was in his corner. I was the only ally he had."

She pauses a moment.

"He was really good-looking," she says, about Walter. "I had a lot of people tell me he looked like Clark Gable. But looks aren't everything." Walter was very abusive, she tells me. When she left him, she left everything she owned in the world behind in that Fort Lauderdale apartment. But she never looked back.

And about Jesse Tafero, Kate adds: "If this asshole is haunting you, put him out of your head and move on. He was a user and a manipulator and when it boiled down to it, he was cold-hearted too."

The next day, on my way to the airport, I drive past the address in Charlotte, North Carolina, provided in police reports for Sunny's parents circa 1976. Four bedrooms, three-point-five baths, an open floor plan, and a pool in a golf-course neighborhood the real estate websites call "prestigious."

I also drop by a house where I believe Alan Jacobs, Sunny's brother, is living. In her book, Sunny wrote that her brother, "Big Al," was the person who introduced her to her boyfriend John, and I've noticed in police reports that Sunny and John were said to have been buying guns together in North Carolina in November 1975, three months before the murders, using a credit card that John's mother later reported stolen. Also, Debbie has just told me that Eric lived with Alan for a while, after his grandparents died in the plane crash. I'm hoping that if there's any aspect of this mystery I'm wrong about, or need to think more about, or have missed, Alan will let me know.

But the man who lives at this address refuses to open the door.

"Who are you?" the man says, from behind the portal.

I tell him. Your sister, Jesse, Walter, the murdered officers, the electric chair.

The man behind the door doesn't tell me I'm at the wrong house, or that he has no idea what I'm talking about. He says: "Go away."

The odd thing is that when you look up Alan Jacobs on the Internet, one of the first things you come across is a video of him demonstrating martial arts skills. He is a security expert offering martial arts classes in personal defense, in person and online. *I'm here with Josh and John and we're going to show you a third-party gun disarm.* And you find lots of photographs of him with Whitney Houston. He was her director of security, for real. The Bodyguard. Doesn't seem like a guy who'd shy away from a private eye.

"Alan?" I call out. "Everybody else has talked to me. I just want to hear anything you have to say."

"Go away, *right now*, or I'm calling the police."

Those are the magic words to get a PI off your porch, by the way. In case you ever need them. But in twenty years, I've almost never heard them spoken, let alone shouted through a locked entryway. Most people at least open the door.

"Okay!" I say instantly. And leave.

On my way to the airport, I get turned around in the aftermath of a thunderstorm—power lines are down across the city and I find myself lost amid ambulances, crashed cars, flooded streets, police roadblocks. I think of going back to Alan's door again, but then I decide, *No. Whatever it is he won't talk to me about, he can keep.*

And I'm not going to try to talk to Jesse and Sunny's daughter, I've finally decided. Tina was ten months old that morning, in the backseat of the Camaro. Innocent. She is forty now. All through this investigation, I've thought about her. I've tried to imagine myself on her doorstep. *Hi, Tina?* I have not been able to do it. *I saw your father die.* I just cannot.

That little girl in the backseat has not had an easy time through life—her father in the electric chair, her mother in prison, her grandparents killed in a plane crash. I do not want to make things any harder by telling her what I now know. It's not my place, anyway. What happened at the rest area is something she can ask her mother about. And what happened at Florida State Prison that morning is for the State of Florida to explain, not me.

I think I might be starting to let go.

It has been such a long time, I think, as I drive. Such a long time since that afternoon out in the Los Angeles desert when I stepped out of my car into *away*. So many days and nights and years of traveling, all the doors I've knocked on, all the time spent with the radio singing me sad songs, with the way the road looks sometimes, shiny and flat, broken edges up ahead, shimmering.

But now it is starting to feel different. Like I could step into a new world where today is today, not a bramble of yesterday and today and tomorrow. I'm not pretending that none of this happened. I know it happened. The murders, the execution. But maybe it is no longer happening. No longer happening *now*.

That would be an incredible relief.

At the airport, it's late afternoon and the terminal is almost empty, a lull before the evening flights begin. I find a seat by the window and watch the wind sweep across the tarmac, gray sheets of rain. It's melancholy, this weather, and it makes me think of Constable Donald Irwin, another person in this I've had to let go of.

I did try to talk with Constable Irwin's family. I wanted to know who he was in life, before this tragedy happened. What his childhood was like, what his dreams were. His wife, Barbara, has passed away, so I could not sit down with her as I had with Grace Black, but I found other family members. I wrote to Irwin's son. I called him. I called the church where Irwin's daughter used to preach. I talked to her briefly by phone. I followed up in writing, as she requested. No response. I reached out to the Ontario Provincial Police and the Ontario Provincial Police Association. I considered driving to Canada. But ultimately I decided no.

Donald Irwin's family does not want to talk to me. Clearly. And although I wish that were not so, I understand why it might be. I know in their place I would find me too much to bear. People have the right to their grief. To be left in peace. I am finally learning that too.

28

Michael J. Satz, State Attorney

In the morning, I arrive early at the Broward County state attorney's suite of offices, on the sixth floor of the courthouse in Fort Lauderdale.

At this moment in September 2015, Michael J. Satz has been state attorney for Florida's Seventeenth Judicial Circuit for thirty-nine years. Satz arrived here in 1968 after graduating from law school and never left. He's in his seventies now. Satz was an assistant state attorney in 1976 when he brought the capital murder cases against Jesse Tafero and Sunny Jacobs, and a week after Sunny's conviction Satz announced his candidacy for the county's top law enforcement job. Getting death sentences against two accused cop killers did not hurt him at the polls. In November 1976, Satz won the election and immediately named as his chief assistant state attorney Ralph Ray, the lawyer who had represented Walter Rhodes. Satz has since been reelected nine consecutive times. This prosecutor is a legend. A fixture. And he's come in for his share of criticism about the case that helped him win his powerful job, particularly from Sunny Jacobs and Walter Rhodes.

At her trial in 1976, Sunny handed a note to reporters referring to Satz as "His Satanic Majesty" and saying Satz "is willing to do anything to win." In 1992, after the U.S. Court of Appeals overturned Sunny's conviction, Sunny's attorneys tried to get Satz disqualified from retrying the case, arguing that the Satz/Ray/Rhodes connection was a serious conflict of interest. In a newspaper interview, one of Sunny's lawyers said at the time that Satz had "made a deal with the wrong person—Rhodes was actually the triggerman."

Walter Rhodes has not been happy with Satz either. In 1991, Walter filed a petition in federal court alleging that Satz had conspired with Ralph Ray to coerce Walter into his plea deal, and in 1997 he sued again, alleging "an ongoing lack of independence" between Satz and Ray that had added up to a miscarriage of justice in the case. "Satz is no dummy. He manipulated me into pleading guilty," Walter told me in prison two months ago.

And in her kitchen in Ireland, Sunny too spoke bitterly about the man who put her and Jesse on death row. "Satz is so dirty and so powerful," Sunny told me. "Withholding evidence in a capital case and allowing the person to be executed? That is murder. He should have been charged with murder."

Now Michael Satz's executive secretary is calling my name.

For nearly a year, I've been a nuisance to this office. Pestering. Asking to see the case files. Asking to see the exhibits. Demanding that they unlock the exhibit warehouse and uncrate the dummies. Along the way, they've asked me pointed questions and have seemed at times to harbor nebulous suspicions about articles I wrote about the case, including the piece that *Time* magazine linked to on the twenty-fifth anniversary of Jesse's execution. "It takes seven minutes before the prison doctor pronounces him dead, seven minutes of heaving, nodding, flames and smoke," I wrote. My calls went to voicemail, I was put on hold, I was told to try back later. I left messages, I waited, I called back. I spent days pacing, worrying, wondering. On two separate occasions this spring, I parked myself in the library here to read through the piles of file boxes, and twice I ordered copies of everything. Every page. I'm sure they're hoping that this will be the day they finally see the last of me.

Inside the office, the vibe is austere. Michael Satz himself greets me, along with Carolyn McCann, head of the State Attorney's Office's appeals unit. McCann worked on Sunny's case in 1992 after the conviction was overturned, and when Sunny agreed to her Alford plea, McCann read the entire plea out loud, word for word, into the court record. I take a seat at Satz's conference table facing a row of windows. The sky outside is so pale it is colorless. I know that if I walked over to the window right now, I would see just to the south the street behind the power plant where Walter's apartment was. That's where I started this search, ten months ago. Where they set out from on that long-ago morning, never to return. Come full circle. Now McCann sits down across the table opposite me, and Satz is at the head of the table, on my right.

Michael Satz is trim and taut, with brown eyes and blunt features. He has a reputation for tenacity and frugality, for being a tough litigator and for being a bit of an enigma too: Newspaper stories portray him as a man of few indulgences, never married, living in the same sparsely furnished condo he's had since forever, going skiing every year at the same Colorado mountain, staying in the same modest hotel there. Today he's wearing a white button-down shirt, gray suit pants, and a bright blue tie, thick in a knot at his throat. And right now, he's sizing me up. I can feel it.

Neither Satz nor McCann has said anything beyond hello—no pleasantries, no *how was your trip*, no *it's warm today isn't it*. This is a chess game, and I know I have to make the first move, but I feel suddenly frozen. Not out of questions, too many questions. And Satz seems preoccupied. Maybe irritated.

"So, I witnessed Jesse Tafero's execution."

They know this. They have no reaction.

"And since then I've spent a quarter of a century reading stories in the newspaper about how he was an innocent man. So I'm here to ask you about his case. I want to know what the truth is."

"Read the transcript," Satz says. He looks like he's ready to get up and walk out.

"I have read the transcript," I tell him. "But there are still some things that I don't understand."

Silence.

"Look, I'm not going to put words in your mouth. I am just trying to find out what actually happened," I say. "That's all. I saw the man die, I want to know."

After that, everybody seems to relax. Me, definitely.

When Jesse testified at Sunny's trial, he was under oath, of course. Jesse told the jury that he witnessed the shots that killed Trooper Black and Constable Irwin that morning, and that Walter Rhodes was the one who fired the gun, from a position at the front of the Camaro.

Over the past year, I have come to my own conclusion about Jesse and his testimony. But I am not actually a forensic expert, and so this is my leadoff question. This prosecutor put Jesse Tafero on death row. I'm finally face-to-face with him. I need to ask.

"Could the shots that murdered the officers have been fired from the front of the Camaro?" I begin.

"Do you know the difference between a revolver and a semi-automatic?" Satz replies.

I do not.

A revolver is a cowboy gun, Satz says. The casing stays in the barrel. With semiautomatics, the casings are dislodged when the gun is fired. That's why you find casings when a semiautomatic has been used. In this case, the murder weapon was a semiautomatic handgun, and there were three casings found at the rest area crime scene. Two of the casings were inside the Camaro, one on a jean jacket just below the front passenger seat and the other on the floorboard of the front passenger wheel well. That casing on top of the jean jacket didn't just climb up there by itself, Satz says. The jacket had to be there first, before the gun ejected the casing on top of it. The third casing was found outside the car, along the curb in front of the front tire on the Camaro's passenger side. The ballistics test showed that those three casings all came from the murder weapon. Next, they tested how that gun ejected casings, and found that the gun ejected casings fifty-four degrees to the right and ten feet to the rear. So if someone was standing and firing the gun at the front of the car, where Tafero testified that Rhodes was firing, the casings could not have landed inside the Camaro or near the front tire on the passenger side, Satz says.

"The three casings were really important," Satz says. "There's no way those casings could have gotten there shooting from the front of the car."

So that's physical evidence point one.

Point two, Satz continues, is the bullet hole in the windshield post of the cruiser. The criminologist "put a metal rod in that hole and the direction was the rear seat of the Camaro. And Pierce Hyman, the truck driver, testified that the first shot came from the Camaro."

"Hyman said all of the shots came from the Camaro," I correct Satz.

Satz looks at me.

"Three," he continues. "The murder weapon was reloaded and strapped to Tafero's waist with two extra magazines. I think one of those was KTW armor-piercing bullets."

"Yes, it was," I say.

"Do you know how semiautomatics are reloaded?"

I do not.

Satz explains. "When you put the magazine in the butt of the gun, you can't immediately pull the trigger. First, you have to pull back the slide to load the bullet into the chamber. As I recall, when they took that gun from Tafero there was a bullet in the chamber. The other gun, the one they took from Rhodes, did not have a chambered round."

I think I get it. Basically, it's that the gun police took from Walter at the roadblock had not been readied to fire, whereas the gun they took from Jesse had a bullet loaded in the chamber, all set to go.

Plus, Jesse Tafero had just reloaded that gun, Satz says. The man whose Cadillac they carjacked, Leonard Levinson, testified that he saw Tafero reloading the gun as they were speeding away.

And then of course there was the Taser, Satz adds.

The Taser, I think to myself. Remembering Sunny's reaction. *I have no clue.* It's the mystery piece of evidence, the weapon nobody who was actually there in the Camaro that day—Walter, Sunny, Eric—seems to know anything about. Or wants to tell me about, certainly. And now here is the prosecutor himself, bringing it up on his own.

"Why was the Taser significant?"

"It was significant because obviously it was fired, the only one who had a Taser was them"—meaning Jesse, Sunny, and Walter—"and there was an empty Taser holster behind the driver's seat of the Camaro where Jacobs was sitting. In the attaché case, there was the Taser, the fired cartridges, and extra cartridges."

"Well, when I talked with Sunny Jacobs, I asked her about the Taser, and she said she had no clue as to what I was talking about."

Satz is waiting, like, *What am I supposed to say to that?*

"Did you mention the Taser at her trial?" I ask.

"I asked Tafero about it, there was the photo of the dart in evidence, we put the attaché case and its contents into evidence. There was a lot of testimony about that," Satz says.

"There was the Taser stipulation in the Alford plea, so even if she didn't remember that it was mentioned at her trial, the plea was read aloud in court," McCann adds.

Satz leans across the table now, right at me.

Sonia Jacobs told the police that her name was Sandy Jenkins and that another woman named Frenchie was with them in the car at the rest area, he says. He's talking about statements that Sunny made to police, right after the murders. "If you didn't do anything wrong, why would you lie? You're in a police station, surrounded by police officers, why wouldn't you say, 'Oh, this terrible thing happened, help me'?"

The Delray Beach substation. February 20, 1976. Sunny Jacobs is being interrogated. The detectives have read her the Miranda rights and she has answered affirmatively that she wishes to proceed with the interview. They've told her that she is being charged with first-degree murder, and she has laughed. Now they want to know more about the guys she was arrested with. Who are they? What are their names? How long has she known them? How did they meet? The guy in the blue shirt—what is his name? Sunny has no response.

"How did you meet this man with the blue shirt?"

"Well, the, he's a friend of the other guy," Sunny says.

"What's the other guy's name?" They're asking about Jesse now.

"I just call him, ah, ah I . . . I . . . I was just calling him, ah, Tone."

"Tone?"

"Tone. Tone."

As Sunny later wrote in her book, "It was a pitiful lie."

That interview was one of three statements Sunny made to police that morning that were ruled inadmissible on appeal. In addition, the appeals court also found that the failure by the State Attorney's Office to disclose Walter's polygraph report was a violation of *Brady v. Maryland*, the important U.S. Supreme Court ruling that requires prosecutors to hand over evidence that is both exculpatory and material to the defense. The court ruling wasn't a total win for Sunny. She lost on one of her key claims, concerning a prosecution witness named Brenda Isham, who testified for the state at Sunny's trial and then years later confessed, in tears on national television, that she had lied on the stand. Regarding Isham, the court found that her "highly significant and dramatic" recantation was credible, but otherwise her testimony was "rife with inconsistencies," and ruled that the prosecution "neither knew or should have known that Isham would commit perjury." But on the basis of the Miranda and *Brady* violations, the court overturned Sunny's conviction and ordered that she be retried.

The second statement ruled inadmissible was one Sunny allegedly made to a trooper at the roadblock. As the officers were leading her and the children away from the Cadillac, Sunny burst free and rushed over to Jesse as he lay handcuffed on the ground. The trooper had been thinking Sunny was a hostage, but after that, he asked her, "Do you like shooting troopers?" and he reported that Sunny said, "We had to." That statement was ruled inadmissible because the trooper had not read Sunny her Miranda rights.

The third statement was one Sunny made to Palm Beach County detective Gary Hill, who transported her and the children from the roadblock to the Delray Beach police station that morning. Hill read Sunny her rights, and then asked her questions after she refused to tell him her name. The court ruled that by refusing to tell Hill her name, Sunny was invoking her right to remain silent, and that therefore any statements Sunny made to Hill were inadmissible. Hill reported that Sunny told him her name was Sandy Jenkins, that she was a hitchhiker, that the men in the orange Cadillac had stopped and asked her if she wanted a ride, that she did not know them and had never seen them before, and that she was their hostage.

After Hill dropped her off at the Delray Beach substation, Detective Lieutenant Angelo Farinato and Captain Valjean Haley read Sunny her Miranda rights again and interrogated her. On appeal, the court ruled that the statement Farinato and Haley obtained was inadmissible because not enough time had elapsed between Sunny's refusal to tell Hill her name and the Farinato/Haley interrogation. It was a win for Sunny and a big loss for the prosecution, because on that tape Sunny tried to mislead the officers about who was in the Camaro at the rest area. She said there had been another woman in the car, who ran off after the shooting. A woman named Frenchie.

Q: What kind of clothes did she have on?
A: Uh, she had on jeans and, uh, a pullover blouse, dark-colored blouse.
Q: Alright, what was her nickname once again? Frenchie?
A: —

Q: You don't know her last name? Do you know where Frenchie
   was from?
A: I have no idea.

Now, in his office, Satz is wondering aloud about that to me.

"I thought it was significant, that she put another woman in
the car. Maybe she felt that somebody saw a woman."

Certainly Walter and Jesse and Sunny knew they'd been observed. Eric was reported to have told a sergeant that it was the
truck driver on his CB radio who notified the police about the
shootings, and that if they'd "wasted" him, they would have made
a clean getaway.

In her book, Sunny acknowledges that she fabricated Frenchie.
No mention of the taped statement, though. Instead, she claims
she was having trouble finding a good attorney and:

> In one of the little notes that Jesse managed to send to me he
> said he did not trust this new lawyer and that I should test him
> in some way. So I made up some fantastic details, which I told
> to him. I said that Rhodes was gay and that his lover, Frenchie,
> a man dressed as a woman, had been in the car with us. The
> story came back to me as the latest police theory. I dismissed
> the attorney.

In her taped interrogation, the Frenchie one later ruled inadmissible, Sunny told the officers that she did not witness the murders. But she claimed the man in the blue shirt—Walter
Rhodes—"was giving the instructions."

That, however, is not what Leonard Levinson—owner of the
carjacked Cadillac—said.

January, earlier this year, back at the beginning. I'd just spent the
day at the Broward County courthouse. I'd returned to our rental
house with a stack of papers from the court files, and Peter and I
were sitting on the couch together, reading.

"Okay, wait," Peter said. He was reading a piece of paper covered in a spidery scrawl. "Hasn't Sunny always said she and Jesse were hostages that morning?"

"Yes, why?"

"Because here is a statement from a guy named Leonard Levinson, and he says he was a hostage too."

I'd never given much thought to Leonard Levinson. He was a retired World War II veteran who'd had the misfortune to be holding the keys to a brand-new Cadillac Coupe de Ville when the stolen police cruiser blasted into his retirement village. After that Cadillac crashed to a halt at the police roadblock, officers found Levinson in the backseat, captive, terrified. What could Levinson know? He wasn't present when the murders took place.

"He says that Jesse Tafero kidnapped him," Peter said, reading.

"So?"

"So, the hostages took a hostage?"

"Let me see that." I snatched the paper out of Peter's hand.

"It's what hostages want most in the world, I've heard," Peter said. "Ask a hostage, any hostage, what they dream of, and the answer is always the same: Get me another hostage."

Leonard Levinson. The third independent eyewitness. Not to the murders, but to the aftermath. The chase. He's gone now, but on February 20, 1976, at exactly the same time as the officers were interrogating Walter, Sunny, and Jesse, Leonard Levinson was giving his own statement to police. There were no fake answers from him. No pitiful lies.

That morning, Leonard Levinson had gone downstairs to get his newspaper and check on his car, and when he saw the highway patrol car pulling into the parking lot he started toward it to see what was up. Maybe someone in the building was having an emergency, he thought. He wanted to help. The cruiser came to a halt and a man with a beard got out of the car, pointed a gun at Levinson, and said, "We're not going to hurt you, we have to get a child to the hospital." Everyone piled out of the cruiser and climbed into Levinson's Cadillac—Walter behind the wheel, Sunny and the two children in the front seat, Levinson and Jesse in the back. The Cadillac took off flying onto Hillsboro Boulevard heading west toward the fields, and Levinson asked them to please slow down because the fog was bad. Jesse said, "He's right, slow it down." As they drove, Jesse and Walter and Sunny were silent, for the most part, and they kept checking out the back window, but occasionally "some words would pass between them," Levinson wrote later. They were talking in code, Levinson thought, "an abbreviation or first letters or cipher of some kind."

Along the way, Jesse, sitting in the back next to Levinson, opened an attaché case, took out an ammunition clip and counted it—"I guess to check to see if the clip was full"—and then loaded more bullets into it. Levinson tried not to look, not to let his eyes stray onto anything they should not see. Jesse told Levinson, "The quicker you forget about what you've seen or heard, the better, because we're not alone." Then Jesse asked Levinson to hand over his wallet.

"Finally the one driving said, 'I think we have a tail,' the other one said, 'Are you sure?' and pushed himself down flat on the seat and made me do the same. Then the driver said, 'I think we have a roadblock ahead.' The other one said, 'Oh no.' I could see them run off the road and then sideswipe the truck. You know the rest."

Leonard Levinson had a very firm idea about who it was who was in charge that morning, according to his statement, and to his testimony later at trial. The man with the beard, sitting next to him.

"I think by the actions of the one beside me, he was the leader," Levinson wrote.

Jesse Tafero.

"Mr. Levinson testified that Tafero was reloading the semiautomatic handgun," Satz is saying now.

"But both Sunny and Eric told me that they saw Rhodes with a gun immediately after the shooting," I say, to Satz. Sunny was so insistent about this to me, and Eric went a step further, saying it was Walter's own gun used in the murders. "Did they ever tell you that?"

Satz looks at me like, *What are you, an idiot?* "I would never have had direct communication with them."

"But was that information ever communicated to you in any way? I didn't see it in the case file, and so I'm wondering if I missed it."

Because it is so exculpatory. Walter Rhodes, chief witness for the prosecution, with a gun in his hand right after the murders—that is something the jury would have needed to know, for sure. In the police station that morning, though, Sunny and Eric both said on tape that they did not see anyone with a gun. I've read the transcripts. I've talked with the officers who obtained those statements. And now I'm asking Satz. For if they did not say Walter had a gun when they were on trial for their lives, then I don't see how I can believe now that it's true.

"That information was never offered to us through their attorney, no," McCann says.

In July 1974, a year and a half before the murders, police officers in South Carolina stopped a van that Sunny and Jesse were driving, Satz says now. He's always thought that traffic stop was just like the one in this case—except that the police officers were not murdered.

This arrest is in the court file. Sunny and Jesse, traveling under the alias Antonio Martes—Tony Tuesday—were in a white van with a cracked windshield. Officers stopped and searched the vehicle and found guns and drugs. In her book, Sunny describes the drugs as "Jesse's party pack—a selection of tablets and good smoke," but actually it was a hundred capsules of amphetamine, plus Ritalin, Quaaludes, barbiturates, benzodiazepines, narcotic pain killers, LSD, and hashish. They both faced charges of drug possession with intent to distribute, and Sunny was charged with having a pistol in her purse. The case file lists Sunny at her parents' home address, and Jesse—as Antonio Martes—at the address for the family's textile business. Herbert Jacobs, Sunny's dad, signed for the property in the case. His signature is on a paper in the file, noting that the guns—a .30 caliber carbine, a .22 caliber rifle, and a .25 automatic pistol, from Sunny's purse—were not returned. Then Sunny and Jesse skipped town and were convicted in absentia.

"This was not a life she was born into," McCann says, about Sunny Jacobs. "This was a life she chose."

We are back to the physical evidence.

"Common sense is, if you're firing a Taser, that would be fired first," Satz says. There's no reason to fire a Taser at the two officers if they're already mortally wounded with gunshot wounds. But a Taser is a little bit tricky. "You'd have to hit them with both darts in order to have electricity go through," Satz says. Trooper Black was demonstrably not hit with both darts, since one of the darts was found in the cruiser's weather stripping.

"Would the dart still hurt, even if it was only one dart?" I ask.

"Yes," Satz says.

And then think of the bullet hole in the windshield post, he says. Back to front, low to high. "If you fire a Taser and it doesn't hit, what do you do next?" Satz asks.

It seems like he's expecting my answer will be *Fire a gun*. But I'm thinking of the notes in Ralph Ray's files, the handwritten ones from an interview with Walter Rhodes.

"Have you seen these?" I ask Satz now, putting the Ray file notes down in front of him. *He doesn't think Sonia shot—thinks maybe Jesse fired all the shots.*

"I would not have had the defense lawyer's notes," Satz says. He sounds shocked at my question. Then he studies the notes so closely that he's bent over almost on top of them. He is reading every single word. Absorbing.

"What if Sunny Jacobs did not fire a gun that morning?" I ask, watching him. "What if she only fired the Taser? Does that change anything—in your view—in terms of her responsibility?"

Satz takes a long moment before answering. He stares down, hands flat on the tabletop in front of him. The room is silent. It's very intense.

"No," Satz says, finally. "It's the same."

"So how did it start, that morning?" I ask him.

"You just have to go by what the testimony was."

But the testimony is from the truck drivers, who didn't see Tafero do any shooting, and from Walter, who doesn't know how it started. *Somebody:* That's who Walter now says fired the first shot.

"I talked to a lot of Palm Beach County troopers and they said they thought maybe Eric fired the Taser," I tell Satz. "Did you consider that?"

"We considered everything. There wasn't any testimony that we had about that. The two truck drivers did not see or hear a Taser."

"Well, in your files, there's a report from Eric's social worker," I say, getting my notes out. "What about 'My mother made me do it'?"

"I don't remember hearing that," Satz says, shaking his head. "I just don't remember that. With Eric, the only thing we knew was what happened afterwards. She told him to shut up."

I have some pages from Walter's memoir with me, and I get them out now too. Pages from the state's star witness.

"I'm just going to share a little bit of this with you," I tell Satz and McCann.

"New Mexico has all kinds of secret shit going on," Walter's reminiscence begins. I'm reading it aloud. It's 1994, he's just been paroled from prison, and he's looking out the window of the house he lives in with Sara. He's already seen a white limo driving around town with dark windows and a CIA license plate, but it's still a little while before the night he comes home drunk, Sara calls the cops, he takes off, and then they both end up on the run in Washington. On this particular evening, it's dusk and there's a man with a dog outside his house, both floating, almost. Walter knows exactly what is going on: It's a Man in Black, a government agent sent to silence people who have seen UFOs. He figures there must be an "interdimensional gateway" nearby.

"Did you hear any of this stuff before the trial?" I ask Satz.

"No," Satz says. He seems unimpressed. "A lot of people thought they saw UFOs in the 1970s."

"Did you meet Walter Rhodes?" I ask.

Yes, Satz says. Never alone of course, he hastens to add— always with Walter's attorney present, and investigator LaGraves. "I never got the impression that he wasn't stable or that he had any mental issues."

"Did you have any doubts about Rhodes—is that why you polygraphed him?"

"I don't think Valjean Haley had any doubts about him, or the Palm Beach Sheriff's Office. And he's the only one who gave a statement at the time about what happened. Her statement, about Frenchie, we know that was definitely not truthful, and we had the physical evidence" as well as the truck driver testimony, Satz says. "We said, Look, let's do everything we can, let's run him and see if he passes. We wanted to do everything we could to make sure."

"But do you know if Rhodes was hypnotized?"

In my pile of papers I find the note from Ray's file that mentions Dr. Gold, the hypnotist, and slide it across now to Satz.

Satz reads it.

"I have never, to my knowledge, worked with a hypnotized witness," Satz says. Fierce. Definite. "I did not hear that Rhodes had been hypnotized, and I didn't know that was something that had been suggested."

What about Walter Rhodes's recantations? I ask.

"All I know is that when anybody interviews him—you or *60 Minutes*—he comes back to the story he told us. All I know is he said right away to check the gun, 'I didn't do any shooting.' What was important to me was the physical evidence, who does that corroborate," he says.

"What evidence?" I ask.

"The Taser, the windshield, who owned the guns, where did they get the guns, who had the most to gain or lose by extracting himself from that situation, who was arrested with the murder weapon. The casings—they were very integral to the case. And those shots, they were all head shots."

But I thought there wasn't much physical evidence in the case, I say.

There was quite a bit of physical evidence, Satz corrects me. In fact "the most important thing was the physical evidence." Why? Because eyewitnesses are unreliable. "The phrase I like to use is, 'Murders don't usually happen in front of a busload of bishops.'"

So take out the testimony, he says. All the testimony. "Just get rid of it."

"You have the three bullet casings. The Taser dart. The hole in the windshield post. The evidence of what gun killed Black and Irwin. The path of the bullets in the body and the death shots. Tafero was arrested with the murder weapon in a pancake holster fully loaded. You have Mr. Levinson's testimony that Jacobs takes the attaché case and gives it to Tafero and Tafero reloads the gun. You know the Taser was fired and you know that the Taser dart was fired. In the attaché case, there was the trooper's gun and the Taser dart and expended Taser cartridge and KTW boxes and KTW ammunition." The green Teflon-coated bullets.

"Now add back in Hyman, the truck driver. He said the shots came from the back of the Camaro. That matches the shot in the windshield post and the Taser dart. Add back in McKenzie, the other truck driver. He also said Rhodes was with his hands up, but had him in a different position. We know Tafero was in violation of his parole. We know Tafero said Rhodes shot from the front of the car, and Tafero said the attaché case belonged to Rhodes. Both lies."

The physical evidence, minus the testimony—that's how you see what happened, Satz says. And about Walter Rhodes, "Our main concern was did he do anything with the shooting. That's where we made him do a polygraph. Then you go to the physical evidence and see what you have."

I think for a minute.

Then I take my notebook and draw an X on the page, to mark where Jesse swore Walter was standing at the front of the Camaro.

"Could the person who murdered the officers have fired the shots from there?" I ask Satz again. Coming back around to where I started the interview. Because this feels so key to me. If Jesse Tafero lied under oath on the stand at a trial where his girlfriend, the mother of his beloved baby daughter, was facing the electric chair, there seems to me just one reason for that. It had to have been because telling the truth about what happened at the rest area that morning would not have helped Sunny—or set her free.

"No," Satz says, answering my question. "Rhodes firing from the front doesn't explain the bullet through the windshield post or the casings in the Camaro—or the Taser dart."

"But Sunny told me that Rhodes moved," I say. I am trying to push this as far as I can. "She told me Walter Rhodes moved from the front of the car to the back of the car. She said she saw that herself."

Satz leans forward again. "She is sitting in court where Tafero's testifying that Rhodes is firing from the front." So if that is what she's saying now, "she knows she is changing her story."

"Well, Sunny Jacobs also told me that Walter Rhodes flunked that polygraph and you covered it up. She said you made a deal with the real killer."

Satz is silent.

"Is that true?" I ask.

"Why do you polygraph someone?" Satz asks.

"To find out if they are telling the truth."

Satz raises his hands with his palms up, like, *Thank you for stating the obvious.*

"Say you're a law enforcement officer and this happened. What do you want?" Satz asks next.

I know this is what Satz does—ask question after question until you the jury reach the conclusion he wants you to. The one he has already reasoned through and reached himself. He's a master at it, clearly. It's been an interesting experience, being here on the hot seat. But still, I find myself hoping that the answer I'm about to give him now is true.

"You want to find out who really did it," I say.

"Yes," Satz says. "That's exactly right. You want to find out what really happened."

"You know on those crime shows, it's always, 'Where is the murder weapon?'" Satz says. We are reaching the end now. "Well, here's the answer: strapped onto Jesse Tafero's waist, in his holster, with two additional cartridges."

"But Sunny and Eric told me that Walter gave Jesse the murder weapon," I say.

"Why would Rhodes give Tafero the murder weapon?" Satz asks.

"I don't know. Maybe it's simply good manners to offer your hostage a gun."

"Hostage?" Satz says.

"They've all said they were hostages."

"They all said they were hostages of each other?" Satz says. Disbelieving.

I've had a thought about that, and now I might as well run it past him.

"But it seems to me they were all acting in concert up right until they hit the roadblock."

"Yes, I agree with that," Satz says.

Bonnie and Clyde, and Clyde's excitable friend.

To the death!

The cocaine, the guns, the UFOs, Jimmy Hoffa, the amphetamines and Thorazine and Quaaludes and the swapped-for beat-up Camaro, the stolen passports and licenses in the attaché case and the rubber mask with the wig in the Camaro's trunk, the hatchet behind the driver's seat, the bayonet, the KTW Teflon-coated bullets, the Taser, one dart, three bullet casings, two small brown paper bags. Half past seven in the morning.

All this sorrow.

"Truth and lies *matter*," I say to Satz.

"Of course they do," the prosecutor replies. Instantly.

"Just so you know, this office did not have to give you those records," McCann says, as we stand up and start to walk out of the office.

"Really?" I assume she's joking.

Later, when I realize this is for real—there is indeed a statutory exemption for investigative materials received by a state law enforcement agency prior to January 25, 1979—I will think of all the phone calls, all the messages, all the silences, all the back-and-forth, all the documents. I will think of the two separate weeks I spent in their library, once to see the state attorney's files and then a second time to review LaGraves's investigative files, the coffee machine behind me slow-toasting that roast all afternoon. The many, many times I acted like they had to kiss my ass on this one, the utter imperiousness with which I marched around and demanded to see things. And the immense amount of information in the records: all the rest-stop interviews, the roadblock interviews, LaGraves's notes and files, the audiotapes, the autopsy reports, the ballistics, the Addis family. The dummies. It will hit me with a force so strong it feels like falling backwards: I almost had to take the word of Walter Rhodes on this. Or Sunny Jacobs. Or the Internet, for God's sake.

I would have had to live with the ghost for the rest of my life.

29

The Truth

The road I take out of Fort Lauderdale after the interview is the same route they drove that morning. North on Interstate 95, west along the parking lot where they kidnapped Leonard Levinson, then north again past the roadblock where they crashed the Cadillac and onward, out across the sugarcane. Green grass, storm light, white birds flying low. I get to the cemetery at five minutes past four o'clock.

Two pillars mark the entrance, here in the small town where Trooper Black grew up. A narrow drive leads up to a circle, and from there, paths radiate outward, patched and torn. The afternoon has turned cloudy and very hot, with the pale lemon glow of coming rain. The trees overhead are completely still, no breeze or breath in the heavy air. I am here to pay my respects to Phillip Black, who has now been beneath the earth here almost exactly as long as he was alive. Fourteen thousand, four hundred, and sixty-seven days.

Up the faded pavement of the central drive, I see a small building that looks like an office. It's closed. There's a paper posted on a bulletin board outside, and I get out of my rental car, hoping it is a map. It's a notice about flowers. I know from the Internet that I am looking for a gray granite headstone near an evergreen shrub. So now I stand for a moment and look out. This cemetery is nearly a hundred years old. Rows upon rows of graves, as far as I can see. From here, every headstone is gray granite, every shrub is evergreen.

No matter, I think. I can find him.

I start in my car, making my way slowly along the widest paths, and then along the narrower ones, and then along the narrowest ones. Finally I get out and walk.

The grass is wet. It soaks through my canvas shoes. The light is fading around me as the rainstorm moves in. Why did I not call ahead? I should have known the office here would close early. Why did I stop for gas? Maybe his grave is in the older section of the cemetery, under the huge live oaks weeping Spanish moss. No one else is here, there's no birdsong or wind in the trees, just all these graves. I feel a gathering sense of—*no*. It's the inner voice I've always promised myself I will listen to. It is speaking now.

No, this is not for you, no, this is private, *no.*

In one instant I decide to leave.

Phillip Black needs to rest in peace, I think, as I drive back down the main path and out onto the county road. He needs his privacy. It's not my place to give any kind of remembrance, I think. Or hallowing. One of the saddest parts of this tragedy is how he and Donald Irwin have gotten lost in it. No wonder I cannot find him now.

Outside the cemetery walls, I get turned around. I'm trying to get to the town where my hotel is, but now for the life of me I do not understand the route on my map app. That never happens. Where am I? I start to head off, but I only get a little bit away when I decide that actually I can't leave here without paying my respects. I turn the car around.

The exit off State Road 60 in this direction has a big sign with the words AVON PARK on it—the name of the prison where I first went to talk to Walter all those years ago—and the ramp leads right to the cemetery. I am starting up the center drive again when I stop.

I have been searching for the truth of this case for nearly a year. I've traveled across three oceans and three continents, to Florida and Ireland and Australia. I've been trying to get as close as I can to the instant those gunshots rang out. I've been trying to understand exactly what happened. For the last twenty-five years, I've been obsessed with knowing the truth. And all along, I see now, the bigger truth was here. Somewhere between the patched and cracked pathways of the cemetery, beneath this lowering sky. I can feel it. A wrenching despair.

Murder.

Phillip Black's life was stolen from him. *That* is the truth of what happened that morning. No amount of going to or through the past will ever make that right, or bring light to it, or bring him back. A beloved husband and father was gunned down in the morning mist. After that morning, Phil Black never took his little boy fishing. He never called home during his shift to say a quick hello to his wife. He never stopped on the side of the road to help a stranded motorist, or checked on a rest area after a cold winter's night. Donald Irwin's life was stolen too. For both men, for their families, for their friends, the joys they would have had, the days they would have shared—all that light stolen away, buried in a field of graves.

And that part of the story is not mine. The heartache part, the wrenching part. The truest part. The dark birds came and bore them across. That will always have happened and can never be changed. It is the darkness at the center of this story.

The violence. The sorrow. The loss.

30

The Heat

The phone number is online, on a website for Jack Murphy's prison ministry, Sonshine Adventures. "To inspire those imprisoned behind bars and those imprisoned with personal limitations to Believe a Man Can Change!" I dial it one afternoon in late December, just before the end of the year.

The day after my trip to the cemetery, I'd stopped by Jack Murphy's house in Florida, but he wasn't home. A big American flag at the cobwebbed front door, and a rusted Hello Kitty umbrella. Patchy grass, scattered sand, peeling paint. Not what I'd expected from the glamorous playboy portrayed in *Vanity Fair*.

"Jack Murphy?" I say now, into the phone.

"Yes." Deep voice. Southern accent. Not friendly.

"I'm writing a book about Jesse Tafero."

"Who?"

"Jesse Tafero."

He does not respond.

"I saw online that you know the man who really killed the officers," I say.

"What is your connection to this?"

"I witnessed Jesse's execution."

A bit of a pause, again.

"That was a tough one," Jack Murphy says.

"Were you there? I wasn't able to tell from what I read if you were there or not."

"No, I was in Boston, praying for him, and my wife was on the phone with Jesse's mother the whole time."

"Oh, Kay, I've heard she was lovely." Thinking of how Marianne Cook described Kay, at the start of this year. "A real lady."

"Yes, she was."

"So I read that you testified in front of the Florida Parole Commission that you knew the real killer in the Tafero case."

"Yes, I did."

And that is how we get to talking.

Jack Murphy. It seems like every time I've dug into anything to do with Jesse Tafero and Walter Rhodes, there he is. Murph the Surf. The star of Miami Beach diving shows, a dazzling beach boy with a brilliant mind and a taste for daring adventure. The cat burglar who stole a legendary sapphire, a flawless ruby, and one of the largest diamonds ever mined in North America. The debonair jewel thief who charmed the press after his arrest. The murderer convicted of killing two young women at Whiskey Creek. The prison preacher who found God and won his freedom. "A stand-up guy," according to Sunny Jacobs.

The lynchpin to Walter's confessions.

Even though I feel certain that Jesse Tafero murdered Trooper Phillip Black and Constable Donald Irwin, I still care about the confessions. I care about them for the same reason I've always cared: Because in this capital murder case, a person other than the man who went to the electric chair confessed to the crime. I care because no matter what the other evidence points to, the fact of the confessions remains—and a confession can seem like the ultimate proof. The smoking gun. I care because the words *before my Creator* had me so convinced at one point that I tracked down the fugitive Walter Rhodes in the far north woods, a reckless journey that I have long regretted. I care because the confessions have always been the crux of the case against Walter Rhodes. I care because Walter confessed. He *confessed.*

Is there something I've missed? As I said, this has never been a guessing game for me. I need to know for sure.

From 1977 until 1982, Walter Rhodes was reported to have confessed at least four times. And it seems to me now that every one of those confessions was linked—directly or indirectly—to Jack Murphy.

In 1977, not quite a year after Jesse's trial, two inmates said Walter confessed to them while in line at a prison amputee clinic. Those inmates went to Murphy for advice, and he helped one of them type up a sworn affidavit for prison officials.

In November 1979, Walter signed another confession. It's the one quoted in *The Exonerated.* Three of Walter's fellow inmates witnessed that confession, and one of those inmates later told La-Graves that he'd heard there was a contract out on Walter's head. Specifically, he'd heard about the contract on Walter from Jack Griffith—Murphy's partner in the Whiskey Creek murders.

In 1982, Walter confessed two more times. One was a typewritten and tape-recorded statement he sent to a Jacksonville newspaper. The other was a forty-eight-page sworn statement taken under oath in deposition by an attorney representing Jesse Tafero. In both those confessions, Walter said he murdered the officers from a position at the driver's-side door of the Camaro. Where Jesse was standing. And he told LaGraves, later, that he'd drawn up that new version with Murphy's advice.

"It just always was a very, very uncomfortable situation," Jack Murphy begins, about Jesse Tafero and Walter Rhodes. "I knew them well," he says. Jesse and Rusty, as he calls them.

Jesse was a "neat guy," Murphy remembers. He first met Jesse at Jesse's 1967 trial on home-invasion, sexual-assault, and robbery charges. Murphy's attorney represented Jesse's codefendant in the case, and one day Murphy stopped into the courtroom to say hello. "The dialogue was something out of a triple-X-rated *Saturday Night Live* routine." Murphy laughs.

Walter was a neat guy, too, at least at first. In the early 1970s, before the murders, Murphy and Walter and Jesse all hung out in prison together. Murphy and Rusty played in a band together, and Murphy and Jesse took karate. Good times, from what Murphy says.

But then Jesse and Rusty got out, met up again, woke up that morning in the rest area, and came back.

"Rusty, from the trauma he went through, he was like a dog that had been hit by a car—he was living a life of fear." And because "Rusty"—Walter—had testified against Jesse and Sunny, when he came back to prison after the murders "he was never really comfortable around my crowd." So Murphy kept tabs on him.

"My friends would meet Rusty where he was and they would talk to him," Murphy says. "They'd say, 'I want to ask you these specific questions,' and then they would tell me what he said. Rusty went from prison to prison, he kept getting beat up, getting in trouble in different places, because of Jesse."

Murphy and Jesse, on the other hand, stayed friends. Even when Jesse was on death row.

"I had some serious meetings with Jesse in the back of the building of death row—they would bring me back up there at eleven o'clock, I'd have to sign up that I wanted to see Jesse, that I was working on his law case. We'd sit in the corner of this long skinny room and there was a stack of law books in the corner. We worked on Jesse's case. We worked on Sonia's case. We'd go back there and visit. We knew a ton of the same people in Miami."

People in the Cravero gang, for one. A top Cravero associate—a drug dealer who was a defendant in the Stanley Harris murder trial—was a defendant along with Murphy in a criminal securities case connected to the Whiskey Creek murders. But that's not what Murphy is reminiscing about now. He's keeping it light. Murph's gal and Jesse's high school girlfriend—"a hot chick, intelligent, with Woodstock written all over her"—used to drive up together from Miami to visit him and Jesse in prison, Murphy is saying. John Clarence Cook, Marianne's husband—"one of the great incredible jewel thieves"—visited too. Had special permission for the visit, even.

"And yeah, didn't you and Jesse both know Jack Griffith?" I say. A pause.

"Jack Griffith," Murphy says slowly. "He was my fall partner on Whiskey Creek."

Murphy talks a little bit about Jack Griffith—"a tough guy"—and is just about wrapping it up with the sad news that his old running partner died in prison as I figure out how, exactly, I am going to ask my question. The question that is the reason for this call.

"So I've read through the files on this case, and I read that Jack Griffith put the word out that there was a thirty- to forty-thousand-dollar price tag on Rhodes's head," I say. "Does that make sense to you?"

"A price tag?" Jack Murphy says. Pause. "It does make sense. Those rumors were around. They probably weren't from Jack Griffith, though. They were from me."

In my preparation for this phone call, I had not considered this possibility. And yet here he is, talking in an utterly matter-of-fact, reasonable tone.

"Wherever Rusty was at, I put the heat on him," Murphy says.

There was heat, for sure.

In May 1976, on the day Jesse was sentenced to death, a drug-dealing Cravero gang member named Marlene Hudson—one of Jesse's main sources of cocaine—was caught on a police wiretap discussing the case. She called Walter "a motherfucking cocksucker" and swore: "I'm going to do everything in my power over that guy."

In September 1976, LaGraves wrote to the assistant superintendent of the state prison medical center, where Walter was incarcerated: "It has come to my attention and to the attention of other law enforcement personnel that threats have been made against Rhodes's life. In most circumstances, threats of this nature can be labeled as 'bluster'; however, it appears that Tafero and his associates have sufficient contacts, in prison and on the street, to lend credence and to present some cause for concern."

In February 1977, Walter wrote to LaGraves. "I must admit that I was afraid the entire time I was in the general population; I felt totally helpless, with no friends." He found a knife under his pillow, and one morning a prison official got word "that I was to be killed" and locked him in a shower for his own protection.

"There is a contract out on me in the event that I do not change my testimony," Walter wrote again, in December 1977. "There has been money put up for this. The vibes are pretty bad. I know I'm in trouble and it's just a matter of time before they get me."

An inmate "who knew Tafero on the streets informed me that there was 'money out on me' from the Crevaro click [sic]," Walter wrote, in May 1978. The letter specifically named the Cravero associate who was charged along with Jack Murphy—and Jack Griffith—with the theft of the securities in the Whiskey Creek case.

"Rhodes's life at this time is in imminent danger," a prison inspector reported in November 1979.

"I was told point-blank that if I didn't play ball I'd be dead," Walter told LaGraves in November 1979.

And Murphy did more than just put heat on Walter. He personally obtained one of Walter's confessions himself. He's telling me about that right now.

It's 1982, Jesse's been scheduled for a clemency hearing, and Walter has been transferred again, this time to Union Correctional Institution, the toughest prison in the system.

"He landed at UCI and he came to see me in the chapel. He

knew I was very hostile toward this whole situation and very pissed off at him," Murphy is saying. Murphy had told Walter, "You need to fess up. I said, 'I got to have this.' He knew I had a very, very serious attitude about this. He said, 'Let me come clean.' "

So Murphy and Walter sat down for "three or four or five different sessions" to work on Walter's confession, Murphy says. Murphy tape-recorded it, edited it to clear it up, and had diagrams drawn up. "It all fit in with the ballistics charges and everything," Murphy tells me.

Shortly after signing that confession, in 1982, Walter told La-Graves that the statement had been "well, well, well constructed" in conferences over "many hours" with Jack Murphy, in preparation for Jesse's clemency hearing. The statement reworked his previous confessions and tied them all in together, Walter said.

"He wrote up this thing . . . which we—I had to memorize, what have you, okay, then we made this tape," Walter said. He called Murphy "the brains behind this whole thing."

"It's gonna look like it makes a lot of sense," Walter warned LaGraves.

"Oh Jesus Christ, oh God, okay," LaGraves said. "How on earth does Murphy have any contact with Jesse? You know, Murphy's in population and Jesse's in death row."

"Very easily done," Walter replied.

Not just inside the prison system, either. Outside too. Because in addition to their contacts behind bars, Murphy and Jesse communicated through Kay Tafero, Walter told LaGraves. "He calls Jesse's mother and everything, man," Walter said.

The proper Welsh matron. A real lady. Such a perfect disguise.

"How come?" I ask Murphy now, about the "heat" he put on Walter.

"Because I wanted to see Rusty." His tone makes the statement seem self-evident.

"Why did you want to see him?"

"So that I could sit down with him and ask him what happened and collaborate what Jesse had told me and to get a deposition that would free Jesse and exonerate Jesse."

Collaborate. Not *corroborate,* a different word entirely.

After we hang up, I take another look at the *Vanity Fair* profile of Murphy. "The 50th Anniversary of New York's Most Sensational Jewel Heist" was the headline. In addition to detailing Murphy's glamorous past as a surfer and jewel thief, and detailing his pious present as a prison minister, the article dipped a toe into the case of Whiskey Creek.

> On that boat ride more than 40 years ago, Murphy says there were five passengers—the two girls, himself, Griffin [*sic*], and a mysterious guy named Rusty. Murphy claims that he was at the wheel when a contentious conversation broke out: "One of the girls said, if we don't get our money we're going to the FBI." On December 8, 1967, the two women's bikini-clad bodies were discovered submerged in the Whiskey Creek canal, weighed down with concrete blocks. They had been stabbed in the stomach and their skulls had been smashed. Murphy insists to me that the shadowy Rusty murdered the women.

The article doesn't name Walter Rhodes. And possibly Murphy has some other "mysterious guy named Rusty" to blame for the Whiskey Creek murders. But if it was Murphy's intention to have Walter Rhodes take the rap for his double murder too, that's interesting. Because in December 1967, Walter "Rusty" Rhodes was in the Maryland House of Corrections, under lock and key and far away from Whiskey Creek. He was seventeen years old and serving a thirty-month sentence for stealing a car. He was still five months away from being paroled, getting out, going on the lam, running away to Florida, stealing another car—and ending up in prison with Jesse Tafero, Jack Griffith, and Jack Murphy, where this story, this tragedy, would begin.

I had asked Walter Rhodes about Jack Murphy, when I went to see him at Jackson Correctional Institution this summer.

"Murphy is an ego-tripping manipulator, very likeable, personable," Walter told me. Charismatic, a showboat, possibly a genius too. When Walter was at Florida State Prison the first time, in the late 1960s, he lived on the same prison wing as Murph, and back then the famous prison playboy had women visitors who brought him drugs, enough to get the whole wing "high as kites," Walter has claimed. His first acid trip was in that prison cellblock, compliments of Murph, Walter said. He and Murph played in their prison rock band together, they knew all the same people, were friends with all the same people. "He was fun to be around, witty, and friendly." Later, after the murders, Murph used to stand on one leg to imitate Walter and his missing leg, and call Walter "Clem Kadiddlehopper," after the simpleminded Red Skelton country bumpkin character.

"I liked him," Walter said to me. "I'll tell you right now, I always did like him. He's also a little scary."

"Did Jack Murphy think that you actually killed those officers?"

"No, of course not. I don't think there was any doubt in his mind. I think he knew Jesse did it. I don't think he had any doubt about that."

So what were Murphy and Griffith trying to do with the recantations?

"To get Jesse off death row. That was the objective," Walter said.

"Just off death row?"

"Well, yeah. Because he knew he was going to be executed. I mean, you don't kill two cops and not get executed in Florida."

I think for a minute.

"But where did you fit into that equation?" I ask. "Because saying Tafero was innocent would mean—"

"Well," Walter said, cutting me off.

It would mean Jesse's friends, the prison in-crowd of drug thugs and karate masters and jewel thieves and lady-killers who used to be Walter's friends too but who made fun of Walter now right to his face, who mocked him, threatened him—it meant these friends thought that if someone was to be electrocuted for the murders of Trooper Black and Constable Irwin, murders that Jesse Tafero committed, let it not be Jesse Tafero. Let it be Walter Rhodes instead.

A couple of months after my visit with Walter, I get a letter from him. He slipped in the shower, the letter says, breaking the hydraulics on his artificial leg and smashing the bones in his left hand and arm. The prison has not yet taken him to a doctor, and in the meantime the bones have fused back together. Without his artificial leg, he cannot walk. He is now a one-armed, one-legged man in a wheelchair, bones knit together in a tangle on his hand, in a prison building with no screens on the windows and no air-conditioning. He has an appointment in a few weeks to see the prison doctor, who will rebreak his hand so it can mend.

"I dread that," the letter says.

"Life is just a flash, and it is over."

Home

The Price of a Lie

In the summer of 1993, I went to see a psychic. It was a classic California experience—wind chimes, bead curtains, sage-scented candles. A friend had some questions about her business that she wanted advice on, and I thought, Hey, I might as well run Jesse Tafero past this lady. Three years after the execution, I was still dreaming about it and I did not know why. Plenty of other reporters went to Q-Wing and then out for a beer with their buddies and left it behind, but here I was, stuck. In my tile work at the time, I was setting a lot of limestone—countertops, walls, floors—and I kept noticing the fossils, tiny living creatures embedded in the stone, frozen forever exactly as they were when disaster hit. I thought, That's me.

I'd been worried that the psychic would say something about past lives or karma, but all she did was close her eyes. Then she told me I was grieving.

"Grieving?" I said.

That had not occurred to me.

I was about to write this off as some New Age bullshit when I realized she might be right. Maybe it was grief I felt whenever I thought of the morning at Starke. A desolate feeling. Bewildering. I hoped naming it would make it go away. But instead it grew more urgent as reports of Jesse Tafero's innocence increased.

On the occasion of the tenth anniversary of *The Exonerated* in 2012, an interview with Sunny Jacobs appeared in *The New Yorker.* She was about to start a one-week run starring as herself onstage.

Q: How did you end up on death row and how did you get off of it?
A: Simply put, I was in the wrong place with the wrong people at the wrong time. We had pulled off the interstate into a rest area—there was no crime going on. We were just resting. But the police came to do a routine check and the driver had a gun, and he was on parole. Having a gun is a violation of parole. In the end, the policemen were dead and the driver was ordering us into the police car with the gun still in his hand. At that point, we became hostages. My partner Jesse was seated in the front. The children, my nine-year-old son and ten-month-old daughter, and I were seated in the back. Ultimately, there was a roadblock, the car was fired upon by a cordon of police armed with rifles, and we crashed. We were all taken into custody. The man who did the shooting immediately requested a plea bargain and received three life sentences in exchange for his testimony against Jesse and me. Jesse's trial took three or four days. He was convicted and sentenced to death. My trial took longer. I was a young mother and a hippie vegetarian type with no history of violence. . . . After seventeen years, and [a] number of confessions by the killer—and the discovery of evidence that had been hidden—we won my appeal and I was released. But not before Jesse was executed, my parents died, and the children grew up as orphans.

There it is, in one paragraph. The Ballad of Sunny and Jesse and Walter, slow and sad and so bittersweet.

For twenty-five years, that ballad resounded around me. In

magazines and newspapers and television shows and legal jour-
nals and spoken-word story hours and books and podcasts and
onstage and online. Low and mournful, marking time, keeping
score. Desolate. Bewildering. Finally it became unbearable, and I
had to find out what was actually true.

At that, I failed.

I do not know exactly what happened at the rest stop that winter morning so many years ago. There are moments of the tragedy
that remain a mystery to me.

But there are a few things I can say for sure right now.

Jesse Tafero was not innocent. On February 20, 1976, Jesse
Tafero murdered Trooper Phillip Black and Constable Donald
Irwin, and on May 4, 1990, he went to the electric chair for his
crimes.

Sunny Jacobs was not a hippie vegetarian in the wrong place at
the wrong time. She and her violent drug-dealing rapist gangster
boyfriend were living "the classic fugitive lifestyle . . . these individuals simply moved from place to place exchanging narcotics for
whatever was available, and living from hand to mouth, day to
day." That is what the report of the pre-sentence investigation for
Sunny said in August 1976, and now I believe it. I also believe
Sunny set off the Taser shot that sparked the murders at the rest
area. I think she fired it herself or she forced her little boy to—
which, to me, is worse.

And Walter Rhodes, star prosecution witness? At two capital
trials, he took the witness stand, swore an oath to tell the truth, and
shared a vivid tale of events that he now remembers differently—
and admits he did not actually see. "You don't always know who is
telling you the truth and who is lying—especially in a situation
like this. I guarantee you, there's some people that can lie so good
that you could not bust them." That is what Walter told me when
I interviewed him in prison before Jesse's execution. It's one thing
he has said that I now know for sure to be true.

But Walter Rhodes did not murder Trooper Black and Constable Irwin, despite what his confessions claimed. Walter's confessions were the product of threats and duress, not the unburdening

of a guilty soul. And while the confessions did not succeed in getting Jesse off death row, as Jesse and his friends clearly hoped they would, they did destroy Walter's credibility as a witness. I believe those false confessions helped set Sunny free.

During the winter of 2015, my laptop broke. I was in Florida at the time, talking to people about Jesse Tafero. Every time I touched my computer, I felt needles piercing my skin. I took it into the Apple store, and the nice Genius there told me there was voltage escaping from the machine. I went back to our bungalow and looked it up. Voltage is what keeps atoms connected together. The electric field. Without voltage, protons and electrons would float free. Two thousand volts in three jolts that morning. Maybe the molecules had gotten swapped around somehow, I thought, looking at the boxes of case papers in my office, the Polaroids from the court files, my notebooks, my notes. Maybe the mystery surrounding Jesse Tafero had literally become a part of me.

But it had not. That's something I know now too. It wasn't fate, or voltage, or even grief that made Jesse Tafero my ghost.

There's an old party game called Two Truths and a Lie. Maybe you've played it. Someone stands up and says a few things about herself, the more outlandish the better. The trick is in guessing which parts are made up and which are true, and the goal of the game is to get you believing something that never happened. To mix fact and fantasy until no one can tell them apart. As played among friends over a few drinks, it's harmless fun. But add an electric chair and put that game on the Internet, and there's a price to be paid. Not by the storyteller. She's living her fairy tale. By everyone else. The listeners. The families. The witnesses. I was trapped in that game for twenty-five years. I paid the price too.

When I started to hear the tale—the myth—of the innocent man two years after Jesse Tafero's execution, beginning with Sunny in tears on television, and first felt that dark slam of dread and grief, I thought it was just me being weak. Or obsessed. I did not yet understand the myth's power. The incredible, intoxicating, madness-

and-mayhem specter of an innocent in flames in the electric chair, how consuming that idea would turn out to be in the culture's imagination, how prurient and alluring. How easily the myth would catch hold, how fast and how far it would fly. How consuming and painful it would be to live with. To not know. And to try to find out. That was painful too.

Over the course of a year, my search stripped me of my illusions, forced me to recognize my own mistakes, reawakened my worst memories, and humbled me in failure. I lived with shame, doubt, fear, and silence. And I kept waking up into Q-Wing, directly into the flames and smoke. All of it, alive. The price of a lie.

In paying that price, I have not been alone.

When I first decided to try to solve this mystery, I did not know if anyone would talk to me. I was afraid it would be a burden to even ask. But on doorstep after doorstep, I only had to say that I was looking into two murders, hoping to find the truth of what really happened, and the person I was talking to finished my sentence for me. *Trooper Black. Constable Irwin. Jesse Tafero.* It was a solace to find out that this secret language I'd been carrying, a language of doubt and pain and sorrow, was a language many other people spoke as well. Two-, four-, six-hour conversations. Communication. Connection. For so long I'd thought I was crazy to care. All that time, others were watching and wondering too.

That was a revelation. I am grateful. It made me realize the power of truth. We needed—all of us caught up in this case—to know for sure. To stop wondering. To find peace. But my long journey also made me realize the power of myth. Everyone I talked to in my year of traveling has been available all along for interviews. I don't have magic powers. All I do is knock, ask, and listen. And it's no secret that the Internet is not a permanent, accurate record. It's a mirror. We know that. But it has not mattered. The myth of Jesse's and Sunny's innocence has an allure that keeps it alive.

In January 2019, seven years after I first read about Sunny's wedding in *The New York Times*, nearly four years after I found my way to her kitchen table and asked her to please just tell me the truth about the man I saw die, after I confronted her about the bullet hole in the police car and the Taser, after she herself told me actually, yes, Jesse Tafero might have been guilty, she gave another interview to the paper's wedding reporter, repeating exactly the same story that had ignited my long and painful search.

"The greatest tool is forgiveness," Sunny told the *Times* this time around, the article illustrated by a full-color photograph of her smiling sweetly, up toward the sky. "If you hold on to that anger and resentment, then there's no room for happiness and love in your heart, and you start destroying your own life." The article made sure to mention that Sunny was a vegetarian hippie when she was arrested, and that "Mr. Rhodes eventually confessed."

The myth lives on, the foolproof brainwashing of merciless repetition, no matter how many cold hard facts out in the real world contradict it, no matter how absurd it might be.

Because it is absurd. A young, wealthy, attractive, sophisticated, well-connected white woman who caught a ride from the wrong person and ended up on death row through absolutely no fault of her own—she didn't even see what happened!—and then was saved by a documentary filmmaker who was also her best friend from childhood. An exonerated woman who now lives in Ireland, where she practices yoga and forgiveness. *Life turned out beautifully*. That is what Sunny told *The Guardian* in 2013.

Maybe life has turned out beautifully for Sunny Jacobs. But the myth has nothing to do with the tragedy of two young fathers gunned down at a rest stop in the Florida mist.

Or with the bleakest realities of the American justice system.

The summer I first testified in hearings about the electric chair—in 1997, one year after I started working as a private detective—I heard about another man on death row who might be innocent. He'd been convicted of killing a police officer, but there was someone else in prison who was confessing to his crime. Those case facts sounded familiar, but this man was from Jacksonville, not Miami. His name was Leo Alexander Jones.

Leo Jones was a Black longshoreman and drug dealer. One night in May 1981, police officer Thomas Szafranski was murdered across the street from Leo's apartment in Jacksonville. Within minutes, police were storming Leo's building. Police kicked in Leo's door, dragged Leo and his cousin out of their beds, and beat them. The beating was not a secret. The police did not deny it. They said they had been forced by necessity to beat Leo Jones because he was "resisting arrest." Police took Leo downtown, interrogated him, took him to the hospital for skull X-rays and treatment of head and facial wounds that included blood trickling from his ear, bruises on his head, and a busted lip, took him back to the police station, and continued the interrogation. After eleven hours in police custody, and without being allowed to see his lawyer—who was there at the station house, searching for him—Leo signed a two-sentence confession, stating that he had used "a gun or rifle" to murder Szafranski. Leo immediately recanted the confession, saying that he'd signed it only because he was in fear for his life, but it was too late. No physical evidence linked Leo Jones to the murder of Thomas Szafranski, but on the basis of his confession Leo went to trial and was convicted, and the conviction stuck even after another man started bragging about having committed the crime. That man's name was Glenn Schofield. He was a widely feared drug dealer, rumored to be a police informant, and he was known to have been in Leo's apartment earlier that evening. But when questioned, Glenn said he was with his friend Shorty that evening. No, he did not remember Shorty's real name.

Over the next decade, the police officers who had obtained Leo's confession resigned amid allegations of brutality—one after beating a woman with his police flashlight, the other accused of arranging a contract murder—and nearly two dozen new witnesses came forward with information linking Glenn Schofield to the murder. Witnesses who swore Schofield confessed to them behind bars. Witnesses who saw Schofield running away from the crime scene that night with a rifle. A Jacksonville policeman broke the code to testify that at roll call the morning after the murder, one of the officers who had arrested Leo bragged about "beating him and beating him and beating him." All that time, Leo's lawyers and investigators searched for Shorty, the alibi witness. Finally, in April

1997, they found him. Roy "Shorty" Williams. Shorty said yes indeed, he was with Glenn Schofield that night. And that night, Shorty said, he personally witnessed Glenn Schofield kneel in a vacant lot beside Leo's apartment building, level his rifle, and fire the shot that took Officer Szafranski's life.

In the summer of 1997, my friend Freya and I went to investigate. We spent a week going door-to-door in Jacksonville—in an old neighborhood underneath a highway, a cast-off world of broken windows, nailed-shut doors, and tall weeds—talking to people about Leo Jones and Glenn Schofield. We talked to Leo's defense team, the police, and the prosecutor. And we talked to Shorty. Shorty told us: "I saw Glenn Schofield shoot the police officer."

But Shorty was uneducated and unsophisticated and impoverished, and his word did not sway the courts. The news stories written about Leo's case—including mine and Freya's, in *The Miami Herald*'s Sunday magazine—never caught on. Nobody was interested in Leo Jones. Just another ghetto drug dealer on death row. Leo Jones was the inmate who brought the suit against the State of Florida after its electric chair caught fire. The state responded by making Leo sit through a dry run of his own execution, to show him that the chair was indeed working. And in March 1998, Leo Jones went to the electric chair and died.

When I was in Florida talking to people about Jesse and Sunny and Walter, I took an afternoon off to meet with Leo Jones's lawyer again. It had been nearly twenty years since I last saw Martin McClain. We went out to a bar for lunch, as I had with Jesse Tafero's attorney. But McClain did not kick back in his chair and laugh about his client's case all these years later, as Jesse's attorney had. McClain did not tell me that his old client was guilty. When I brought up Leo Jones's name, McClain went pale and looked stricken. And then, as we talked about Leo Jones in that crowded bar, thronged with sunburned tourists on their second margarita of the afternoon, Martin McClain covered his face with his hands and wept.

Americans know that the foundation of our justice system, and our society, is the principle of equality under the law. We also know that inequality and injustice and racism continue to be tragic realities in our country. The appeal of the Ballad of Jesse and Sunny and Walter is that it takes the unconscionable atrocities that haunt our judicial system and turns them into a sentimental story with a feel-good ending. It's a story that is notably absent of any meaningful mention of its victims, Phillip A. Black and Donald Robert Irwin. It's a story that glosses over the intransigencies, the heartbreak, and the shattering violence of what a death penalty case actually involves. And it's a story that, in the end, evades the difficult questions around capital punishment.

In the years that I worked on this book, I came to despise Jesse Tafero. A killer, a rapist, a liar, with his cold eyes and his cowardice, he was a dangerous and selfish and guilty man.

But I still ended up uneasy about his case.

Innocence is the star around which our discussion of capital punishment now orbits. But Jesse Tafero was not innocent. He was a murderer. Does it matter, then, that the prosecution's key witness at trial testified to things he did not actually see? Is it okay that this key witness told his own attorney a version of events that contradicted his trial testimony? Should a police captain have been allowed to feed this key witness a mixture of facts and lies about the case, rehashing his memories as new evidence came in? Is it acceptable that the prosecution withheld from Jesse Tafero's defense lawyers the damning—to use the appeals court's own language—polygraph report that undermined what this witness told the jury? Is it a concern that Jesse Tafero's primary defense lawyer did not call any witnesses on his behalf and was a few years later disbarred? And is it troubling that after the trial, the key prosecution witness was caught pretending to be a spaceman imprisoned in the Florida system? That incident involved the bilking of an elderly pen pal and an inquiry by the U.S. Postal Inspection Service, and it resulted in a finding of conspiracy to defraud against Walter Rhodes years before the first death warrant was signed against Jesse Tafero. Plenty of time for the State of Florida to have second thoughts about the integrity of the conviction. But the reckoning never happened. The execution went forward anyway.

Some people say—they've said it to me—that Jesse Tafero deserved to die as he did. On fire in the electric chair. But I have spent half my life thinking about him and his crimes and his death, entangled in a tragic mystery of guilt and innocence, and I come now, finally, to bear witness. That morning at Starke, I witnessed a guilty man in an electric chair and, at six minutes past seven o'clock, an act of infinite cruelty. And I say we need to be better than that.

Still, I have realized something good in all of this. There was a door in the back of my world that blew open all those years ago, a door that let the night wind in. And now I have found that door and pulled it closed. That is what finally sorting truth from lies feels like. What owning up to myself and my own mistakes feels like. It feels like the start of something brand-new. Freedom.

One morning, on the beach near our house in Michigan, I say that out loud to Peter.

It's a wild and windswept place, this beach, an arc of blue lake water and silver dunes shimmering north as far as it is possible to see. For such a long time, even out here, I felt the shadow. Now it's gone.

"Already it all seems so long ago," I tell him. "Thank you."

"Anytime," Peter says.

And he reaches over to put his hand in mine.

Acknowledgments

I am grateful to my agent, Mollie Glick, for her unshakeable faith in this story and for everything she has done over many years to bring it to life. I've had lightning in my corner.

It has also been my extraordinary good fortune to have had a home at Random House while working on this book. To everyone whose desk these pages passed across, I give my thanks. In particular, thank you to David Ebershoff for saying yes to my quest and, with genius and generosity, helping it take shape. I am so grateful to Andy Ward for his steady patience and for the gift of time; to Tom Perry for inspiring me to do better; and to Robin Desser for kind encouragement. I am grateful too to Andrea Walker and Anna Pitoniak, for their hard work on my behalf, their commitment and creativity, and their editorial expertise. Many thanks to Carlos Beltran and Jo Anne Metsch for their beautiful designs, Deborah Dwyer and Loren Noveck for their exacting and thoughtful copyediting and production work, and Rachel Rokicki and Katie Tull for their enthusiasm, advocacy, and support. Thank you too to Matthew Martin for his meticulous review. And I am deeply indebted to Clio Seraphim, who helped me find this story's true heart.

For his friendship and advice I thank Mitch Langberg, whose wise insights and honest opinions greatly improved these pages. I am lucky to know Jacqueline Tully, who welcomed me years ago into her cool group of women investigators and has been generous ever since with both assistance and camaraderie; I am grateful to her and to Nancy Pemberton for sharing their deep knowledge of the death penalty. Sue Carswell was a valued ally; her steely precision made these pages shine. I am thankful for the inspiration and fellowship of Jane Moss and Kath Morgan at The Writing Retreat in Cornwall. And my teacher Tom Parker's voice is always with me.

I am grateful to Martin McClain for talking with me again about Leo Jones. And without the decision of the Broward County State Attorney's Office to grant me access to their case files, I could not have written this book. Thank you.

All along I have relied on my excellent friends. I am grateful to Carol Anshaw, Jason Friedman, Kim Lile, Jane Moss, Sharyn Saslafsky, and John Sullivan for their astute comments on early drafts. Jean Bahle, Julia Barrie, Larry Block, Jesse Ewing, Jeffrey Friedman, Bill Gleave, Tim Kingston, Edward Kiszenia, Robert McDonald, Max Moses, Chuck Prestidge, Rob Rebigea, Darren Reynolds, Kari Richardson, Christine Stroyan, Kevin Vanden-Bergh, and Alan Williams asked, listened, advised, endured, and made me laugh. Thank you to my Lorrimar friends and neighbors for all the good cheer. To Lynn Stubbs and Karen Williams, I offer my heartfelt gratitude for guidance and healing. You have shown me the bright world.

As I worked to understand the tragedy at the center of this story, I came to imagine all of us who'd been caught up in it as ripples on a pond, overlapping, extending outward from the central pain. It has been my profound privilege to meet and speak with so many people, from all different parts of the story we share. With some of you I had brief conversations; with others, we spent hours together. Some of your names appear here, but many do not, else this book would have been one thousand pages long. I thank every single one of you now. For opening your doors to this stranger, for taking the time to talk, and for listening too. In sharing your stories you have helped me reclaim my days, and that means much more to me than I can say.

In particular, I thank Grace and Christian Black for their kindness in talking with me.

To my family: You are all amazing and you inspire me every day.

And to Peter: Thank you for our life. I love you so much.

ABOUT THE AUTHOR

ELLEN McGARRAHAN worked for a decade as an investigative reporter at newspapers in New York City, Miami, and San Francisco before accidentally finding her calling as a private detective.

ABOUT THE TYPE

This book was set in Photina, a typeface designed by José Mendoza in 1971. It is a very elegant design with high legibility, and its close character fit has made it a popular choice for use in quality magazines and art gallery publications.